WARLORDS OF CHINA
700BC TO AD1662

WARLORDS OF CHINA
700BC TO AD1662

CHRIS PEERS

ARMS AND
ARMOUR

Arms and Armour Press
An Imprint of the Cassell Group
Wellington House, 125 Strand, London WC2R 0BB

Distributed in the USA by Sterling Publishing
Co. Inc., 387 Park Avenue South, New York,
NY 10016-8810.

British Library Cataloguing-in-Publication Data:
a catalogue record for this book is available from
the British Library

ISBN 1-85409-401-7

Designed and edited by DAG Publications Ltd.
Designed by David Gibbons; layout by Anthony
A. Evans; edited by John Gilbert; printed and
bound in Great Britain.

CONTENTS

INTRODUCTION

What exactly is a 'warlord'? The word itself is often associated in the popular mind with China, and with good reason. According to the Oxford English Dictionary it is Chinese in origin, being a direct translation of the term *junfa*. This was the name given to the military commanders who set up a number of de facto independent states in China in the chaotic period between 1916 and 1928. Nowadays, by extension, a 'warlord' has come to mean a 'military commander having a regional power base and ruling independently of the central government'. This is in addition to its more general meaning of 'a military commander or commander-in-chief'.

The 'warlords' whose stories are told in this book all fell under one of the above definitions at some stage in their careers, but otherwise they are a fairly diverse group. They came from widely differing backgrounds, and operated in very different periods of China's history. Some were born to greatness; others fought their way up from obscure beginnings. Some led their troops in desperate acts of valour on the battlefield. Some preferred to lay their plans in secret councils, while others did the fighting for them. A few of them destroyed or founded dynasties; the rest had to be content with local pre-eminence, or with serving greater masters.

What these men do have in common is that all were deeply involved in both the military and political struggles of their times. Hence their stories are of interest not only on a personal level, but for the light that they shed on some of the most dramatic episodes of China's long history. Unpopular though the habit of emphasising personalities may have become among academic historians, it has in the present case two great advantages:

it reflects the way the Chinese themselves have always seen these matters; and it provides an easy way for the general reader to gain an overview of one of the most monumental chunks of human experience – more than three and a half thousand years of Chinese history, from the Shang dynasty to the People's Republic.

Three and a half millennia of continuous history is not an easy concept for the Western mind to grasp. Europe, three and a half thousand years ago, was still firmly prehistoric: its peoples are known to us not by names, but by archaeological labels – Mound People, Urnfield Culture, Middle Helladic III. Egypt and Iraq possess the remains of civilisations even older than China's, but any sense of continuity that their present-day inhabitants feel is an artefact of modern nationalism. Their languages and religions are now utterly different, and their very awareness of the ancient past is mainly due to Western archaeology. The nearest equivalent to the Chinese experience is perhaps that of the Jewish people, but their moment of glory as a great military power was very brief, and even their independent political existence has been interrupted for extended periods.

In China, on the other hand, the whole of this immense past is still very much alive in the national consciousness, and is often regarded as applicable to today's problems. This applies not only to intellectuals in the traditional mould, but even to the most radical of revolutionaries. When Mao Tse-tung observed that 'We are not the Duke of Sung', he was referring to that gentleman's famous blunder in a battle fought in 638BC. But Mao's entourage of twentieth-century Communists would have understood at once the meaning and relevance of his remark.

Dynasties

Scholars attempt to make this expanse of time more manageable by dividing it up into 'dynasties'. These are usually named after the imperial family which provided the country's rulers during that period, and which in turn often took its name from its place of origin. However, in AD1260, when the Mongol conqueror Kubilai Khan established his own regime, he broke with tradition and adopted for this dynasty the name 'Yuan', or 'Origin' – signifying, as he saw it, a new beginning. The succeeding regimes of the Ming ('Brilliant') and Ch'ing ('Pure') followed his example in using a descriptive rather than a geographical title.

Unlike the dynasties of ancient Egypt, those of China are not the artificial creations of more recent historians, but reflect the situation roughly as people saw it at the time. Unfortunately, because this system is based on political reality, it is not very tidy. China was not always united under one ruler, and so at times several dynasties ran concurrently in different regions. The transfer of power between one ruling house and another was often protracted and bloody, so that the date of the end of one regime rarely corresponds exactly with the founding of its successor. What is more, the power of some dynasties was more real than that of others: the rulers of the Chou dynasty, for example, had lost all real authority by the end of the eighth century BC, but were permitted to persist as figureheads for another five hundred years, while their nominal vassals functioned effectively as independent states.

It is generally considered that the earliest date in Chinese records which can be precisely correlated with our Western calendar is 841BC. Before that, different chronologies give different dates, even for major events. The fall of the Shang dynasty, for example, is variously dated to 1122 or 1027BC, depending on whether one follows Ssu-ma Ch'ien's Han period *Shih Chih*, or the text known as the *Bamboo Annals*. The dates indicated by a question mark below are currently the best available guesses.

?2000–?1750BC   HSIA

The Hsia was long thought to be mythical, although recent archaeological discoveries suggest that some sort of organised state or states did precede the Shang. Before that, traditional accounts describe a succession of emperors who are best regarded as mythological culture heroes, rather than as historical figures.

?1750–?1050 BC   SHANG
?1050–256BC   CHOU
?1050–771 BC   Western Chou
771–256BC   Eastern Chou

Temporarily split into two parts in 771BC, the kingdom was reunited in 750. Then in 707, it fragmented into numerous independent states. This period is traditionally divided into:

771–480BC   'Springs and Autumns'
480–221BC   'The Warring States'
221–207 BC   CH'IN

The earliest true imperial dynasty; its founder was the first to adopt the title of *Huang-ti*, or 'Emperor'.

202BC–AD220   HAN
202BC–AD9   Western Han

AD9–23 Short-lived 'Hsin' dynasty of Wang Mang, generally not recognised as legitimate by traditional scholarship.

23–220   Eastern Han
221–265   'The Three Kingdoms'

The Three Kingdoms were:

221–265   Wei
221–265   Shu Han
221–280   Wu
265–316   TSIN

316–589 'The Northern and Southern Dynasties'. This was a period of political division. Several 'barbarian' peoples set up states in north China, while a succession of weak native dynasties held the south. Some of the most important regimes were:

In the north:

304–329   Former Chao
319–350   Later Chao
337–370   Former Yen
351–394   Former Ch'in
386–535   Northern (or Toba) Wei
535–550   Eastern Wei

535–557	Western Wei
550–577	Northern Ch'i
557–581	Northern Chou

In the south:

317–420	Eastern Tsin
420–479	Liu Sung
479–502	Southern Ch'i
502–557	Liang
557–589	Ch'en
581–618	SUI
618–907	T'ANG

690–705 'Chou' dynasty established by the Empress Wu. Like Wang Mang's 'Hsin', this is not normally accorded official recognition.

907–959 'The Five Dynasties and Ten Kingdoms'. Another period of division, this time with the south partitioned among several independent native warlords (the 'Ten Kingdoms'), while the north saw a series of mainly Turkish dynasties in the Yellow River plain, with the far north-east occupied by the 'Liao' regime of the Manchurian Khitan people. The fiction was maintained by scholars that these northern rulers were the 'true' emperors, but this was not universally accepted at the time. The succession in the north was:

907–1125	Liao
907–923	Later Liang
923–936	Later T'ang
936–946	Later Chin
946–951	Later Han
951–959	Later Chou
960–1279	SUNG
960–1126	Northern Sung
1127–1279	Southern Sung

The Sung never succeeded in controlling all of north China, parts of which were occupied at various times by the Liao and two other 'barbarian' dynasties, the second of which overthrew and replaced the Liao:

1038–1227	Western Hsia (Tangut)
1125–1235	Kin (Jurchen)
1260–1368	YUAN (Mongol)
1368–1644	MING
1644–1911	CH'ING (Manchu)

In 1911 a Republic was established, bringing to an end the imperial phase of Chinese history.

Nomenclature and Transcription

Written Chinese is not easy to transcribe into our alphabet, and several different systems have been tried over the years. None of them has proved to be entirely satisfactory. The Wade-Giles system followed here has been in use for the last century, and is still employed by the majority of academic and popular works. Its only current rival is the Pinyin system, which is endorsed by the present regime in the People's Republic of China, but otherwise has little to recommend it. In particular, the pronunciation of many of the consonants can be misleading to English speakers. If the following basic rules are observed, terms in the Wade-Giles system can be pronounced, if not entirely accurately, at least comprehensibly:

CH' = English CH	CH = English J
P' = English P	P = English B
T' = English T	T = English D

The study of Chinese history is further complicated by the often inconsistent procedure for naming both people and places. A ruler, on taking the throne, would generally adopt a different name: thus Hsiao-pi is better known to history as Duke Huan, and Chu Yuan-chang as the Hung-wu Emperor. Therefore it has sometimes been found necessary to refer to the same individual by different names at different stages in his career. I have attempted to keep this to a minimum, and also to indicate where necessary any further names or titles by which a subject may appear in other works. Thus Li Yuan is often referred to as the Duke of T'ang, and Liu Pang as the Governor of P'ei. The special case of the 'Dukes' of the Springs and Autumns period is discussed in Chapter 2.

Places also change their names. The names of the states of the Springs and Autumns and Warring States eras continue to crop up as geographical terms for many centuries after they lost all political identity. This is particularly true of the topographically distinct regions of Ch'in and Ch'i.

Towns and cities were routinely renamed every time they changed hands between different regimes. The city which we now know as Beijing or Peking, for example, was known under the Kin dynasty as Chung-tu, then as Ta-tu when it became the capital of the Mongol Yuan. The Ming renamed it first Pei-ping, and then Pei-ching, which means 'Northern Capital'. In general, I have used the contemporary names for the period under discussion, indicating the modern equivalent where appropriate.

A strategic map of China

Like any other country in the world, China's development has been fundamentally influenced by its geography. Even a brief study of military campaigns throughout those three and a half thousand years of history will show that the same battlefields, the same mountain passes and the same strategic configurations appear again and again. The accompanying map attempts to show some of the permanent geographical factors which have constrained Chinese commanders throughout the ages.

KEY:

(i) Approximate course of the lower Yellow River in the time of Duke Huan of Ch'i. Because of the load of silt which it brings down from the interior, the Yellow River is notoriously unstable. It floods frequently, and is inclined to change its course at unpredictable intervals. Its reputation as 'China's Sorrow' is well known, but the impetus given to large-scale public works by the need to control its floods was probably a crucial factor in the rise of early Chinese civilisation. From a military point of view, the Yellow River has always been an obstacle, rather than an artery of communication.[1]

(ii) Approximate course of the Yellow River in the time of Li Shih-min. Over the centuries, the river has wandered about the plain, shifting its direction of flow generally southwards. This has not been a gentle or gradual process, however. Long periods of relative stability have been punctuated by sudden and catastrophic diversions into a new course. Changes in AD11 and 1194 caused especially heavy loss of life, and seriously undermined the governments of the times.

A strategic map of China, showing the main geographical influences on the conduct of military operations throughout the region's history. See text for explanation.

(iii) Course of the Yellow River in the time of Chu Yuan-chang. In 1289 the river underwent an even more dramatic change, taking a course south of the Mount T'ai massif to join the Huai River. It continued to flow in this general direction until 1853, when it again swung northwards. In 1939 another drastic change of course took place. This time it was deliberately engineered by the Chinese government, which ordered the dikes to be broken in a desperate attempt to disrupt a Japanese offensive.

A The 'Land Within the Passes'; ancient Ch'in, later known by the name of Kuan-chung. The fertile valley of the Wei River, protected by encircling rivers and mountains, was a natural stronghold, of which it was said that twenty thousand men could hold the passes against a million. Here the state of Ch'in, which eventually unified China under its first imperial dynasty, was able to nurture its strength in safety. The great dynasties of Han and T'ang also had their power bases and seats of government here. The area lost much of its strategic significance in Sung times, when it was overrun by invaders from the west. Many centuries of intensive agriculture had by then eroded the soil and impoverished the region, so that it never regained its former importance. Similar environmental destruction, of course, contributed to the decline of ancient civilisations in places as diverse as Iraq, Italy and Mexico. Luckily for China, however, it was able to survive by developing new territory – notably in the Yangtze valley, and later along the southern coast.

B The modern province of Shantung; ancient Ch'i. 'A Ch'in in the east as well as in the west', as it was described by a Han period commentator. Though less secure than its western counterpart, Ch'i was often regarded as a strategic counterweight to the 'Land Within the Passes'. Protected by the sea, flanking rivers, and the Mount T'ai massif, this region was also economically important from early times because of its salt industry.

C The Szechwan Plain; ancient Shu. The third of the great enclosed strategic bases, the Szechwan region was accessible only via the Yangtze Gorges, or the precarious 'Gallery Road' across the mountains from the north. Both were extremely difficult for armies to traverse, although the feat was achieved on several occasions. The region was conquered by Ch'in in the late fourth century BC, but was not brought fully into the sphere of Chinese civilisation until the imperial age. The irrigated plain is today the third great centre of population in the country, but before the Sung period it was relatively undeveloped. Thus, although in times of disunity it was often the seat of independent powers, these seldom succeeded in holding out against the rest of a unified empire. The strategic significance of Szechwan was re-emphasised during the Second World War, when it became the Nationalist seat of government, following the loss of Peking and the coastal regions to the Japanese.

D The Ordos Steppe. North of the Wei valley, the country becomes drier, merging gradually into the grassy steppes of Central Asia. The steppe area within the great loop of the Yellow River is known as the Ordos, and has at various times served as an advanced base for both Chinese and Central Asian armies in their campaigns against each other. The Ordos region is discussed further in Chapter 11.

E The modern province of Fukien; ancient Min-Yueh. In classical times, this whole area was beyond the reach of Chinese civilisation. The Wu Yi mountains prevented easy access by land, and it was not until late in the Han period that it was brought under imperial control. Even then, it remained remote and thinly populated for many centuries. Like most of the south, the Fukien region was infected with malaria and other tropical diseases, and was regarded by soldiers and officials from the north as a hardship post. It was not until Sung times that it began to

The modern provinces of China. Although this particular arrangement dates only from the eighteenth century, the modern names are a useful guide to the general location of places mentioned in the text. They have been used where appropriate throughout this book.

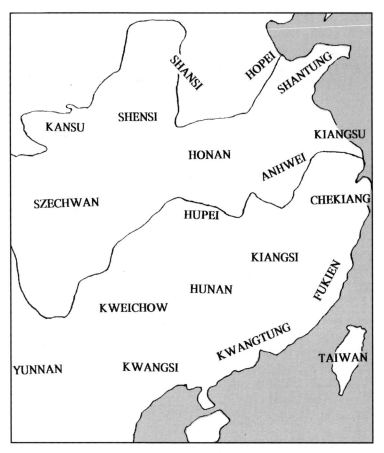

support a dense population, most of whom lived by fishing and maritime trade. The strategic role of the area was most significant during the Manchu conquest in the seventeenth century, when it served as a base for Ming loyalists.

F The T'ong Pass. The main access route into the 'Land Within the Passes', this is probably the most fought-over battlefield in the whole of China, if not the world. An inscribed stone which is still to be seen at the entrance to the pass gives details of just a few of the dozens of engagements which have taken place on that spot. Perhaps the best known is the battle of AD756, during the An Lu-shan Rebellion. On that occasion the armies of the T'ang dynasty bungled their defence of the pass, permitting the rebels to break through and sack the capital, Ch'ang-an.

G The Yangtze Gorges. The Yangtze is much more reliable for navigation than the Yellow River, largely because the two great lakes, Tung-t'ing and P'o-yang, help to even out the seasonal variations in its flow. Its lower course is therefore a vital strategic waterway, and most powers based in the Yangtze valley have maintained navies and emphasised the role of water transport. The gorges, however, form a natural barrier to riverborne traffic, and have often been further strengthened by fortifications. On several occasions - notably in AD36 and 1371 – they have been the scene of heavy fighting, when imperial fleets from the east attempted to fight their way through to invade Szechwan.

H The Grand Canal. This artificial waterway links the Peking region in the north with Hangchow Bay in the south. It is 1100 miles long, and was constructed over a period of centuries between the Sui and Ming dynasties. Its primary purpose was to transport the agricultural produce of the south to the seat of government in the north, without having to resort to the dangerous sea route around the Shantung Peninsula. In later imperial times the canal became a major strategic prize, and was often the scene of military operations. Most of the fighting in the Ming civil war of 1399 to 1402 took place along the line of the canal.

THE CHARIOT IN CHINESE WARFARE

The introduction of the war chariot

The armies of the Hsia and early Shang dynasties fought exclusively on foot. In western Asia, meanwhile, the war chariot had become the decisive arm in warfare as early as 1600BC. The greatest exponents of chariot fighting – and perhaps its inventors – were the Hurrians, a people originating from the Caucasus region. Here they were ideally placed to combine the craftsmanship of Mesopotamia with the horse-breeding skills of the northern steppes. Like any successful weapon of war, the new invention spread rapidly, and by the middle of the second millennium BC it was in use as far afield as north-western Europe. At about the same time, the Aryan invaders introduced it into India.

Chariots, however, do not appear in the Chinese archaeological record until around 1300BC, when great nobles of the Shang began to be buried with their vehicles. It is generally assumed that knowledge of the chariot system must have arrived in the Yellow River valley from the west, rather than being a coincidental local development. This diffusionist theory has gained support from the existence of ancient rock carvings of wheeled vehicles in Mongolia, along the route by which it would presumably have been transmitted.

Against this theory is the fact that other Chinese borrowings from the west during this period are virtually unknown. The focus of Shang power in north China lay thousands of miles from the nearest centres of civilisation in the Middle East, and much of the intervening territory was barren steppe and mountain, populated only sparsely by primitive tribes. On the other hand, a new weapon

of great mobility might have been one of the few inventions of the settled people which the steppe tribes could adapt to their own way of life, and thus would be likely to transmit over long distances. For a better known example of this type of phenomenon, one could point to the spread of the horse among North American Indians. The animals quickly outpaced the white men who had introduced them, and were soon being adopted enthusiastically by tribes who had no idea of their ultimate origin.

There is no reason, therefore, to suspect that warriors from the Middle East ever actually arrived in China. Certainly, Chinese sources contain no record of them. But by the twelfth or thirteenth century BC, the chariot had clearly become central to the power and prestige of the Shang aristocracy, just as it had done elsewhere in Eurasia. It was not restricted to the Shang, however. Chariots were also used by many of their neighbours, who although living within what is now China, were then considered to be 'barbarians', outside the pale of Chinese civilisation. Both Shang and later Chou inscriptions record the capture of wheeled 'vehicles' during campaigns against such enemies.

As might be expected, there were differences between the Chinese vehicles and their presumed western prototypes. Most of our knowledge of early chariots comes from remains found in excavated tombs, where they were often buried along with other items which might be of use to the deceased in the next world. Shang vehicles usually had a team of two horses, although four were used on occasion. They had a low, open-fronted cab, enclosed only by rails, although it is probable that leather panels

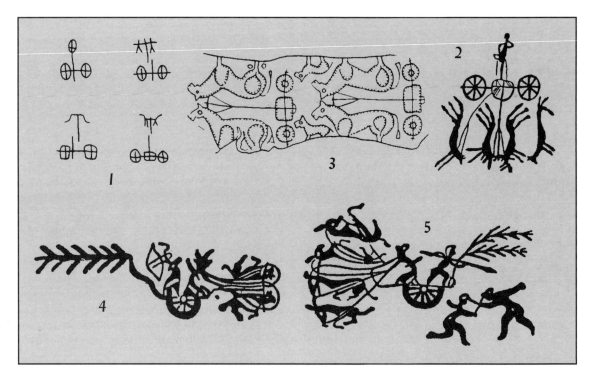

Two- and four-horse chariots, as represented in early Chinese art. 1) Pictographs on incised bones from the Shang dynasty. 2), 3), 4) and 5) Chou dynasty carvings, and representations on pottery and bronze vessels.

were lashed to the rails to protect the crew from missiles, as was the practice in Chou times. Wheels were up to five feet in diameter, and of sophisticated design, with eighteen or more spokes. The axle-caps, decorative plaques on the harness, and the finals on yokes and flagpoles, were bronze. Many examples of these items have survived. The rest of the vehicle was made of wood, which can often only be reconstructed from the impressions which it has left in the soil.[1]

The Chou period

The Chou, who replaced the Shang, lived originally in the far west of China, on the edge of the steppe. They had long been famous as charioteers and horse-breeders. A probably fourth-century text, the *Ssu-ma Fa*, distinguishes between the vehicles of the early dynasties, although its attribution of chariots to the Hsia tends to cast doubt on its reliability. 'As for their war chariots,' we are told, 'those of the rulers of the Hsia were called "hook chariots" for they put uprightness first. Those of the Shang were called "chariots of the new moon" for they put speed first. Those of the Chou were called "the source of weapons" for they put excellence first.'[2]

There may, however, be some truth in the idea that the Chou emphasised armament rather than speed. During the Western Chou period a larger, four-horse chariot became the norm. It was crewed by a driver; an archer, who stood on the left; and a spearman on the right. All three men were usually protected by coats of tough rhinoceros-hide armour. The vehicles tended to be heavy and cumbersome, and were often weighed down with an excessive quantity of bronze plaques and bells, as well as large numbers of colourful flags. This reinforces the impression gained from written sources that tactical mobility was not considered to be their primary function.

Chariots were not usually capable of riding down formed infantry, and so tended to deploy on the flanks of an army or as a skirmish line in front, where they could be matched against the vehicles of the enemy. Their role in battle was to enable the nobility on either side to skirmish with each other, and to overawe the enemy by their spectacular appearance. Serrated bronze blades were sometimes attached to the wheels, but there is no evidence that they were intended to be used as the Persian scythed chariots were, to break up infantry formations by sacrificial charges.

In difficult terrain, chariots were often outmanoeuvred by lightly equipped infantry. For example, the *Tso Chuan* describes the nervousness of the charioteers of the state of Cheng, when facing the Jung barbarians in 713BC. They were apparently worried that the enemy, who although entirely on foot were 'light and nimble', would be able to outmanoeuvre their chariots and capture them: 'They are footmen, while we have chariots. The fear is lest they fall suddenly upon us.'[3] Likewise, in 613BC a force of 800 chariots sent to restore the ruler of the state of Tsu was destroyed by the peasant infantry who had deposed him.

As warfare spread beyond the Yellow River plain into regions where the terrain was less suitable for wheeled vehicles, their importance declined. For example, the state of Wu, which was based in the marshy lower Yangtze region, never used them to any great extent, preferring to rely

The other main source for early Chinese chariots is archaeology. The vehicles were often interred in tombs with their wealthy owners. This is a chariot burial of the Warring States period, discovered on the outskirts of the city of Lo-yang. (After Su Ping-ch'i et al.)

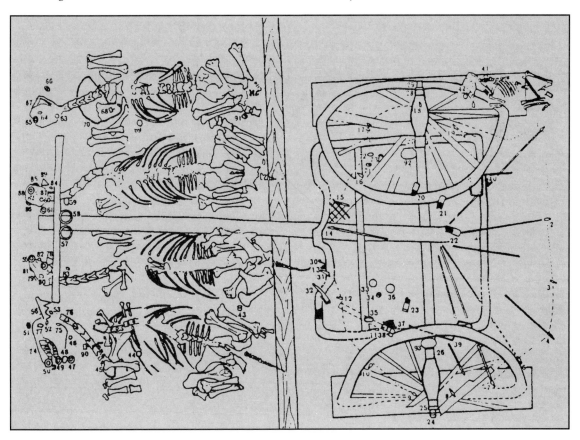

on its well-disciplined infantry. Eventually even the northerners began to realise the limitations of the chariot, although the aristocracy continued to cling to them for the sake of prestige. In a famous battle in 540BC, Tsin charioteers defending a mountain pass were ordered to dismount and fight on foot. The nobles objected to this, and their commander was forced to behead one of their number before the order was obeyed.

Even as their tactical inadequacies were becoming apparent, however, the sheer numbers of chariots available continued to grow. By the sixth century BC, the larger states often fielded them in thousands, and it was common to rate the strength of a state in terms of the numbers of vehicles which it could muster. The rise of Ch'i, for example, was marked by the expansion of its chariot force from about a hundred in the 720s, to more than four thousand by 500BC.

Specialist variants

Some of the theoretical military texts of the Warring States era detail the roles of a variety of different types of chariot. The best example is the *Six Secret Teachings*, a work which is generally thought to be of Warring States origin, although it is traditionally ascribed to the eleventh century BC. Here, among others, are listed:

> Martial Protective Large 'Fu-hsu' Chariots...The chariots have eight-foot wheels... Martial Flanking Large Covered Spear and Halberd 'Fu-hsu' Chariots... They have five-foot wheels and winch-powered linked crossbows which shoot multiple arrows for self-protection... Great Yellow Triple-linked Crossbow Large 'Fu-hsu' Chariots...In the daytime they display pennants of red silk six feet long by six inches wide, which shimmer in the light. At night they hang pennants of white silk ... which appear like meteors. They are used to penetrate solid formations, to defeat infantry and cavalry.[4]

There was also a mobile observation post – the *ch'ao ch'e* or 'crow's nest chariot' – which we know was used at the battle of Yen-ling, in 575BC. This was a vehicle equipped with a tower on to which a man could climb, in order to observe the enemy from above the dust which manoeuvring armies inevitably raised. Otherwise there is little evidence, from either archaeology or contemporary battle accounts such as those in the *Tso Chuan*, for significant variations in construction or function between different sorts of chariots. It is by no means clear how, if at all, the passage from the *Six Secret Teachings* relates to actual battlefield practice. Nevertheless, there is nothing inherently unlikely about the idea of mounting heavy multiple crossbows on chariots, for such weapons were in widespread use during the Warring States period.

The decline of the chariot

It was probably the crossbow which precipitated the decline of the chariot in China. It is often claimed that chariots in general were very vulnerable to archery, being large targets and requiring only one horse to be brought down for the whole team to be put out of action. This is a misconception, since horses and crews were typically well armoured, and in any case a horse was rarely killed outright by an arrow. What usually happened was that the pain would cause the animal to run out of control or throw a rider. But if it was part of a team, securely harnessed both to its neighbours and to a heavy vehicle, its options in this respect would be severely limited.

The chariot's real disadvantages are its expense, and its lack of mobility. Four cavalrymen riding their horses represent much the same fighting power as a four-horse chariot with four crew, and are far more mobile, especially over rough ground. In the West, therefore, the appearance of the ridden horse around 1000BC was the principal factor which caused the chariot to become obsolete. In China, however, the situation was different. Horses were not commonly ridden in battle until the very end of the fourth century BC, yet the chariot had declined in significance long before that. This was partly due to the rise of immense conscript armies, with the associated increase in the importance of infantry, and partly, as we have seen, to the extension of military operations to areas where the terrain was unfavourable. But at about the same time the crossbow was also coming into use. This weapon had a much greater draw weight than an ordinary bow, and probably was capable of killing or knocking over a horse, thus stopping a vehicle in its tracks with a single shot. To carry the weight of armour thick enough to keep out bolts shot with this sort of force was obviously impossible.

From the early fourth century BC onwards, therefore, the numbers of chariots in the armies of the various states declined steadily. They are still found in the terracotta army of the First Emperor of Ch'in, who died in 209BC, and appear in the records of the early Han, up to around 90BC. But by then they were used mainly as mobile command posts, or even unhitched and arranged as a sort of defensive wagon laager. Some of their ancient prestige still lingered, but the role of the mounted manoeuvre force in battle had long since passed to the cavalry.

A reconstruction of the cab of a Ch'in dynasty chariot in the museum at Xian. Based on remains found in association with the terracotta army of Ch'in Shih Huang-ti. (Duncan Head)

DUKE HUAN AND DUKE WEN: THE FIRST HEGEMONS

'Well-ordered states are always prosperous while disorderly states are always poor. Therefore those skilled in ruling will first enrich the people, and thereafter impose their government on them.' – Kuan Chung

The era of the Spring and Autumn Annals

The Western Chou dynasty, which replaced the Shang in about 1050BC, has always had a special place in Chinese tradition. The Confucians, especially, looked back on it as a golden age of enlightened government. The *Rituals of Chou*, a classic supposedly setting out the principles of that government, was used as a theoretical basis for successive regimes as late as the nineteenth-century Taipings.

Much of this tradition is a later idealisation. On the other hand, the early Chou rulers do seem to have tried to emphasise ritual and correct behaviour, rather than naked force, as the basis of their authority. The *Ssu-ma Fa* illustrates the difference from previous styles of government with a striking metaphor: 'For insignia the Hsia used the sun and moon, valuing brightness. The Shang used the tiger, esteeming awesomeness. The Chou used the dragon, esteeming culture.'[1] This change of emphasis, however, was probably an un-avoidable consequence of the weakness of the system of government which the Chou established.

The Chou regime is often described as 'feudal', and although their system was different in many ways from the more familiar feudalism of medieval Europe, the label remains a useful one. Most of the terri-tory of the kingdom was parcelled out among the descendants of the Chou and Shang nobility, who were too powerful to suppress altogether. These magnates were obliged, in return for the lands and titles which they held, to provide troops to supplement the royal army when required.

In the traditional system introduced by the Chou, there were five grades of semi-independent rulers. Their titles are often rendered in English by rough equivalents, as follows:

In descending order of rank, the grades were: *Kung*, or Duke; *Hou*, or Marquis; *Po*, or Earl; *Tzu*, or Viscount; and *Nan*, or Baron. The titles went with the feudal 'states', rather than being hereditary in the strict sense, and reflected the relative importance of the ruling families at the time of the original Chou settlement. Thus the rulers of Sung, who were descended from the Shang royal family, were dukes, while the lords of Tsin, which was much larger in area, were merely marquises. All ranks were subordinate to the Chou ruler, who was the only one entitled to call himself *Wang*, or King.

As time went on, however, the states pros-pered or declined at different rates, and soon the titles bore little relationship to the actual hierarchy of power. In particular, those who were situated on what had once been the periphery of the Chou kingdom were able to expand and incorporate neighbouring 'barbarian' peoples, gradually coming to dominate their more centrally placed rivals. Ch'i in the east, Tsin in the north, and Ch'u in the south were soon strong enough to rival the central Chou power itself. As early as the tenth century BC, kings Chao and Mu were obliged to lead a series of campaigns against

Ch'u. The rulers of remote Ch'u – officially viscounts – were in the habit of styling themselves 'kings', and had to be forced from time to time to renounce the title and acknowledge Chou sovereignty. There is a further complication to this system of ranks: it became customary to refer to all rulers after their deaths by the honorary title of 'Duke'. Thus Huan and Wen, the heroes of this chapter, were during their lifetimes only marquises, but have been referred to as dukes ever since.

Eventually, the ramshackle Chou government fell apart. In 771BC the barbarian Jung tribes sacked the Chou capital at Hao, and forced the court to flee eastwards down the Yellow River to Lo-yang. Most of the king's vassals failed to support him in this crisis. This is the context for the famous story about the foolish emperor who called out his nobles with their troops for a joke, to amuse his concubine, so that when a real invasion occurred they no longer took any notice. Whatever the truth of this, the Chou ruler could no longer rely on his over-mighty subjects.

The *coup de grâce* came in 707, when Chuang, the Earl of Cheng, rose in revolt, and defeated King Huan in a battle at Hsu-ko. The Chou remained in control of a small territory around Lo-yang, and for a long time continued to be treated with the outward forms of deference, but their authority over the rest of the country had vanished. Their vassals became in effect independent states, and at once started to devour one another. This was a process that continued for centuries, slowly gathering pace. In 707 there were about 170 such states; 300 years later, there were eight. By 221BC, as we shall see, only one survived.

The first part of this age of internal strife – roughly between 707 and 480BC – is known as the 'Springs and Autumns' period, after the *Annals* of the state of Lu, which recorded events under these seasonal headings. The *Annals* were allegedly compiled or edited by the famous sage Confucius, and together with the commentary known as the *Tso Chuan*, written by Tso Ch'u-ming, they are our main source for the events of the period. They tell a complex tale of incessant warfare and constantly shifting alliances, but two major themes can be said to run through them. The first of these concerns the gradually increasing scale and sophistication of the contending states, and also of the wars which they conducted.

Analysis of the *Tso Chuan* has shown that between about 700 and 500BC, the larger states developed organised bureaucracies in which ministers took over much of the day-to-day government from the rulers. They also greatly extended the frequency and range of their long-distance diplomatic and trading missions.[2] Population and economic activity increased dramatically. So did the size of armies, and the distances covered in their campaigns. We have already seen how states which could muster just a few hundred chariots at the beginning of the 'Springs and Autumns' era were fielding them in thousands by its end. At the same time, infantry forces were expanding even faster as they began to replace the chariot as the main offensive arm.

The other outstanding theme of the period was the struggle for dominance between two great power blocs – one based in the north, among the states of the Yellow River valley, and the other in the south, centred on Ch'u. At the end of the eighth century Earl Chuang of Cheng took the lead in organising resistance to Chu's expansionist plans, and over the next 200 years the leadership of the north was assumed in turn by the leaders of several of the larger states. This pre-eminence was sometimes officially recognised by the Chou kings, but remained largely informal, based on military strength and force of personality. It became the custom to refer to these leaders by the term *pa*, which is variously translated as 'hegemon', or as 'protector' of the Chou monarchy. After the death of Earl Chuang, this position passed to one of the most famous political figures in classical Chinese history – Duke Huan of Ch'i.

Upheaval in Ch'i

The land of Ch'i was situated on the north-east coast, around the base of what is now the Shantung Peninsula. At the beginning of the seventh century it was already a powerful state, having expanded into fertile and mineral-rich territory formerly controlled by the Yi barbarians. Because of its coastal situation it was also prominent in the salt trade, which it operated as a state monopoly. Another advantage enjoyed by Ch'i was the natural barrier formed by the sacred Mount T'ai and its associated hills, which forced any invading army to negotiate a series of easily defensible defiles.

However, Marquis Hsiang, who was the ruler of Ch'i from 696 to 685BC, was not the man to make the most of these advantages. He had a knack for making himself unpopular. The *Tso Chuan* records that even before he came to power he was despised by the people for his unspecified 'irregularities' of behaviour. As marquis, he demoted many officers who had been favoured by his predecessor, and drove others into exile. Eventually a plot was hatched against him, under the leadership of one of the disgraced officers, Hsiang's own cousin Wu-che.

The *Tso Chuan* provides us with the details of the coup. One day in the winter of 685, the marquis was out hunting. He encountered a wild boar at close quarters, and received such a shock that he fell down in his chariot. (The story that the animal stood up on its hind legs and howled at him is presumably just an excuse for his cowardly behaviour.) Unnoticed in the heat of the moment, one of Hsiang's shoes came off. On his return to the palace, he ordered a servant called Pe to bring him the shoe. When the man could not find it, the infuriated marquis flogged him until his back was running with blood. As Pe staggered out of the palace gate, he met a band of assassins waiting outside. They grabbed the unfortunate servant, who pulled off his jacket and showed them his back. His still bleeding wounds spoke for themselves. 'Why should I oppose you?' he asked.

The assassins, assuming that Pe was now sympathetic to their cause, let him go. But Hsiang had in Pe a more loyal servant than he deserved. Pe ran back inside the palace to warn the marquis, then returned to the gate, through which the attackers were now pouring. He and some others tried to stop them, and were quickly cut down. The assassins then ransacked the palace. Spotting the marquis's foot protruding from behind a door, they dragged him from his hiding place and murdered him.

Wu-che appropriated for himself the title of Marquis of Ch'i, but was assassinated in his turn only a month later. A deputation from Ch'i then went to the neighbouring state of Lu to ask for help in establishing Prince Chiu, a brother of Hsiang, as the new ruler. Nothing is said of this in the sources, but the fact that this outside assistance had to be invoked suggests that Chiu was not a universally popular choice. Nevertheless, Lu agreed to back him, and an army took the field.

It was already too late. There was another brother, Hsiao-pi, who had fled into exile in 696 when Hsiang came to power. What the background was to this event we are not told, but Hsiao-pi must have enjoyed considerable popular support, and perhaps even then Hsiang had feared him as a potential rival. Now, Hsiao-pi returned home and proclaimed himself marquis. This man, until now almost unknown to history, was to rule the state of Ch'i for the next four decades, under the name of Marquis (and later Duke) Huan.

At this time, Huan was about thirty-five years old. His father was Marquis He, who had governed Ch'i between 720 and 696BC. From Tso Ch'u-ming's account of how, in the year 650, he was offered special privileges by the Chou king 'in consideration of his seventy years', we can deduce that Huan was born around the time of his father's accession. According to Confucius, he 'had integrity, and was not crafty'.[3] By Huan's own admission, according to a later work, he had many personal failings: he was avaricious, lustful, and addicted to drink. The extravagance of his harem was to pass into legend; within his palace, it was said, he had seven market places and 700 compounds for his women.

But Huan also had considerable political skill, and he knew when to act decisively. His first recorded act was to establish his legitimacy by burying the late Marquis Hsiang with all the appropriate ceremonies. Then he called out the troops, and hurried to meet the Lu army.

Marquis Chuang of Lu was disastrously defeated at Kan-she, within the borders of Ch'i, and was lucky to escape with his life. He lost his chariot, and two officers who took the marquis's flag into their own vehicle were overtaken and killed by the Ch'i soldiers. Huan had also had a close call – during the battle, an arrow shot from close range had hit his belt buckle, but glanced off. Soon after the battle, the Ch'i army entered Lu and demanded the surrender of Prince Chiu and two of his leading followers, Shao Hu and Kuan Chung. The demoralised Marquis Chuang personally put Chiu and Shao to death, and handed over Kuan Chung to the victorious Huan.

The rule of Duke Huan

Kuan Chung already had a reputation as an extremely talented official, and he had powerful friends in Huan's entourage to speak up for him. Even so, his prospects cannot have looked good when he brazenly confessed to Huan that it was he who had shot him on the field of Kan-she. And yet Huan not only pardoned him, but appointed him as his chief minister. This proved to be the most far-reaching decision of the duke's career.

In the *Analects* of Confucius, written a couple of centuries later, the relationship between Duke Huan and Kuan Chung is treated as a prime example of the conflict between personal morality and the requirements of statecraft. The argument was put to the master that Kuan was not a man to be admired, because he had betrayed his ruler.

'Not only did he not die for Prince Chiu,' said Tzu-kung, 'but he lived to help Duke Huan, who had the prince killed.' Confucius, however, took a wider view. His verdict is worth quoting:

> Kuan Chung helped Duke Huan to become the leader of the feudal lords and to save the empire from collapse. To this day, the common people still enjoy the benefit of his acts... Surely he was not like the common man or woman who, in their petty faithfulness, commit suicide in a ditch without anyone taking any notice.[4]

Many scholars consider that Kuan Chung was the true architect of the reforms which were now put into effect in Ch'i, and that without him, Huan would never have attained the status of hegemon. In fact it is difficult from the early sources to distinguish the individual contributions of the two men. It was a partnership, and an extraordinarily fruitful one. Because Kuan Chung could rely completely on the support of his master, he was able to break the power of the feudal aristocracy within Ch'i, and to establish the first truly centralised state in China's history. The economy was boosted by state involvement in such areas as irrigation schemes, manufacture of farm tools, price controls, and the casting of coins. The salt monopoly was reinforced, and the trade expanded.

With the economic base thus strengthened, the population was reorganised, and a formal system of conscription introduced. Ch'i was divided into three provinces, each with five districts. These supplied the manpower for three armies, each consisting of five divisions. The armies were commanded respectively by the duke, the heir-apparent, and the duke's second son. Within the districts, each family had to nominate one member as a soldier, who was always on call if required for military service. Infantry in Duke Huan's day fought in solid formations – usually five deep – and were armed with spears or halberds. Bronze daggers were widely used, but swords would not become popular until the end of the sixth century. The *Tso Chuan* mentions archery only in connection with chariot-fighting, but it is usually assumed that some infantrymen also fought with the bow, as they certainly had in Shang times, and would do in later centuries. It appears that iron was known in Ch'i in the seventh century, but techniques for working the 'ugly metal', as it was known, were still imperfect, and it was not yet in use for weapons.

The new system provided a guaranteed source of troops, and enabled them to be mobilised quickly and with minimal disruption to agriculture. When compared with the haphazard methods employed in other states, this alone accounts for much of Ch'i's military predominance in the seventh century BC.

Duke Huan's first major campaign, however, was a disaster. In 683 he invaded Lu, and was routed at the battle of Ch'ang-choh. This defeat was attributed to a villager named Ts'ao Kuei, who advised the duke of Lu to stand on the defensive until the Ch'i drums had sounded the advance three times, and only then to beat his own drums and charge. The idea was that the first roll of the drums raised the morale of the soldiers, but the second produced diminishing returns, and by the third they were exhausted. This seems odd, but perhaps we should consider the volume of noise which could be produced by the simultaneous beating of hundreds of drums, accompanied no doubt by bells and gongs, and by the yelling of tens of thousands of men. Such a deafening racket could be inspiring, but it might also produce confusion and disorientation if repeated too often. In any case, the stratagem passed into folklore, and is repeated in several of the later military classics. But Huan was not to be caught out that way again.

The next year, Huan requested and received the

A bronze halberd blade from the Warring States era. Also shown is the ferrule which was originally attached to the butt of the shaft. Such weapons were widely used in the Eastern Chou period (eighth to third centuries BC), by both foot-soldiers and charioteers. (British Museum)

hand of the Princess Ke, a daughter of the Chou king, in marriage. Traditionally it was not considered appropriate for the king himself to enter into such negotiations, so he had to enlist the aid of one of the rulers of the states as a go-between. On a previous occasion when a marquis of Ch'i had married a royal princess, it had been the marquis of Lu who had been entrusted with the task. Therefore the king asked Lu to act for him again, and it was from Lu that the lady Ke travelled to meet her husband-to-be.

The hostilities between Lu and Ch'i were not permitted to interfere with ceremonial matters. In fact they were soon allowed to lapse, because Huan was becoming increasingly distracted by affairs in another neighbouring state – Sung. A certain Nan-kung Chang-wan, an officer of Sung, had been wounded and taken prisoner in a battle against Lu, then subsequently released. The duke of Sung treated him with contempt for allowing himself to be captured, so Chang-wan, who seems to have been a fairly tough character, first murdered the duke, then killed another officer who tried to intervene with his bare hands. Sung, left leaderless, dissolved into civil war. Nan-kung Chang-wan fled to a nearby state, but was handed back wrapped in a rhinoceros hide to the people of Sung, who – in the terse account of the *Tso Chuan* – 'made pickle of him'.

Hegemon

This drastic retribution, however, did not settle the disorder in Sung, and in the spring of 680 Duke Huan decided to call a meeting to resolve the conflict. This encounter took place at Pi-hang in Ch'i, and is generally regarded as marking Huan's assumption of the role of *pa*, or hegemon. Exactly what authority he had for summoning his fellow rulers like this is unclear, as no formal acknowledgement of his status is recorded until two years later. It seems that the system was as yet completely informal, and that it was Huan's ability to take the lead in organising alliances among the states which brought him the title, and not vice versa.

What mattered was that he called on the parties to attend, and they obeyed him.

The meeting itself decided nothing. The people of Sung renounced the agreement which was made, and in 679 Ch'i and its allies invaded Sung. Only at the end of that year was the country brought firmly within Duke Huan's sphere of influence. At the subsequent summit meeting, which was held at Kuen in the state of Wei, the rulers of Sung, Wei and Cheng agreed to recognise Huan's authority. Also present was the Earl of Shen, a representative of the Chou king, who brought the royal seal of approval for Huan's activities. As this was the first time that a Chou monarch had acknowledged the pre-eminence of one of the rulers, Huan is traditionally regarded as having been the first 'official' hegemon, notwithstanding the prior claims of the Earl of Cheng.

Throughout his reign, the duke was engaged in almost incessant warfare. Although he seems personally to have been more interested in domestic administration than in a military career, it was impossible in such turbulent times to maintain the alliance by diplomacy alone. Large states often had to be invaded several times in order to bring them to heel, while smaller states were frequently extinguished completely, and their territory annexed by Ch'i, or given to one of the other allies. The *Wei Liao-tzu*, a work written perhaps three centuries after Huan's death, mentions him as the first of a list of generals whose methods should be emulated: 'Who led a mass of one hundred thousand and no one under Heaven opposed him? Duke Huan.'[5] The 'hundred thousand' is doubtless a figure of speech rather than an exact statistic – the forces of the Springs and Autumns period seldom exceeded a third of that number – but the passage shows how the invincible reputation of the Ch'i armies had passed into popular memory.

Nevertheless, Huan's hegemony rested on more than naked force. Relations between states in the Springs and Autumns period were governed, at least in theory, by a complicated system of rule and ritual. Huan was happy to break specific rules when it suited him, but he eagerly exploited the idea, first introduced by the early Chou rulers, of a cultural as well as a political leadership. For example, regular ceremonies of sacrifice to the guardian spirits of the land were a feature of all states. Normally they were purely domestic affairs, but Huan used the festivities as an opportunity for a series of spectacular military reviews. Spectators from other states were made welcome, and no doubt returned home suitably impressed by Ch'i's power, as well as its hospitality. The marquis of Lu was once rebuked by a minister for going to witness the event, for it was contrary to the traditional rules for a head of state to attend the ceremonies of other countries, but there is no reason to suppose that his lapse was unique.

On another occasion, Huan defeated an army of the Jung barbarians, who had been harassing Lu, and presented the spoils to the ruler of that state. The later commentators on the *Spring and Autumn Annals* have plenty to say about this. It was considered very bad form, as only the Chou king himself was strictly entitled to receive such trophies. But in the politics of the real world, Huan's action made more sense: it not only offered some compensation to the injured party, but it was also a good opportunity to publicise the success of Ch'i arms, and perhaps subtly to put the marquis of Lu in his place.

The Jung and Ti 'barbarians' presented the most intractable of all Huan's problems. They inhabited the northern and western fringes of the Chinese world, and frequently raided as far as the Yellow River and even beyond. The state of Wei seems to have suffered especially badly from their attentions in this era. These 'barbarians' are not necessarily to be regarded as primitive savages: they had agricultural communities and even cities, and often maintained diplomatic relations with the Chinese states. Their languages may have been different, but there was in any case no standardised Chinese language at this time. A man of Ch'u and a man of Tsin would have had almost as much

difficulty in understanding each other as either would in conversing with the Jung or Ti. Some of the outsiders eventually adopted Chinese customs, and their lands came to be recognised as part of the Middle Kingdom – Chung-shan, north of the Yellow River, was one such state.

Yet to traditionalist Chinese of the seventh century BC, the Jung and Ti remained beyond the pale. They dressed differently, and they disdained even nominal allegiance to the Chou king. Kuan Chung made the distinction forcefully:

> The Ti and Jung are wolves, to whom no indulgence should be given: within the states of the Great Land (i.e., China proper), all are nearly related, and none should be abandoned...

Already in Kuan Chung's day the barbarians had been driven into marginal lands in the mountains and steppes, and poverty no doubt encouraged their propensity to raid. They appear to have fought mainly on foot, although chariots were not unknown among them. Duke Huan was forced to campaign almost incessantly against their incursions, which continued unabated as late as the 640s. Confucius went so far as to claim that these campaigns had saved Chinese civilisation, though giving the credit mainly to Huan's chief minister. 'Had it not been for Kuan Chung,' observed the sage, referring to the barbarians' outlandish mode of dress, 'we might well be wearing our hair down and folding our robes to the left.'[6]

Confucius was surely exaggerating the threat, but at times it was serious enough. In 660, the Ti overran the minor state of Hing. In the following year, they went after larger prey. At the battle of Yung they smashed the army of Wei, captured many of its great officers, then went on to storm the capital. (According to Tso Ch'u-ming, the marquis of Wei was an eccentric who was crazy about storks. He even provided the birds with official carriages. When he called out the people to fight the invaders, they joked bitterly that he should have asked the storks to defend him instead, since they had been receiving all the privileges!)

Only a few hundred of the citizens of Wei escaped this disaster. They fled, and took refuge in Sung. Duke Huan immediately sent his eldest son, Wu-k'uei, with 3000 troops and 300 chariots to try to halt the barbarians. Then, in 658, he despatched a large allied army to restore both Hing and Wei to their rightful rulers. No battle is mentioned in the context of this campaign, and it seems likely that the Ti, whose aim was usually loot and not the conquest of territory, withdrew without a fight.

As in the case of many of these expeditions, we are not told whether Huan was personally in charge of the army. The *Annals* simply refers to 'an army of Ch'i', which has led most commentators to infer that the duke was not present. After the war leading to his succession, we have no more anecdotes about his personal adventures in battle. But on at least one more occasion, Huan had been confronted with the threat of violent death.

This, paradoxically, was a result of his attempt to make a final peace with Lu, in 680. Marquis Chuang of Lu had agreed to hand over to Ch'i the city and district of Sui, and the two rulers met to seal the agreement at a place called K'o, where an altar had been set up on top of a mound. Attending Chuang was an officer named Ts'ao Mei – who according to one account was the same man as the Ts'ao Kuei whose advice had won the battle of Ch'ang-choh for Lu. However, another source – Ssu-ma Ch'ien's biography of Ts'ao Mei in his *Shih Chih* – tells us that Ts'ao's fortunes as a general had subsequently been in decline. He had fought three more battles against Ch'i, and had been defeated on each occasion. Nevertheless, he retained the favour of Marquis Chuang, who confided to him before the meeting at K'o that he regarded the terms as a humiliation. 'It were better for me to die than to live,' Chuang lamented.

So Ts'ao Mei decided upon drastic action to reverse his country's defeat. After Chuang and Huan had sworn the oath at the altar, Ts'ao suddenly pulled out a dagger and threatened Huan with it. From the somewhat staid accounts in our sources it is unclear how violent this threat was, but we are told that neither the duke nor his attendants dared to move. Perhaps we should imagine Ts'ao actually pressing the sharp bronze against Huan's throat. Then one of the Ch'i entourage – according to one source, it was Kuan Chung himself – stepped forward and asked, 'What is it you want?'

Ts'ao could not resist delivering a lecture on the iniquity of Huan's conduct. 'Ch'i is powerful,' he said, 'and Lu is weak. You and your mighty state – how deeply have you penetrated into the territory of Lu! If the walls of the Lu capital were to collapse, they would come crashing down on the very borders of Ch'i! Perhaps, my lord, you would give this some thought.' Huan, it appears, retained his composure, whatever he might have been thinking. After all, assassination attempts on heads of state were by no means rare occurrences.

Once again, Kuan Chung asked Ts'ao Mei what he wanted. Ts'ao's demand was simple: the restitution of the territory which Ch'i had just taken from Lu. Kuan looked at his master, who signalled his agreement. As soon as the covenant was sworn, Ts'ao Mei threw down his dagger and walked back to his place among the other officers, facing north in the correct ritual position for a subordinate. He was outwardly completely calm, we are told, and his voice and his features showed no sign of emotion. But he can hardly have expected to escape with his own life, let alone retain the concessions that he had extorted. For a covenant sworn under duress was not binding, and Ch'i was still the stronger power, in a position to dictate whatever terms it wished.

Yet Huan's reaction was surprising, if perhaps in a way characteristic. Ssu-ma Ch'ien's account has him proposing to repudiate the agreement, and Kuan Chung talking him out of it. Others attribute the decision to Huan alone. Either way, it was decided that Ch'i would abide by its promise, and return the territory in question to Lu. Thus, Huan argued, Lu had demonstrated the courage of its officials, and Ch'i would prove its good faith. The news of this agreement quickly spread throughout the country, and greatly enhanced Huan's prestige. As for Ts'ao Mei, he had retrieved his own reputation and regained what he had lost in his last three battles. Duke Huan held no grudge against him, and did not demand that he be punished. And so the long-standing hostility between Ch'i and Lu was brought to an end.

The alliance against Ch'u

There remained, however, a much bigger cloud on Huan's horizon. The southern state of Ch'u not only remained stubbornly outside Ch'i's sphere of influence, but repeatedly attacked the states on its northern borders in an attempt to build up its own regional hegemony. Time and again Ch'u's victims had to be relieved and defended, and retaliatory expeditions sent into the south. One of the largest was in 655, when an army consisting of contingents from Ch'i, Sung,

Wei, Cheng and Ts'ao, among others, invaded the Yangtze valley.

On this occasion, we know that both Huan and Kuan Chung were present. The self-styled 'King' Ch'ing of Ch'u sent a messenger to Huan, in effect proposing that they agree to divide the entire country between them: 'Your Lordship's place is by the northern sea, and mine is by the southern.' Kuan Chung's reply is interesting, for it shows that there had been a deliberate attempt to base Huan's position on more than brute force. It presents a case for the authority, not just of Duke Huan, but of the entire ruling house of Ch'i, based on an admittedly rather dubious historical precedent. The first ruler of Ch'i, the T'ai-kung, was supposed to have received from the

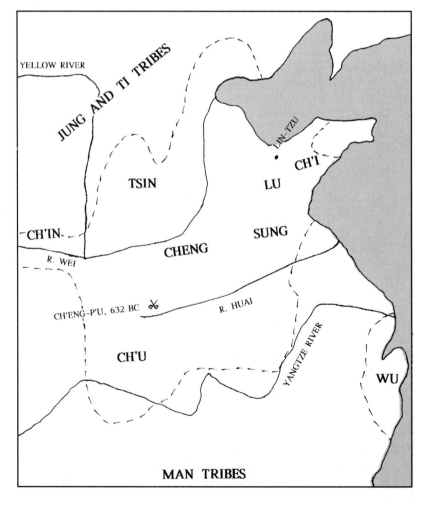

China in the time of Dukes Huan of Ch'i and Wen of Tsin. The dotted line indicates the approximate limits of literate, urban civilisation in the seventh century BC. Those peoples living outside these limits, although in some cases closely related to the Chinese themselves, were traditionally dismissed as 'barbarians'.

founder of the Chou dynasty both hegemony over the entire country, and the task of punishing any wrongdoers among the other princes. There is no reason to believe that any of this was true, but it no doubt seemed a persuasive argument at the time – although perhaps more among Ch'i's own allies than in the case of Ch'u, which notoriously had never been very amenable to Chou authority.

Kuan then went on to inform the Ch'u ruler that the allies had come to investigate the disappearance of King Ch'ao, a Chou monarch who had drowned in mysterious circumstances while campaigning in the south. As this event had taken place about three centuries earlier, it seems absurd to bring it up at this stage. But it was no doubt part of what had obviously become a policy of legitimising Huan's authority, by giving it roots in the venerated past.

On this occasion, King Ch'ing came to terms without the need for a battle. But Ch'u was not overawed for long, and Huan continued to have to organise coalitions to counter its expansionist plans. In 645 another huge army – supplied by Ch'i, Sung, Ch'en, Wei, Cheng and Ts'ao – attempted unsuccessfully to relieve the little state of Hsu, which was being victimised because of its attempts to join the northern alliance.

Elder statesman

By this time, Huan had become widely revered as a long-standing institution in his own right. In the summer of 650 he held another summit meeting, at K'uei-k'eu in Sung, at which the leaders of the northern states reaffirmed their commitment to 'banish everything contrary to good relations among us'. Also present at K'uei-k'eu was the chief minister of the Chou king, who presented to Huan a portion of the sacrifice which the king had recently offered to his own ancestors.

This in itself was a great honour. It was customary on such occasions for the recipient to kneel and show appropriate reverence, and this Huan prepared to do. But the Chou minister stopped him. 'There was another command,' he said. 'The Son of Heaven charged me to say that, in consideration of his uncle's seventy years, he confers on him an additional degree of distinction – that he shall not descend and do obeisance.' 'No,' replied Huan. 'The majesty of the king must be upheld. I dare not but descend and do obeisance'. And so, before he would receive the gift, he knelt as a loyal subject should.

In 645, the faithful Kuan Chung died. By this time, Huan had ruled in Ch'i for more than forty years, and was well into his seventies. His own imminent death, it seems, was widely expected. In the same year strange omens occurred in Sung – stones fell from the sky, and hawks were seen flying backwards. The Duke of Sung asked a visiting scholar what this foretold. The man later confessed that he did not believe in omens, and only replied bcause he did not wish to disagree with the duke. So he made what must have seemed to him a safe prediction: 'Next year Ch'i will be all in disorder.' At the end of 645, Huan summoned his fellow rulers to his fifteenth summit meeting. Sure enough, it was to be his last.

In his capital at Lin-tzu, Huan was surrounded by the leading scholars and craftsmen of the age – many of them attracted from neighbouring states by the reputation of his regime. He had three wives and countless concubines, of whom, according to the *Tso Chuan*, 'there were six who were to him as wives'. Each of these six women bore him a son, but he had no sons by any of his official consorts. This situation would inevitably lead to trouble on his death.

When Kuan Chung died, five of the six sons had approached the duke, asking to be proclaimed as his heir. One of the boys – Ch'ao, the son of a lady called Ke – had in fact already been selected, and had been sent away to live at the court of the Duke of Sung. But the eldest son, Wu-k'uei, had strong support among some of the officials. When in the winter of 643 Duke Huan finally died, his sons immediately came to blows over the succession. In the chaos, even the burial of their father's body was forgotten.

Wu-k'uei's partisans entered the palace and slaughtered everyone who was thought to be opposed to them, then set up their nominee as ruler. But Ch'ao, who had now returned to Ch'i, escaped and enlisted the help of the Duke of Sung, who invaded Ch'i on his behalf. Wu-k'uei was soon killed, but the other four sons raised their own claims against that of Ch'ao. Lu also became involved – although on the side of which candidate is unclear – and even the Ti barbarians could not resist the temptation to intervene. For several months, the prosperous state of Ch'i became a battleground. Eventually the Sung army, supported by many of the common people of Ch'i, defeated its opponents and placed Ch'ao on the throne.

The new ruler's first task was to bury Huan's body. It had been lying unburied for eight or nine months, and the state it was now in can be imagined: worms could be seen crawling under the door of the room in which it had been locked. To the Chinese, who regarded respect for one's parents – whether alive or dead – as the very foundation of civilisation, this was a scandal. That the greatest statesman of his age should have been treated in this way has been seen ever since as the clearest possible illustration of the transience of power.

Another postscript to Huan's career was almost farcical. The advantage of having a single leader who could bring the northern states together was obvious. At a conference shortly after Huan's death, in what must have been a moving speech, Marquis Mu of Ch'en 'asked that a good understanding should be cultivated between the princes of the various states, and that they should not forget the virtue and services of Huan of Ch'i'. But the personal qualities required to replace the late hegemon were in short supply.

Duke Hsiang of Sung decided that he himself was the best candidate to succeed to the position, and duly called a summit meeting. No one turned up. A few years later, in 638, Hsiang tried to take on the responsibility of defending the north whether it wanted him or not, and brought out his army to oppose a Ch'u invasion at the battle of the Hung River. The southerners were still crossing the river when the Sung troops deployed, and Hsiang was urged to attack them while they were thus divided and in disorder. He refused to take what he regarded as an unfair advantage, saying, 'Though I am but the poor representative of a fallen dynasty (i.e. the Shang), I would not sound my drums to attack an unformed host.' The Ch'u army thus deployed at its leisure, then charged and quickly routed its opponents. Hsiang's Minister of War analysed the defeat succinctly. 'Your Grace,' he told him to his face, 'does not know the rules of fighting.' It was to be another three years before Duke Huan found a worthy successor.

The exile of Ch'ung-erh

It was in the year 655 that civil strife had first broken out in the large state of Tsin, north of the Yellow River. The reigning marquis, Kuei-chu, had three sons by his first wife. After her death he had taken another consort, Le Ke, with whom he was said to be completely obsessed. This woman plotted to make her own son, a boy named He-ts'e, heir to the state. When the marquis's eldest son, Shin-sang, performed a sacrifice to his late mother and sent some of the meat as a gift to his father, Le Ke poisoned the meat in order to frame Shin-sang. Kuei-chu – no doubt as a routine precaution – gave some of the meat to a dog, which died.

Le Ke, of course, had no difficulty in persuading the besotted marquis that it was Shin-sang who had tried to poison him, and that his other two sons by his first wife, E-wu and Ch'ung-erh, were also implicated in the plot. When Kuei-chu's officials arrived to investigate the charges, Shen-sang, knowing that his father would never take his word against that of his consort, committed suicide. E-wu escaped into exile. Ch'ung-erh was in the town of P'u when they came for him. According to the *Tso Chuan*, out of respect for his father he refused to permit his followers to resist the troops, and allowed them into the town unopposed.

This is but the first of many occasions on which Ch'ung-erh's actions are ascribed by the chroniclers to the most honourable and pious motives, but as usual there is an alternative interpretation. Contrasting him with Duke Huan, Confucius said of Ch'ung-erh that he 'was crafty and lacked integrity'. Tso Ch'u-ming tells us that there had previously been something of a scandal over the fortifications of P'u, which had been shoddily built and consisted of no more than a layer of faggots between two brick walls, rather than the normal solid-rammed earth. Perhaps Ch'ung-erh simply realised that the place was indefensible. At any rate, he climbed over the wall and escaped, although his pursuers were so close behind him that their leader struck at him as he scrambled over, and cut off the sleeve of his robe.

With a handful of followers Ch'ung-erh fled to the country of the Ti barbarians. They received him hospitably, and even presented him with a captured princess as a wife. He remained with the Ti for twelve years. Meanwhile, in 650, Marquis Kuei-chu had died. He-ts'e succeeded him, as Le Ke had wished, but was soon afterwards assassinated by supporters of E-wu and Ch'ung-erh. E-wu, who as the second son of Kuei-chu was now the rightful heir, canvassed support in Ch'i and Ch'in, and the armies of these two states helped to place him on the throne. E-wu's response to these services was to ignore the promises he had made to Ch'in in return for its support, and to eliminate the partisans who had killed He-ts'e and so made his own succession possible.

No doubt wisely in such circumstances, Ch'ung-erh did not return to Tsin. In fact E-wu later had him declared an outlaw, although what crime he was supposed to have committed is unclear. In 643 he took leave of his Ti hosts and travelled to Ch'i, leaving his wife with instructions to wait for him for twenty-five years. If he was not back by then, he told her, she was free to marry again! En route to his destination, Ch'ung-erh passed through the state of Wei. This experience was not a happy one: the ruler 'treated him discourteously', as the *Tso Chuan* puts it, and he was even forced to beg for his food. On one occasion, a peasant responded by throwing a lump of earth at him. Ch'ung-erh was about to give the yokel a good flogging with his whip, until one of his companions persuaded him to treat this 'gift' of the soil of Wei as a good omen. But the young prince had a long memory. Wei had stored up trouble for the future.

In Ch'i, by contrast, his sojourn was so happy that he was reluctant to leave. He got on well with the ageing Duke Huan, who gave him another wife, and twenty four-horse chariot teams. However, his companions became impatient and, with the connivance of his new wife, they got him drunk and carried him away with them. Several passages in the *Tso Chuan* mention the favourable impression made by Ch'ung-erh's followers, including many men of ability who later served him as ministers on his return to Tsin. It seems quite likely that they were the real driving force behind the subsequent events.

Passing through several other states, whose rulers welcomed them with varying degrees of enthusiasm, the exiles came at last to Ch'u. (Ch'ing, the ruler of Ch'u, was already referring to himself as a king, relishing its implication of total independence from the house of Chou. One of his predecessors, Wu, had appropriated the title in 703, and despite the offence which this gave to the Chou monarch, no one could persuade his successors to give it up.) Ch'ing gave Ch'ung-erh a great feast, at which the king finally voiced the thought which must have been in everyone's mind. 'If you return to Tsin, and become its marquis,' he asked, 'how will you recompense my kindness to you?' Ch'ung-erh tried at first to evade the issue, replying with extravagant praise of his host's wealth. 'Feathers, hair, ivory and hides, are all produced in Your Lordship's country; those of them that come to Tsin, are but your superabundance. What then should

I have with which to recompense your kindness?'

But Ch'ing was not so easily put off. He pressed him again, and eventually Ch'ung-erh agreed to an extraordinary bargain. If Ch'u helped him to take the throne of Tsin, and if ever in the future the two states should go to war with each other, he would withdraw three times in front of the Ch'u armies. Each stage of the retreat would cover thirty *li* (i.e. about ten miles, or roughly a day's march). 'If then I do not receive your commands,' the young prince continued in the high-flown language typical of the age, 'with my whip and my bow in my left hand, and my quiver and my bow-case on my right, I will manoeuvre with Your Lordship.'

Ch'ing was impressed. One of his officers, a man named Tzu-yu, suggested that he should put Ch'ung-erh to death for his apparent insolence, but the king refused. 'The prince of Tsin,' he said, 'is a grand character, and yet distinguished by moderation, highly accomplished and courteous. His followers are severely grave and yet generous, loyal and of untiring ability. The present marquis of Tsin has none who are attached to him... When Heaven intends to prosper a man, who can stop him?'

In the event, it was not Ch'u to which Ch'ung-erh was to owe his return to Tsin. Earl Mu of Ch'in, who was Tsin's neighbour on the west, had lost patience with E-wu and was only too happy to see him deposed, Knowing this, King Ch'ing provided his guest with an escort and sent him on to Ch'in. Here, for an instant, we see a less savoury side of the young hero. He was presented with five noblewomen to attend him, including the earl's daughter. For some reason which we are not told, he behaved with extraordinary arrogance towards this lady. He ordered her to pour out some water from a goblet so that he could wash, and then imperiously waved her away, splashing her with water from his wet hands. She was so upset by this discourtesy that Ch'ung-erh had to humble himself publicly to undo the damage, 'putting off his robes', as the *Tso*

Chuan tells us, 'and assuming the garb of a prisoner'.

Return to Tsin

This gaffe, nevertheless, did no permanent harm to Ch'ung-erh's cause. In the spring of 635, a Ch'in army took the field with the aim of placing him on the throne of Tsin. The operation was not seriously opposed. When the Tsin troops came out to meet the invaders, their commanders were persuaded to meet with Ch'ung-erh for negotiations. Evidently E-wu's rule had become very unpopular, because as soon as the talks began, his army deserted to his brother en masse. Ch'ung-erh entered the marquis's palace in triumph, captured E-wu, and had him put to death. Then he set himself up as marquis. His throne name was Wen, and it is as Duke Wen that he has become known to posterity.

It was time for the new ruler to settle old scores. One of the first suppliants to arrive at the palace was a certain P'e – the man who had cut off his sleeve during his escape from P'u, nineteen years earlier. The new ruler initially sent him away, commenting that although P'e could not be blamed for having carried out his then ruler's instructions, he did not have to be so zealous about it.

P'e sent back a detailed justification of his actions, explaining that 'It is the ancient rule that, when an officer receives his ruler's commands, he think of no other individual'. He reminded Wen of his friend Duke Huan of Ch'i, who had forgiven Kuan Chung for trying to kill him, and pointed out that, if the new ruler dismissed everyone who had served his predecessors well, he would have few good officials left. Wen then agreed to see him – an act of magnanimity which brought its own reward. P'e was able to give him details of a plot by E-wu's followers to burn the palace and assassinate him. So when, on the appointed day, the plotters burst in under cover of the flames, they found their quarry gone. They fled, only to be arrested by Ch'in soldiers and executed.

During the events that led to his accession, Ch'ung-erh seems to have formed an unfavourable impression of the battleworthiness of the Tsin troops. For a year he devoted himself to training them and fostering their loyalty, before testing them in a limited campaign against the small neighbouring state of Yuen. Even then his minister Tze-fan considered that they were not yet ready for major operations, and it was another year before they took the field again.

War broke out between Tsin and Ch'u in the spring of 632. The circumstances recall the complex system of interlocking alliances which amplified a minor quarrel in the Balkans into global disaster in 1914. After his defeat at the Hung River, Duke Hsiang of Sung had transferred his allegiance to Ch'u. However, his successor, Duke Ch'ing, had been favourably impressed by Ch'ung-erh when the exiled prince had passed through the state on his travels, and had recently been inclining towards Tsin. The king of Ch'u now sent an army to bring Sung to heel, and Ch'ing naturally appealed to Duke Wen for help.

Tsin proposed to retaliate by attacking the minor pro-Ch'u state of Ts'ao, but this strategy required the troops to pass through territory controlled by Wei. This Wei's ruler refused to allow. Wen, who of course already had reason to dislike the people of Wei, quickly struck with overwhelming force, and overran the country. He then added Ts'ao to his conquests without meeting any further resistance.

At the same time, Tsin was also active on the diplomatic front. The states of Ch'i and Ch'in were known to be unhappy at the prospect of Ch'u extending its power into the Yellow River plain, but had so far been reluctant to join a military alliance. Duke Wen persuaded the Duke of Sung to send gifts to the two rulers, and to ask them to intercede with Ch'u on his behalf. He then leaked to Ch'u the news that he was proposing to dismember Wei and Ts'ao, and give parts of their territory to Sung. So infuriated was King Ch'ing by this that he angrily dismissed the attempts of Ch'i and Ch'in to mediate. This did the trick. Soon contingents from both these states were marching to join Tsin's coalition.

At the same time, a great Ch'u army was marching northwards. In command was Tzu-yu – the same man who many years before had urged his master to put Ch'ung-erh to death. It appears that when he realised the strength of the alliance against him, Ch'ing sent orders to Tzu-yu to abandon Sung, rather than let himself be drawn into a battle. But either Tzu-yu was a glory-seeker, or else he had some personal score to settle with Wen, because he responded by sending back a message begging the king for permission to fight. At this critical point Ch'ing chose the worst of both worlds: he gave Tzu-yu his head, but sent him only a handful of reinforcements, not wishing to risk losing more of his men.

The Ch'eng-p'u campaign

The clash came on the border of Wei and Ts'ao, south of the Yellow River. Just as he had promised King Ch'ing, Wen withdrew three times in front of Tzu-yu, ignoring the protests of his officers. The latter argued that it was undignified for a ruler to retreat before a mere subject – and that furthermore the Ch'u troops were already tired by their long march, and could be easily defeated.

The minister Tze-fan explained his master's reasoning: 'It is the goodness of its cause which makes an army strong... If the marquis showed ingratitude ... we should be in the wrong and Ch'u would be in the right.' This is traditionally put forward as a prime example of the chivalrous approach to warfare which is supposed to have characterised the age. However, it could also be interpreted as another example of Wen's famous 'craftiness'. We are not told when the allied contingents arrived to link up with the Tsin army, but they must have had a long distance to travel, and bringing together a number of independent forces at the right moment was a tricky manoeuvre, given the communications of the period. The few days'

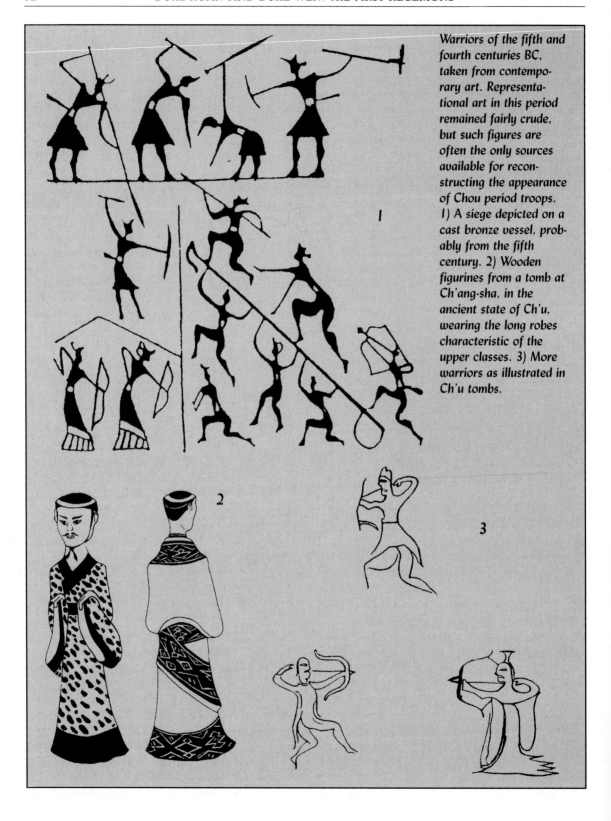

Warriors of the fifth and fourth centuries BC, taken from contemporary art. Representational art in this period remained fairly crude, but such figures are often the only sources available for reconstructing the appearance of Chou period troops. 1) A siege depicted on a cast bronze vessel, probably from the fifth century. 2) Wooden figurines from a tomb at Ch'ang-sha, in the ancient state of Ch'u, wearing the long robes characteristic of the upper classes. 3) More warriors as illustrated in Ch'u tombs.

delay could well have been calculated to give them the extra time they needed to reach the scene of operations.

Whatever the real motives behind all this manoeuvring, the alliance was fully in place when the northern army finally halted at Ch'eng-p'u. There were contingents from Tsin, Ch'i, Ch'in and Sung, under the overall command of Duke Wen. The latter is supposed to have been persuaded to fight at last by a prophetic dream, but given his record there is no reason to believe that more rational considerations were not paramount. Tzu-yu, who had followed up his enemy's withdrawal closely despite his instructions, sent a message to the Tsin camp, couched in the customary chivalrous terms:

> 'Let me have a game with your men. Your Lordship can lean on the crossboard of your carriage and look on, and I will be there to see you.'

Wen sent back this reply:

> 'I have heard your commands. I dared not to forget the kindness of the lord of Ch'u, and therefore I am here. I retired before his officer; should I have dared to oppose himself? Since I have not received your orders not to fight, I will trouble you, Sir, to say to your leaders, "Prepare your chariots; see reverently to your prince's business." Tomorrow morning I will see you.'[7]

Unfortunately, we have no details of the relative strengths of the opposing armies, although it seems certain that the Tsin alliance was by far the stronger. We do know that Tsin fielded 700 chariots, many of which were deployed on the left flank under an officer named Seu Shin. These immediately charged the Ch'u right and shattered it, driving their opponents from the field. Meanwhile, the Tsin right appeared to fall back in disorder, concealed behind a screen of chariots dragging branches behind them to raise dust. Tzu-yu was convinced by the ruse, and sent his left wing chasing after their opponents in a wild charge. They rushed straight into Wen's trap. The charging Ch'u chariots were struck in the flank by the main Tsin force, while those who had been retiring in front of them turned around and completed their envelopment.

With both wings of his army gone, Tzu-yu realised that his cause was lost. He rallied the infantry in the centre, and attempted to lead them away intact. Few can have succeeded in escaping. The victors captured at least a hundred chariots and a thousand foot soldiers – these were the numbers that Wen presented to the Chou king after the battle. The left ears of the Ch'u dead were cut off and taken back to Tsin, to be displayed in the temple there. The Tsin troops and their allies also captured the Ch'u camp, with supplies of food for three days. Tzu-yu subsequently died in circumstances which are unclear, but he probably committed suicide.

Chief of the princes

In the aftermath of the battle, the Tsin ruler went to see the Chou king, and presented his captives. In return the king laid on a feast for him, and bestowed on him the trappings of 'chief of the princes' – in other words hegemon, in the footsteps of Duke Huan, although Huan had never enjoyed an official inauguration on this scale. The gifts which the new hegemon received included a set of robes, two bows – one red and one black – and 300 lifeguards to attend him. The king then formally appointed Wen as his protector, concluding with the words: 'Reverently discharge the king's commands, so as to give tranquillity to the states in every quarter, and drive far away all who are ill-affected to the king.'

In accordance with protocol, Wen three times declined the honour, but eventually agreed to accept, saying: 'I, Ch'ung-erh, venture twice to do obeisance, with my head bowed to the earth – and so do I receive and will maintain the great, distinguished, excellent charge of the Son of Heaven.' The appointment was later confirmed in writing by the king's ministers. Of course, this ritual could not disguise the real political situation. The duke had attained his position not by the grace of the king, but by force of arms. He was now the real power in northern China, and the Chou monarch could do no more than acknowledge this fact.

In his campaigns as ruler of Tsin, Wen was always greatly concerned about the public impression he was making. On occasion he displayed a scrupulous attitude which was much admired by the chroniclers. The *Tso Chuan* tells, for example, of his conduct at the siege of Yuen. As his men had only three days' provisions left, he announced that if the city did not surrender within the three days, he would raise the siege and return home. On the third day, however, his spies reported that the garrison was planning to surrender on the following evening. Naturally, his officers suggested that he should wait one more day, but he refused. 'Good faith,' he said, 'is the precious jewel of a state, and what the people depend upon. If I get Yuen and lose my good faith ... my loss would be much greater than my gain.' So he ordered the withdrawal, as he had promised. Before the Tsin army had retired more than a day's march, a delegation from Yuen – suitably impressed – caught up with it, and offered their surrender.

Wen could now devote his energies to consolidating the alliance of the northern states that he had brought about. He convened a summit meeting at Wan – at which, among others, were representatives from Ch'i, Sung and Ch'in. This, incidentally, was the first time that the still semi-barbarous Ch'in had been recognised as fully belonging to the Chinese diplomatic community. No one present at Wan could have foreseen the consequences, but his invitation to Ch'in to send troops 'east of the passes' into central China was ultimately to be Duke Wen's most lasting – and most unwelcome – legacy.

Both Wei and Ts'ao now swore allegiance to Tsin, and their rulers were restored. Outright annexation, which was to become the normal policy of expansionist states in subsequent centuries, was not yet on Tsin's agenda. As far as the northern borders of Ch'u itself, the minor states of central China

also flocked to join the alliance. Only the tiny city-state of Hsu remained obdurate, and towards the end of 632 Tsin led its allies to besiege it.

It was at this point that things began to go wrong for Wen. He fell ill during the siege, which seems not to have been prosecuted with much vigour. Two years later, Hsu was still holding out. The duke therefore decided instead to attack Cheng, whose earl was trying to play off Tsin and Ch'u against each other. While he was preoccupied with making plans for Cheng, the Ti barbarians invaded Ch'i. Duke Huan had cemented his position as hegemon by protecting the other states from such incursions, but Wen was too busy to do anything about this one. By the time he moved against Cheng in 629, the Ch'i troops had returned home to defend their country, and only a detachment under Earl Mu of Ch'in remained behind to support the Tsin army.

Earl Wan of Cheng was a wily old politician, who had maintained his country's independence for more than forty years – although surrounded by many stronger rivals – by his astute diplomacy. In this he was more than a match for Duke Wen. Seeing the combined forces of Tsin and Ch'in encamped outside his walls, Wan had a messenger let down from the walls at night by a rope. This man went secretly to the Ch'in camp, and gained an audience with Earl Mu.

'If the ruin of Cheng were to benefit Your Lordship,' the messenger told him, 'I should not dare to speak to you.' But he pointed out that Ch'in was separated from Cheng by the territory of Tsin, and so could hardly exert much control over any cities which it might gain at Cheng's expense. On the other hand, a well-disposed and free Cheng could be a useful supply base for Ch'in troops when they ventured east. Besides, the emissary went on, it was well known that Ch'ung-erh had double-crossed Mu before: Ch'in had still not received the lands that it had been promised in return for helping him to power. The messenger concluded:

'Tsin is insatiable. Having made Cheng its boundary on the east, it will go on to want to enlarge its border on the west. And how will it be able to do that except by taking territory from Ch'in? To diminish Ch'in in order to advantage Tsin – this is a matter for Your Lordship to think about.'

Earl Mu did indeed think about it. Without informing his ally, he made a separate treaty with Cheng, and then marched off home. Wen had no choice but to raise the siege and do likewise. Clearly this was a humiliation for the 'leader of the states', but we are not told of his reaction. In 629 the duke is described as holding a great review of all his troops, whom he reorganised into five armies in place of the original three. This, we are told, was 'to resist the Ti', but nothing is said of any campaign against them. Instead it was an expedition from Wei, provoked by an attack on its capital, which struck back at the Ti, invaded their homeland, and finally forced them to sue for peace.

Duke Wen's last recorded act, early in 628, was to make a formal peace with Ch'u. The next entry in the *Spring and Autumn Annals* records simply: 'In winter, in the twelfth month ... Ch'ung-erh, marquis of Tsin, died.' This was fairly sudden, and seems to have been unexpected, but no explanation is given. (The cause of his death, of course, may well have been the illness that he contracted while besieging Hsu.) But despite the brevity of his reign, Wen is remembered in Chinese tradition as almost the equal of his illustrious predecessor, Duke Huan.

The *Tso Chuan* has a weird postscript to Ch'ung-erh's life. As his coffin was being placed in the ancestral temple, a noise was heard coming from it, which was described as being like the bellowing of a bull. A diviner named Yen listened to the sound for a while, and then announced to the assembled officials: 'His Lordship is charging us about a great affair. There will be an army of the west passing by us; we shall smite it, and obtain a great victory.'

There was indeed a great army approaching secretly from the west. It had been despatched by Earl Mu of Ch'in, and its mission was to seize Cheng by a *coup de main*. Mu had remained in contact with disaffected elements in Cheng, who had promised to open the gates of the capital to his troops. We are not told the size of the Ch'in army, but it must have been very large. It passed by the gates of Lo-yang, where it infuriated the Chou king by its disregard for the usual forms of respect: the Ch'in officers merely jumped down from their chariots, took off their helmets, then remounted and drove on without stopping. Next, the Ch'in warriors came to the little state of Hua, which they casually destroyed.

By this time, however, Cheng had been warned of the danger, and realising that surprise had been lost, the Ch'in commanders decided to turn back. Waiting for them at a spot known as Hsiao, where the road ran between two ridges, was the new marquis of Tsin, Ch'ung-erh's son Hsiang, with the battle-hardened army which his father had trained. The Tsin army had been raised in such haste that Hsiang was still wearing his black-stained mourning robes.

There was some dispute among the Tsin ministers over what should be done, but it was clearly Duke Wen's last wish that they should avenge the humiliation that he had suffered at the siege of Cheng. 'I have heard that if you let your enemy go a single day,' said one, 'you are preparing the misfortunes of several generations.'

So, with Hsiang at their head, the Tsin troops swept over the ridges, and charged into the unsuspecting men of Ch'in. The latter were taken by surprise, and completely defeated. Their three principal generals were carried back as prisoners to Tsin. Ch'ung-erh had repaid the last of his debts, even from beyond the grave.

3

SCHOLARS, PHILOSOPHERS AND SOLDIERS

The era of the *Spring and Autumn Annals*, with the subsequent Warring States period – roughly from the seventh to the third centuries BC – together constituted one of the most intellectually exciting periods in world history. In every sphere of human activity, the Chinese were breaking new ground, speculating and experimenting on a massive scale in fields as diverse as philosophy, government, technology and art. Far from being a deliberately planned programme, this progress was so successful precisely because it was spontaneous. The intellectual ferment of these centuries has often been contrasted with the more restrictive climate that sometimes prevailed in subsequent ages – especially under the later empire, when a centralised government was able to exert closer control over ideology.

In fact, one of the most important factors that encouraged the flowering of ideas was the political fragmentation of the period. With dozens of competing states and rulers, each having their own traditions and theories of government, no single ideology could become sufficiently powerful to suppress the others. And yet at the same time, there was enough cultural unity – in language and a shared historical heritage, for example – to permit extensive cross-fertilisation. This is a phenomenon that is also familiar from other times and countries which have become famous for their originality: Classical Greece and Renaissance Italy are among the most obvious examples.

The feverish atmosphere of the times inevitably had its

Lao Tzu, the traditional founder of Taoism, as depicted in a medieval portrait. This humble old man riding on a water buffalo is surely the antithesis of militarism, but Taoist ideas had a fundamental influence, via Sun Tzu and his followers, on Chinese military thought.

impact on the conduct of war. During this period, the scale and ferocity of conflict increased dramatically. Already in Duke Huan's day it was becoming acceptable for the larger states to expand at the expense of their less powerful neighbours, although the outright destruction of an eminent ruling house was still looked upon with disfavour. By the early fifth century, no one had any compunction about exterminating even long-established and respected states whenever the opportunity offered, and around this time some of the leading players of the Springs and Autumns period start to disappear from the record. Ch'en was overthrown by Ch'u in 478; in 473, the south-eastern state of Wu fell to Yueh; twenty years later mighty Tsin collapsed, split by feuding clans into the three successor states of Han, Wei and Chao. And in the 390s, even the ancient and prestigious lands of Lu and Cheng fell victims to the greed of their neighbours, and lost their independence forever.

Naturally the rulers of the remaining states were well aware that the same thing could happen to them, and they were willing to employ every possible means to gain an advantage over their current or potential enemies. Therefore there were always good prospects of employment for the growing class of *shih*, or gentlemen-scholars, who wandered from one court to another, offering advice on matters of government. This advice, however, did not constitute a single coherent body of knowledge. The theories on offer were diverse and often mutually contradictory, derived from one of several contemporary schools of philosophy, or from the alleged practices of a semi-mythical ancient dynasty such as the Hsia. The wandering sage with his store of antique wisdom, searching for a pupil worthy of receiving it, became a stock figure of the age, but few of the *shih* actually lived up to this image. Themselves products of the unprincipled atmosphere of the Warring States, they did not hesitate to leave their countries of origin in order to serve rival states, or even to work for two or more at a time, playing them off against one another, or selling their ideas to the highest bidder.

Inevitably, military affairs were prominent among the concerns of these men and their employers. As the opening paragraph of Sun Tzu's *Art of War* remarks: 'War is a matter of vital importance to the state; the province of life or death; the road to survival or ruin. It is mandatory that it be thoroughly studied.' And as might be expected, the ideas that were circulating on the conduct of warfare reflected the diversity of the Chinese cultural environment as a whole.

The Taoist influence

The most famous of all Chinese military writers, Sun Tzu, echoes many of the themes of Lao Tzu's *Tao Te Ching*, the first classic of Taoism – a work which probably dates from about the fifth century BC. Even the imagery in the two works is often the same – for instance the use of water as a metaphor for strength hidden behind outward weakness. Just as Lao Tzu counsels the prospective ruler, Sun Tzu advises the general how to manipulate the hearts and minds of his troops without them being aware of it. Even an enemy can often be controlled in the same way, and his strengths, if carried to excess, can be turned against him. For Sun Tzu, as for the Taoists, things are not always what they seem. Subtlety, deception, and the interplay of opposites are the keys to his military thought.

Thus Lao Tzu:

I have heard it said that one who excels in safeguarding his own life does not meet with rhinoceros or tiger when travelling on land, nor is he touched by weapons when charging into an army. There is nowhere for the rhinoceros to pitch its horn; there is nowhere for the tiger to place its claws; there is nowhere for the weapon to lodge its blade.[1]

Compare Sun Tzu's description of the attributes of the ideal commander:

Against those skilled in attack, an enemy does not know where to defend; against the experts in defence, the enemy does not know where to attack... Subtle and insubstantial, the expert leaves no trace; divinely mysterious, he is inaudible. Thus he is master of his enemy's fate.[2]

For Lao Tzu's disciples, the secret of success in any enterprise is the *Tao*, the 'Way' – impossible to define or describe, predating and underpinning morality, law, ritual and all the other supposed fundamentals of human society. Sun Pin, who as we shall see was perhaps the most eminent practitioner of the theories of Sun Tzu, refers explicitly in his own work to the '*Tao* of warfare'. Naturally, this approach does not lend itself to rigidly prescribed formations and tactics, and in general these are not to be found in the writings of Sun Tzu's school. The master himself states :

Therefore, when I have won a victory I do not repeat my tactics but respond to circumstances in an infinite variety of ways... And as water has no constant form, there are in war no constant conditions. Thus, one able to gain the victory by modifying his tactics in accordance with the enemy situation may be said to be divine.[3]

Another strategist of the Warring States period, Wu Ch'i, is perhaps second only to Sun Tzu in the reputation that he has enjoyed down to modern times. Wu Ch'i flourished during the first two decades of the fourth century, at various times serving the rulers of the states of Lu, Wei and Ch'u. His book on the *Art of War* also survives, and has many elements in common with Sun Tzu. Once again, its main themes are the need to understand and manipulate one's enemies, and the fundamental role of deception.

The Mohists

Another philosopher whose influence on the conduct of war was considerable in his own day, if less so in later eras, was Mo Tzu, who died in 381BC. His followers were known as Mohists. Mo Tzu condemned aggressive war altogether, denouncing it as nothing more than robbery and murder on a large scale. He was far from being a conventional pacifist, however, and in his writings he expounded a number of practical techniques that the victims of aggression could use to defend themselves. During the wars of the fourth century BC, groups of Mohists often went to the rescue of small states which were being victimised by larger ones.

On one occasion, Mo Tzu himself is said to have deterred an attacker by demonstrating the devices that he would if necessary make available to the victim. These included pulleys and counterweight engines for defending city walls, methods for detecting besiegers' tunnels by sound location, and poisonous smoke which could be blown down the tunnels to suffocate the attackers.

The Confucians

Rather less practical was Hsun Tzu, a third-century follower of Confucius, who was a believer in the innate benevolence of human beings. Hsun Tzu strongly disapproved of the duplicity inherent in the Taoist approach. Instead, he tried unsuccessfully to apply his master's love of ritual and correct behaviour to the brutal business of war. In stark contrast to Sun Tzu, he insisted that 'the armies of the benevolent man cannot use deceit'. Hsun Tzu considered that if a ruler was sufficiently enlightened, and treated the common people with benevolence, the enemy's soldiers would learn of his reputation and would refuse to fight against him. According to the Confucian view of history, this had been the basis on which the early Chou kings had established their authority.

Not surprisingly, the leaders of the Warring States, struggling to survive in the chaos left by the collapse of Chou rule, were less than impressed by this argument. A record survives of an extraordinary debate at the court of King Hsiao-ch'eng of Chao in 260, when the all-conquering armies of Ch'in were almost at the gates. Hsun Tzu expounded his usual 'hearts and minds' approach, but was opposed by a general of the Sun Tzu school named Lin Wu-chun. Lin advocated hiring mercenaries, and employing generals with a sound knowledge of strategy. This in itself would be a deterrent to Ch'in. 'When Sun and Wu (i.e. Sun Tzu and Wu Ch'i) led armies,' he said, 'they had no enemies in the whole country.' In the event, the entire debate proved to be a waste of time. Ch'in gave Hsiao-ch'eng no opportunity to put either policy into effect, and Chao suffered a disastrous defeat, from which it never recovered.

The Legalists

More popular, with statesmen, both at the time and later, were the ideas of the Legalists, whose name is derived from their uncompromising insistence on the rule of law. They were, in fact, early totalitarians, who had little interest in individual morality, and who saw their sole aim as the strengthening of the state. This was to be achieved through efficient, centralised administration, coupled with an inflexible and utterly ruthless system of rewards and punishments. This school of thought had its roots in the reforms of men such as Kuan Chung in Ch'i, and Sheng Pu-hai, who was chief minister of the state of Han in the early fourth century BC. Its most famous exponent, however, was Shang Yang, or Lord Shang, who between about 350 and 338BC reorganised the state of Ch'in along Legalist lines. The terrible results of this experiment are explored in Chapter 6.

Another Legalist, Han Fei-tzu, whose career is discussed in the same chapter, was an outspoken critic of the school of Sun Tzu. In his book entitled *Five Vermin*, Han includes among the 'enemies of the state' those people who kept copies of the works of Sun Tzu and Wu Ch'i. He advocated destroying the offending books, and abandoning the strategies of their authors – the reason being, presumably, that by discussing ways in which skill could overcome numerical strength, they might enable dissident groups to resist the armies of the all-powerful state in which Han Fei-tzu was such a passionate believer.

After the Warring States period, the teachings of the classical philosophers enjoyed varying fortunes. Mohism virtually disappeared. Taoism declined into a collection of popular superstitions concerned with such matters as the prolongation of life. Sun Tzu in particular continued to be revered, but the philosophical basis of his ideas was increasingly obscured. The Legalists enjoyed a brief period of unchallenged supremacy with the reunification of China by the Ch'in dynasty in 221BC, but the savagery of Ch'in rule helped to discredit them. The institutions of the succeeding Han dynasty still owed much to Legalist thought, but over later centuries it was the Confucians whose influence came to dominate. From the beginning of the seventh century AD, the Sui and T'ang dynasties began to institute the civil service system, in which government office was reserved for those who passed examinations in the Confucian classics. Ultimately, this victory of the Confucianists was one of the factors behind the decreasing status of the military in China.

4

SUN PIN: THE TAO OF WARFARE

'Know the enemy and know yourself; in a hundred battles you will never be in peril.'
Sun Tzu

The Warring States

According to his biography in Ssu-ma Ch'ien's *Shih Chih*, Sun Pin was a descendant of Sun Tzu, the author of the classic *Sun Tzu Ping Fa*, or *Master Sun's Art of War*. Sun Tzu, however, is an elusive figure who – despite the fame of his book and the plethora of later traditions concerning his life – is difficult to pin down to any historical time or place. Both Ssu-ma Ch'ien, and the late and not very credible *Spring and Autumn Annals of Wu and Yueh*, identify him with a certain Sun Wu, who is said to have served the king of the south-eastern state of Wu, around the end of the sixth century BC.

It is known, however, that the family of Sun Pin was a branch of the aristocracy of Ch'i. The Suns were apparently related to the ruling house of Ch'i, and had a long tradition of involvement in the military affairs of that state. It is of course by no means impossible that one of their number took employment in Wu, nor that he incorporated some of the accumulated experience of the Sun clan into the book that bears his name. The possible influence of Sun Tzu on Sun Pin's military thought – and vice versa – will be discussed below.

So we can imagine the young Sun Pin being brought up with stories of the achievements of his forebears, and perhaps being groomed from an early age for a military career. A popular tradition has it that he studied military strategy under the legendary expert Kuei Ku-tzu, who recognised him as an exceptional pupil, and so entrusted him with the secrets of his ancestor's *Sun Tzu Ping Fa*. Unfortunately, our sources tell us almost nothing else about his early life. Even his original name is unknown: 'Pin' is a nick-

name that he must have received later, as we shall see. Sun was born in Ch'i, in what is now the western part of Shantung province, at some time during the early fourth century BC. This places him in the middle of the Warring States era, and in a region that saw some of the most extensive fighting of that troubled age.

The descendants of Duke Huan had succeeded in retaining power in Ch'i until 390BC. In that year the reigning marquis, K'ang, was overthrown in a coup led by a nobleman named T'ien Ho, who was the leader of the T'ien clan. This family came originally from Ch'en, but had for many years been a leading force in the politics of Ch'i. In 386 T'ien Ho took the title of marquis, and later his successor, Wei, made himself king. (The date of Wei's accession is not certain, as two different sources give inconsistent dates. According to the data in the *Bamboo Annals*, which seems the most plausible, King Wei reigned between 357 and 320BC. This would place the whole of Sun Pin's recorded military career in his reign. Ssu-ma Ch'ien's chronology, however, implies that Wei died in 343, two years before Sun Pin's final victory at Ma Ling.)

Under the rule of the T'ien family, Ch'i embarked on a series of largely unsuccessful wars with the neighbouring states of Wei and Yen, which ended in the loss of much territory. Western Shantung was traversed by invading armies on several occasions during the 370s and 360s BC, and it is inconceivable that the young Sun Pin's life was unaffected by these upheavals. Like many of his contemporaries, no doubt, he stood at the roadside with his family to watch the great armies passing by, and perhaps overheard his elders lamenting that great Ch'i had been reduced to such a state.

Officer of Wei

And yet when we first hear of Sun Pin in public life, it is in the service of the ruler of a rival state – King Hui of Wei. As we have seen, there was nothing unusual at that time in a man seeking employment outside his homeland. Perhaps – his family background notwithstanding – there was no suitable vacancy for him in the Ch'i army. When he arrived in Wei, Sun discovered that among King Hui's generals was a man named P'ang Chuan, who had apparently studied with him under Kuei Ku-tzu. It is possible that P'ang had helped Sun to obtain the appointment in Wei, although in view of subsequent relations between the two men this would appear unlikely.

At this point Ssu-ma Ch'ien takes up the story. On his arrival in Wei, Sun was interviewed by P'ang Chuan, who soon realised that the newcomer knew far more about the military art than he did himself. Fearing for his own position, P'ang managed somehow to have Sun framed for some imaginary crime. As a result of P'ang's false accusations, Sun was arrested, put on trial and found guilty. Exactly what he was supposed to have done we are not told, but it must have been fairly serious. He was sentenced to one of the lesser degrees of mutilation, which involved having his face branded and his feet cut off. This cruel sentence was duly carried out, and in accordance with the usual procedure for mutilated convicts, Sun was also banished from the court.

It may reasonably be wondered why, if Sun was so much of a threat, P'ang Chuan had not simply arranged to have him executed. Other degrees of punishment involved decapitation or castration. The latter was virtually equivalent to a death sentence, since the victim was expected to commit suicide rather than endure the disgrace of being unable to perpetuate his family. One modern authority speculates that P'ang intended to put the blame for the injustice on to someone else, and to present himself as the man who had saved Sun from the death penalty, so earning his gratitude. Then, with the young military genius effectively housebound and out of sight of the king, P'ang could benefit from his expert advice, and gain all the credit for the subsequent victories.

Whatever the truth about P'ang's motives, his malicious plan backfired drastically. Sun Pin seems to have been in no doubt about who was responsible for his sufferings. One day an emissary from Ch'i arrived in Wei, and Sun managed to get a message to him. The ambassador went to see his fellow-countryman, immediately recognised him as a man of exceptional talent, and smuggled him into his own enclosed carriage. When he returned to Ch'i, Sun secretly went with him. It may be assumed that it was about this time that he received the name that would thereafter distinguish him from the other members of the Sun family living in Ch'i – Sun Pin, or 'Sun the Footless'.

General of Ch'i

At King Wei's capital – the same Lin-tzu where Duke Huan had held his court – Sun Pin was introduced to T'ien Chi, the supreme commander of the Ch'i army. The general was just as impressed with Sun as the ambassador had been, and took him into his entourage. T'ien Chi was a keen gambler, who liked to race his horses against those of the royal princes, but had so far enjoyed only moderate success. One day, he took Sun along to a race meeting. The exact form of this event is not clear from the sources. We are not told whether the horses were ridden, or raced in teams pulling chariots, but at any rate there seem to have been three separate events – one for the best horses, one for the second-best, and the third for the slowest. Sun Pin, watching the races, realised that there was little to choose between the quality of the horses in each category. So he took T'ien Chi aside and said, 'Bet again, my lord, for I can make you win.'

Such was T'ien's confidence in Sun that he did not even ask for an explanation. He

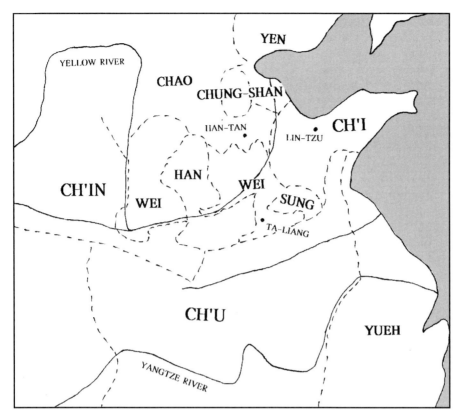

China in Sun Pin's day, c.350BC, showing the approximate boundaries of the rival states. Note especially the awkward strategic situation of Wei and Han, which would inevitably bring them into conflict.

immediately wagered a thousand gold pieces on the next set of races, on a 'best of three' basis. Sun then told him, 'Put your slowest team of horses against their best; your best team against their middle one; and your middle team against their lowest one.' This seems rather underhand, but as no one appears to have thought of the scheme before, there was presumably no regulation specifically forbidding it. T'ien Chi lost badly in the first race, but won the last two easily, and so came out on top overall.

When he went to collect his winnings he presented Sun Pin to King Wei, who questioned him further. Once again, Sun made a very favourable impression – so much so that the king wanted to promote him on the spot to the post of commander-in-chief of the Ch'i armed forces. Sun, however, declined, on the grounds that he was physically unfit, and in any case was still technically a convict, which should disqualify him from office. No doubt

he was also understandably reluctant to upset his mentor, T'ien Chi.

So in the event, when war broke out with the state of Wei soon afterwards, T'ien was given the supreme command, with Sun in the informal position of chief of staff. It appears that Sun's lack of mobility was no real obstacle to the performance of his duties. When on campaign, he travelled in a screened horse-drawn carriage, like any other important official of the day. If necessary, he could also have made use of a litter carried by soldiers.

The Kuei-ling campaign

Wei was one of the three states which had been formed in the fifth century BC, from the breakup of the old northern power of Tsin. Under the rule of Marquis Wen (434–396BC), assisted by the famous strategist Wu Ch'i, Wei had become the dominant military power in the region. However, its fortunes had since suffered a relative decline. Wei's strategic situation was particularly difficult. The chaotic collapse of Tsin had left Wei and Han with long, convoluted and quite indefensible borders, whose complexity is best explained by reference to the map (page 42). A narrow corridor of Han territory cut Wei into two parts, while Han was similarly almost bisected by Wei. This made communication, and especially military deployments, very difficult for both parties. It was thus inevitable that Wei and Han would become either the very closest of allies, or the deadliest of enemies.

Sun Pin's first employer, King Hui, who ascended the throne of Wei in 370BC, chose enmity. In fact he would have been well advised to seek good relations with his nearest neighbours, as he was already threatened on three sides by other powers. To the east was Ch'i, which could always be relied on to intervene in order to prevent the reunification of its ancient rival, Tsin. To the south, the Yangtze valley state of Ch'u was again expanding aggressively in these years, and was now beginning to impinge on Wei's borders. And from the west, the warlike frontier state of Ch'in – until now despised by the more sophisticated peoples of central China – was turning eastwards under the direction of its ruthless chief minister, Lord Shang.

In 354BC, war broke out between Wei and the third of the Tsin successor states, Chao. Chao had defied Wei's claim to regional hegemony by annexing one of Wei's small client states, and also by entering into an alliance with Ch'i. King Hui promptly responded by invading Chao and placing its capital, Han-tan, under siege. Chao was by far the weaker of the two opponents. With only about a third of Wei's military strength at its command, Chao stood little chance of defending itself unaided. In desperation, its ruler appealed to Ch'i for help.

Details of a conference held in Ch'i by King Wei and his ministers have been preserved in a not always reliable later source – the *Chan-kuo Ts'e*, or *Intrigues of the Warring States*. It appears that at first there was a general feeling that Chao should be left

to its fate, but it was eventually realised that as Ch'i was bound by treaty to stand by Chao, it dared not risk losing the respect of the other states by doing nothing. But the self-interest of Ch'i was to be paramount; it would be dangerous to allow either Wei or Chao to emerge even stronger following a decisive victory.

Consequently, no attempt was made to relieve Han-tan. Instead, a limited diversionary attack was made into Wei, in the direction of the city of Hsiang-ling. The Chao capital fell to the Wei armies after a siege lasting about a year, which left both the antagonists weakened. Only then – with calculated cynicism – did King Wei allow the main Ch'i forces to intervene. The Wei army was still formidable, however, and Sun Pin had been asked to devise a plan to counter it. It must have added considerably to his enthusiasm for this undertaking when he discovered that the supreme commander of the enemy forces was none other than his old acquaintance, P'ang Chuan.

Sun's plan involved dividing his already inferior forces into three parts. This, of course, violates every accepted rule of military strategy, but in the tradition of Sun Tzu's thought, there was an even more important principle – 'Know the enemy and know yourself'. P'ang Chuan had always been impetuous, and had a tendency to underestimate his enemies. Sun Pin, who had studied with P'ang in his youth, must have been thoroughly familiar with this failing.

The first of the three Ch'i detachments, it appears, was deliberately sacrificed. It was sent against the town of P'ing-ling, a minor but strongly-held military base north of the Wei city of Ta-liang. The advance of this small force left its supply route exposed, and it advanced without reconnaissance into an area that was swarming with Wei troops, in transit to the Chao front in the north. Inevitably, it was quickly crushed. Sun Pin's own comment on this plan, preserved in his own work on the *Art of War*, the *Sun Pin Ping Fa*, demonstrates his purpose: 'We will show them,' he explained to a bewildered T'ien

Chi, 'that we do not understand military affairs.'[1]

The next stage of the plan was to send a second small mobile force against Ta-liang. This city may have been the Wei capital at the time – the records are contradictory – and it was certainly the most important town in the eastern half of the country. It seems unlikely that a detachment of light troops could have posed much of a threat to the place, but the potential political damage if it did succeed would have been too serious to risk. Besides, it was already obvious that the Ch'i strategists did not know what they were doing. So P'ang Chuan, whose army was still deployed in the north near Han-tan, decided to move swiftly to eliminate this nuisance.

Leaving his supply train and his heavy infantry behind, P'ang raced southwards at the head of the rest of the army. As he advanced by punishing forced marches, the Wei troops became more and more strung out. Those men who did manage to keep up with their hot-headed commander quickly became exhausted. It was with just such situations in mind that Sun Tzu had advised: 'Close to the field of battle, they await an enemy coming from afar; at rest, an exhausted enemy; with well-fed troops, hungry ones. This is control of the physical factor.'[2]

But it was Sun Pin, and not P'ang Chuan, it will be remembered, who had been considered worthy of studying Sun Tzu's book. There was only one road from Han-tan to Ta-liang, and Sun Pin knew it well. It passed very close to the border of Ch'i, at a spot known as Kuei-ling. Here, Sun and T'ien Chi were able to bring their main army out of hidden positions on their own side of the border, and deploy it astride the Han-tan–Ta-liang road with days to spare. By the time P'ang Chuan arrived, the waiting Ch'i troops were rested, well-fed, and firmly established in fortified positions.

The *Sun Pin Ping Fa* describes his method of constructing field fortifications, although in the context of a later battle. Ditches were dug, and metal caltrops placed in front of them to impede enemy chariots. Apparently the defenders' own chariots were deployed – with the horses presumably unhitched – as additional obstacles. Shields were placed along the top of the defences 'as battlements', in order to protect the defenders from missiles. Behind them, spears and swords were stacked ready for use against any enemy who broke through, while crossbowmen stood further back, with instructions to shoot over their own front ranks into the attackers as they bunched up in front of the obstacles.[3]

It must have been just such a position that faced P'ang Chuan on the road at Kuei-ling. He surely realised that without the heavy troops whom he had left behind, he had no chance of assaulting it. In the event he was given no opportunity even to try. While he hesitated, the Ch'i soldiers launched a sudden attack on the disordered and straggling Wei army. The battle was over almost at once, as the Wei troops broke and scattered in panic.

According to the account in the opening chapter of the *Sun Pin Ping Fa*, P'ang Chuan was captured at this battle, but it is not clear what happened to him afterwards. In the Ma-ling campaign thirteen years later, P'ang is found still in command of the Wei army. No doubt Sun Pin would have liked to have had a frank discussion with him about false accusations, but it seems that on this occasion he was denied the satisfaction. Perhaps P'ang's release was one of the stipulations of the peace agreement which concluded the war. Even then, the Wei commander was surely lucky to have escaped punishment by his own master for his recklessness and incompetence. His fate, however, had merely been postponed.

Consummation at Ma-ling

The next war between Ch'i and Wei broke out in 341BC. On this occasion, Wei had decided to victimise Han, which naturally followed the example of Chao, and sent to Ch'i for aid. Again the matter was debated at the Ch'i court, and according to Ssu-ma Ch'ien's account, Sun Pin and T'ien Chi argued persuasively for a repeat of the previous successful strategy. This the king eventually agreed to. So Han was allowed to fight on alone for a while – losing no fewer than five successive battles – until both Han and Wei had suffered heavy losses. Then Sun Pin and T'ien Chi mobilised their forces and advanced towards Ta-liang.

According to Sun Pin's reasoning, the Wei troops were contemptuous of their counterparts in Ch'i, whom they were accustomed to regard as cowardly. It had been more than a decade since the battle of Kuei-ling, and perhaps few of the Wei veterans of that war were left to warn their comrades against accepting this verdict at face value. The best course of action would therefore be to confirm their prejudices. (Not everyone, incidentally, shared this opinion of the Ch'i soldiers. In another of Ssu-ma Ch'ien's biographies, the historian quotes a remark that we can hardly be expected to take literally, but which suggests that they were not only respected, but widely feared: 'They eat people and cook the bones...' we are told. 'These are the troops of Sun Pin.')[4]

The Ch'i army marched into Wei, and proceeded westwards for three days. On the first night the men lit 100,000 cooking fires; on the second, only 50,000; and on the third, 30,000. (These are Ssu-ma Ch'ien's figures. The actual size of the army is not known, but the principle is clear enough.)[5] When his scouts reported this to P'ang Chuan, who was now on his way to the east from the theatre of war in Han, he jumped to the predictable conclusion. The 'cowardly' Ch'i soldiers were already deserting in terror at the news of his approach.

Almost incredibly, P'ang repeated his mistake of thirteen years before. His one fear seems to have been that the enemy would escape back over the border before he could catch them and destroy them in battle. So he put himself at the head of his more mobile troops – the chariots and light infantry – and drove them hard in pursuit. The supply train and heavy infantry were left to follow as best

they could. These units remained under the command of P'ang's superior, Prince Shen, who was a son of the king. It may be that Shen was only too happy to lag behind. According to a story in the *Chan-kuo Ts'e*, Shen had been warned by a neutral – a citizen of neighbouring Sung – that Sun Pin and T'ien Chi were once again in command of the Ch'i army. Clearly, by now their reputation was well known.

Sun Pin had been born not far from his chosen battlefield. This was situated in a narrow, wooded valley known as Ma-ling. Once again, Sun must have known the terrain intimately. According to his calculations, P'ang Chuan would arrive at this spot around dusk. So Sun deployed 10,000 crossbowmen in ambush positions on both sides of the road, with orders to shoot as soon as they saw a light. As at Kuei-ling, the troops were apparently protected by field fortifications.

This, incidentally, is the first mention in Chinese history of the use of the crossbow in open battle, rather than in sieges. But there is no suggestion that it was unknown to the enemy. The victory was to be due not to any secret weapon, but to the application of the well established tactical principles of the school of Sun Tzu.

As Ssu-ma Ch'ien tells the dramatic story, P'ang Chuan did indeed arrive at Ma-ling just as it was getting dark. Ahead of him, he saw a white patch on a tree trunk, where the bark had been scraped off. He could see characters written on the exposed wood, but it was already too dark to decipher them. So P'ang lit a torch, and held it close to the trunk in order to read the message. It said, 'P'ang Chuan will die under this tree.' And at that moment, 10,000 crossbow bolts came flying out of the darkness. Those Wei soldiers who were not hit were taken completely by surprise, and were thrown into utter confusion. Then the Ch'i warriors charged.

P'ang Chuan had somehow survived the first deadly volley, but it did not matter. As the enemy closed in, he cut his own throat in order to avoid capture. According to Ssu-ma Ch'ien, his last words were: 'So I have

In the fourth century BC the beleaguered state of Wei built a series of long walls to protect itself from hostile neighbours. Although constructed only of earth packed hard by repeated pounding, they have proved astonishingly durable, and sections such as this remain recognisable even today. (Cultural Relics Publishing House, Beijing)

contributed to the fame of that wretch!' – meaning, presumably, his old enemy Sun Pin. Neither did Prince Shen escape the débâcle. The retreating remnants of P'ang's force collided with his men as he came up in the rear, and threw them too into disorder. The victorious Ch'i army enveloped them, and many were captured. Shen's own fate is uncertain. According to Ssu-ma Ch'ien he was taken prisoner by Sun Pin and T'ien Chi, but King Hui of Wei apparently later told the philosopher Mencius that the prince had died in the disaster. The two statements are of course not necessarily incompatible: Shen may have been wounded, taken alive, and subsequently died of his wounds. Such an occurrence must have been common in

ancient times, when there was no reliable means of combating infection.

In any case, the outcome was disastrous for Wei. Soon afterwards King Hui was forced to sue for peace, abandon his campaign against Han, and acknowledge the hegemony of Ch'i. But even Sun Pin's foresight had its limitations. In the longer term, a weakened Wei was forced to cede its territories west of the Yellow River to its neighbour on the western side – Ch'in. And as we shall see, the strengthening of Ch'in was not an outcome that should have been welcomed, even in Ch'i.

Later life
The sequel to the victorious campaign can only be pieced together from a couple of tantalising references in the *Chan-kuo ts'e*. It appears that Tsou Chi, the Lord of Ch'eng, who was Chief Minister in Ch'i, resented T'ien Chi's success, and was plotting against him. Sun Pin was aware of this, and advised T'ien to take the army back to Ch'i and mount a *coup d'état*; thus he might be able to force Tsou to flee before he could put his own plot

into effect. Sun even produced a detailed plan for an attack on the capital, but for reasons that are not explained, T'ien did not take his advice.[6]

As Sun had feared, Tsou Chi succeeded in bringing a charge of treason against T'ien, who was driven into exile. He took refuge in Ch'u, and lived there until after the death of King Wei. We do not know whether Sun Pin accompanied him. In fact, our sources record no more of Sun's life after his hour of triumph at Ma-ling. And yet the book that bears his name contains references to battles fought as late as the last decade of the fourth century. Victories by Ch''i forces over the states of Yen and Ch'u are mentioned: these probably took place in 314 and 301BC respectively.

It is of course possible that a later editor might have inserted this material, and there are certainly elements in the text that must have been added in the third century or even later. But it is tempting to think that Sun may have lived on for another forty years or so in honourable retirement, working on his book, and reminiscing about the two great battles which had earned him his place in history.

Sun Pin's Art of War

In the long run, Sun Pin's writing was surely his most significant legacy. The book attributed to him has the same title as the earlier work of Sun Tzu – the *Sun Pin Ping Fa*, or *Sun Pin's Art of War*. It appears to have been widely read until the late Han dynasty, but was subsequently lost. It was known only by reputation for 2000 years, until a copy was discovered in a Han tomb in 1972. In some ways it is even more interesting than the *Sun Tzu*, as it represents the thinking of a historical commander whose practical record on the battlefield is confirmed by independent sources.

The *Sun Pin Ping Fa* begins with an account of the battle of Kuei-ling – to establish the author's credentials, as it were. It continues with a series of discussions between Sun and King Wei, in which the former answers the latter's questions, and those of T'ien Chi, on a series of general and specific military issues:

King Wei asked: 'How do we attack someone of equal strength?' Sun Pin said: 'Confuse them so that they disperse their forces...'[7]

King Wei said: 'Is there a way for one to attack ten?' Sun Pin said: 'There is. Attack where they are unprepared; go forth where they will not expect it.'[8]

T'ien Chi asked Sun Pin: 'What about the Awl Formation? What about the Wild Geese Formation? How does one select the troops and strong officers?'... Sun Pin said; 'The Awl Formation is the means by which to penetrate solid formations and destroy élite units... The Wild Geese Formation is the means by which to abruptly assault the enemy's flanks...'[9]

Subsequent chapters deal with a variety of subjects, varying from the abstract or metaphorical:

To be lustful, yet scrupulous; to be a dragon, yet respectful; to be weak, yet strong; to be pliant, yet firm, this is the Tao of arising.[10]

To the concrete and specific:

Three men are emplaced in a chariot; five men are emplaced in the squad of five; ten men make a line; a hundred men make a company; a thousand men have a drum...[11]

Several passages clearly reflect the tactics which the author had successfully used in his campaigns. For example:

Those who excel in warfare can cause the enemy to roll up his armour and race far off; to travel two days' normal distance at a time; to be exhausted and sick but unable to rest; to be hungry and thirsty but unable to eat. An enemy emaciated in this way certainly will not be victorious! Sated, we await his hunger; resting in our emplacement, we await his fatigue; in true tranquillity, we await his movement.[12]

This, of course, is exactly what Sun Pin did to P'ang Chuan in the Kuei-ling campaign. It is also a tactic expounded by Sun's predecessor Sun Tzu, whose *Art of War* contains an almost identical passage. In many respects the philosophies of Sun Pin and Sun Tzu are very similar – a fact which has encouraged speculation that there is more to their relationship than is apparent from Ssu-ma Ch'ien's account.

Sun Pin and Sun Tzu

Sun Tzu simply means 'The Master Sun'. It is a title rather than a name, and could plausibly be applied to any revered member of the Sun family. It does not in itself help much towards the identification of this mysterious figure. The traditional story of his life is based mainly on Ssu-ma Ch'ien, who discusses Sun Tzu in the same chapter as his fellow masters of the art of strategy: Sun Pin and Wu Ch'i. There is a very similar account in a book called *The Spring and Autumn Annals of Wu and Yueh*, but this is thought to be largely a forgery of the Han period or later, and so cannot be relied upon as an independent source.

Sun Tzu, so Ssu-ma Ch'ien tells us, was born in Ch'i, wrote a book in thirteen chapters on the art of war, and on the strength of this work gained employment with King Ho-lu of Wu, who reigned between 513 and 494BC. Because of his association with that state, the master is also sometimes referred to as Sun Wu. His biographer then goes on to relate a well-known story about Sun drilling the king's concubines, then provides this frustratingly brief resumé of the rest of his career:

> Sun Tzu defeated the strong state of Ch'u to the west and entered Ying (i.e. the Ch'u capital); to the north he intimidated Ch'i and Tsin. That the name of Wu was illustrious among the feudal lords was partly due to his achievements.

The other major chronicler of this period, Tso Ch'u-ming – who otherwise deals with the affairs of Wu in considerable detail – fails to mention Sun Tzu at all. There are no autobiographical details in the *Art of War* attributed to Sun. A further difficulty is that, from internal evidence, the *Sun Tzu Ping Fa* cannot be as early as the beginning of the fifth century. Taking into account factors that it discusses such as the size of the armies; the length and intensity of the campaigns; the sophisticated methods of command, and the familiar references to the crossbow, it seems to be more characteristic of the second half of the fourth century. These considerations have led some authorities to go so far as to deny the existence of Sun Tzu altogether, and to suggest that the book which bears his name was written by a later author – none other than Sun Pin himself![13]

That Sun Pin is known to have written another book on a similar theme can hardly be an argument against this theory. It was common practice in the Warring States period to seek extra respectability for a work by attributing it to some mythical ancestor, and hence to what was believed to have been a golden age of wisdom. Military works in particular were almost routinely ascribed to an impossibly early date – in some cases, as far back as the beginning of the Chou. Perhaps Sun Pin wished to distinguish that part of his writings which was directly inspired by family tradition from his own developments of the theme.

But of course it is not necessary to suppose that he composed both *Arts of War* from scratch. We know that there was a long tradition of military studies in Ch'i, and that manuals of some sort were available at least as early as the sixth century BC. Perhaps Sun Pin edited a mass of earlier material, introducing examples from his own time where he thought it necessary. Perhaps some of this material had originally been produced by his own ancestors. Perhaps one of these ancestors had indeed seen service in Wu, and had been fortuitously overlooked by earlier chroniclers.

On the other hand, Ssu-ma Ch'ien is a remarkably accurate chronicler, and is usually vindicated when his account can be checked from other sources. His history of the Shang dynasty, for example, was for a long time dismissed as myth, until archae-ologists began to excavate the long-lost cities of the Shang. The historian, it turned out, was even correct about the names of many of the Shang kings – confirmed in modern times from inscriptions on bones which had been used for divination – although he was writing more than a thou-sand years after the event. So to dismiss his biography of a much more recent figure would seem to be going too far. All that can be said with certainty is that the *Sun Tzu Ping Fa* was edited and revised at some time during the fourth century or later, and that Sun Pin is as likely as anyone else to have been involved in the task.

Anything further is speculation. That Sun Pin *was* Sun Tzu is a contention that can be neither proved nor disproved. But it is a fasci-nating thought that the author, or editor, of the most influential of all the Chinese mili-tary classics may have put his own teachings into practice in two of the most spectacularly successful campaigns of the age. For Sun Pin's record is surely enough to qualify him in his own right as one of the greatest commanders of the East.

One final comment is worth making in this connection. For this was an age excep-tionally rich in military genius, not only in China, but also in the West. As Sun Pin entered middle age, Alexander the Great was embarking on his spectacular career of conquest, which would take his armies half-way from the Mediterranean to the North China Plain. The following hundred years or so would witness the careers of many of the other great figures in the history of warfare: Pyrrhus of Epirus, Chandragupta Maurya, Hannibal, Scipio Africanus, to name but a few.

Why such a sudden flowering of the art of war? Two factors are worth considering. First, in both East and West, social and economic structures had developed by that time to the extent that armies of many tens of thousands of men could be raised, supplied, and kept in the field for extended periods. There was therefore naturally a demand for new tech-niques of commanding these forces. But the growth of large and cohesive states had not yet reached its logical conclusion – the point where single monolithic empires controlled entire regions of civilisation. This would occur within a few more generations, with the establishment of the Ch'in empire in China in 221BC, and the conquest of the Greeks and Carthaginians by the Romans in 146BC.

Once that stage had been reached, and the 'civilised' armies became concerned mainly with defending the frontiers against less technically sophisticated opponents, genius on the field of battle was perhaps less in demand than common sense and a will-ingness to stick to 'the book'. An example can be found in the career of Huo Chu-ping, the 'Swift Cavalry General' of the Han dynasty, who was notorious for rejecting the classical 'Sun Tzu' tradition of generalship, but who nevertheless enjoyed considerable success against the nomadic barbarians.

Sun Pin, Alexander and Hannibal, however, found themselves pitted against foes who were at least as numerous and well-equipped, and often nearly as well-organ-ised, as were their own armies. In that situation, the personal skill of the commander-in-chief became crucial. Perhaps we should let Sun Pin himself have the last word:

Thus when those who excel at warfare discern an enemy's strength, they know where he has a shortcoming. When they discern an enemy's insufficiency, they know where he has a surplus. They perceive victory as easily as seeing the sun and moon. Their measures for victory are like using water to conquer fire.[14]

CAVALRY AND CROSSBOWS

During the fourth century BC, two major new developments began to make their mark on warfare in China – cavalry, and the crossbow.

Cavalry came very late to the region. The use of the ridden horse in warfare had spread through Western Asia and Europe not long after 1000BC, and within the next few centuries extended eastwards across Central Asia, following the route thought to have been travelled earlier by the chariot. It has been suggested, based on the distances covered during their campaign, that the Hsien-yun barbarians who invaded China in 823BC were already mounted, but it is not until about 400BC that we have hard evidence for horse-riding tribes on China's northern borders – tribes known to the Chinese by the generic name of 'Hu'.

By that time, a few individuals within China were already riding horses – the *Tso Chuan* gives several instances from as early as the sixth century BC – but no organised cavalry units yet existed. Although apparently early manuals like that attributed to Wu Ch'i do refer to cavalry, these are likely to be later additions to the text. Sun Tzu describes only infantry and chariots.

Wu-ling and the cavalry of Chao

It was partly the association of riding with the despised Hu, whose outlandish costume and predatory habits so disgusted the Chinese, that delayed the adoption of cavalry in China.

The earliest role of Chinese cavalry was as mounted archers. This carving from the Han dynasty appears to show such a horseman using his superior mobility in combat against a chariot. (British Museum)

Before the end of the third century BC, cavalrymen were beginning to adopt armour, and close-combat weapons such as swords and lances. This reproduction of one of the famous Ch'in terracotta warriors shows the type of armour worn by élite cavalry of the period. (Royal Armouries)

According to the traditional account, which seems too detailed and circumstantial to discard, the decisive step was taken in 307BC by King Wu-ling of Chao, a state which was situated on the edge of the steppe, and so was particularly exposed to nomad influence. Wu-ling was seeking a method of extending his territories at the expense of his neighbours, and so set out to form units of mounted archers – an action that caused a furore among his more conservative relatives and ministers. The *Chan-kuo Ts'e* describes the controversy that resulted.[1]

The problem was that the Chinese costume of the time, which consisted of a long robe tied at the waist by a belt, was completely unsuited to horse-riding. It was therefore necessary to adopt the jacket and trousers of the Hu. But clothing had always been regarded as one of the fundamental differences between Chinese and 'barbarians', and in the eyes of many people, to dress like a barbarian was tantamount to abandoning one's own people and in a sense becoming a barbarian.

As Kung-tzu Ch'eng argued, China was 'a land looked up to from afar, and a model of behaviour for the barbarian. But now the king would discard all this and wear the habit of foreign regions. Let him think carefully, for he is changing the teachings of our ancients, turning from the ways of former times, going counter to the desires of his people, offending scholars, and ceasing to be part of the Middle Kingdoms'.

Wu-ling realised that the only way to induce his subjects to change their mode of dress would be to set an example himself. He knew that he would face not only opposition but ridicule in some quarters. He is quoted as saying:

'My only qualm is to hear the laughter of the empire... If the empire goes with me there is no end to the advantages of the Hu costume; and even though all China laughs, I shall have me the land of the Hu and Chung-shan.'

So he forced through his reform, and established his corps of mounted archers.

Later developments

Wu-ling, of course, was completely vindicated. Cavalry soon became a vital part of the forces of all the states and, within another century, had replaced the chariots as the mobile striking arm of the armies. By that time the original light mounted archers, based on the Hu model, had been supplemented by heavier cavalry, wearing armour and equipped with swords and possibly crossbows. Crossbows, halberds and long spears, as well as bows, were the characteristic weapons of the cavalrymen of the Han dynasty.

Detail of a saddle and horse furniture of the Ch'in period, from the same source.

A chapter, perhaps of Han date, which has become associated with Sun Pin's *Art of War*, lists ten tactical functions of the cavalry, including advancing to seize positions ahead of an enemy, operating against his flanks and rear, severing his lines of communication, capturing his supplies, and moving swiftly to surprise him while he is unprepared.[2] Not mentioned, it will be noted, is the shock role that we commonly associate with heavy cavalry. It is not until the sixth century AD, when lances, stirrups and horse armour had become available under yet another wave of barbarian influence, that we read of horsemen winning battles by frontal charges against formed troops.

The crossbow

Unlike the cavalry, the crossbow appears to have been an indigenous Chinese invention, though roughly paralleling its first use by the Greeks in the West. A late Han text attributes the device to a man named Ch'in, who allegedly lived in Ch'u in the sixth century BC. This may not be reliable, but the approx-

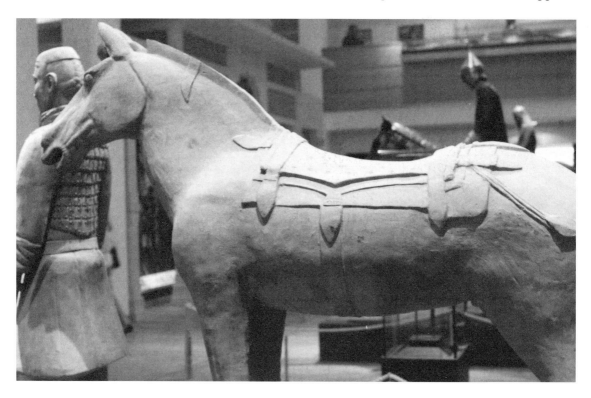

imate date seems correct. Certainly by the time that Sun Tzu wrote his *Art of War*, the weapon was familiar enough to be used as a metaphor. 'The momentum of one skilled in war is overwhelming,' we are told, 'and his attack precisely regulated. His potential is that of a fully drawn crossbow; his timing, the release of the trigger.'[3] Clearly, the author must have expected his readers to be already conversant with the crossbow and its trigger mechanism.

The crossbow remained one of the most popular weapons of Chinese soldiers for thousands of years. The favoured method of drawing the heavy bow, however, changed over time. 1) In the Warring States period and the Han dynasty, archers placed both feet on the bow before pulling up the string. This method is shown here in a relief from a Han tomb at I-nan. 2) By the time of the Sung dynasty, the introduction of a stirrup enabled the bow to be cocked using only one foot. This drawing, from the Wu Pei Chih of 1621, shows this technique being employed by a Ming crossbowman.

As discussed in Chapter 4, crossbows were used to decisive effect at the battle of Ma-ling in 341BC. They became increasingly popular thereafter, as evidenced by numerous mentions in the *Chan-kuo Ts'e*, and their appearance alongside the terracotta warriors of Ch'in Shih Huang-ti. According to a passage in *Chan-kuo Ts'e*:

> The most powerful bows and the staunchest crossbows in the world come from Han (i.e. the Warring States country of Han – not to be confused with the imperial Han dynasty) ... all of which can shoot further than six hundred paces. And when Han troops brace their feet against the bows to cock and shoot them, they can shoot a hundred bolts without pause.[4]

The crossbow was the most prominent weapon of the Han dynasty, when it was in widespread use by both infantry and cavalry. Some of the bows had draw-weights of up to 350 pounds, and could only be cocked by men of exceptional strength. These élite

troops were known as *chueh chang*. Cavalry crossbows, on the other hand, were lighter, and some could apparently be cocked while mounted and shot with one hand.

For the tactical employment of the crossbow in the Warring States period, we could do worse than consult its leading practical exponent, Sun Pin. In the *Sun Pin Ping Fa*, he mentions crossbow-armed soldiers in response to several of King Wei's questions. In defence against a more numerous enemy, mobile detachments of crossbowmen should be formed to give support to threatened points. Behind fortifications, they should shoot over the heads of the men defending the obstacles. In the event of an unexpected encounter with the enemy while on the march, bowmen and crossbowmen should quickly deploy into line, in order to screen the rest of the army and permit it to form up unmolested.

Carvings of crossbowmen are a common feature of Han dynasty tombs, and are usually supposed to have been placed there as a warning to prospective tomb-robbers. They are often depicted in the characteristic pose of cocking the weapon – both feet on the bow, on either side of the stock, pulling up the string with both arms, with the bolt held in the teeth, ready for loading. This procedure was necessary because the draw-weights were generally much higher than for ordinary bows. The idea behind the carvings may have been to warn illiterate bandits that the tombs were booby-trapped: real crossbows could be set up inside, sited so that they could be discharged by a trip-wire. According to Ssu-ma Ch'ien, the as yet unexcavated tomb of the First Emperor, Ch'in Shih Huang-ti, was protected in this way.[5]

The crossbow fell somewhat from favour during the barbarian invasions of the fourth to sixth centuries AD, when the composite bow of the steppe tribes became the principal missile weapon, especially for the cavalry. This trend continued under the Turkish-influenced T'ang dynasty: one list of equipment for a notional army of 12,500 men includes 12,500 bows, the same number of spears (which of course does not necessarily mean one for each man – it would make sense to carry spare weapons in case of breakages, and two bows each was quite common for cavalry), but only 2500 crossbows.[6] A slightly later text states that the T'ang placed little reliance on the crossbow, and so also equipped their users with halberds as a second line of defence.

The main reason for the loss of confidence in the weapon was probably its slow rate of fire. On the other hand, a crossbow bolt had much greater penetrating power than a normal arrow, and was much less dependent on the strength of the shooter. We have already seen in Chapter 1 how this factor probably contributed to the demise of the chariot. The effective range of the crossbow was also considerably greater than for other types of hand-held missile weapon. In T'ang archery contests, the 'far-killing crossbow' was regularly used at a range of 300 'double paces', and a Sung version was said to be able to 'pierce a large elm from a distance of 140 paces'.

Under the Sung dynasty, the crossbow was restored to its old prominence. In Tseng Kung-liang's *Wu Ching Tsung Yao*, a military manual dating from AD1044, the weapon is described as 'the strongest weapon of China and what the four kinds of barbarian most fear and obey'. The author goes on to explain how crossbowmen should be deployed in independent units, which employed a kind of circulating formation, with men advancing to shoot and then retiring to reload. This formation, he assures his readers, could defeat even impetuous cavalry charges by firepower alone, and so did not require men armed with other weapons to support it. In fact, mixing in such weapons would lessen the density of shooting and so weaken the unit.

The crossbow continued to be used by later Chinese armies. The Mongolian Yuan dynasty even had a separate corps known as the *Nu Chun*, or 'Crossbow Army'. Even the appearance of effective hand firearms did not entirely supersede them, and modern museum collections contain many examples of crossbows which were still in front-line use in the nineteenth century.

SHIH HUANG-TI – THE TIGER OF CH'IN

'The whole universe is Ch'in Shih Huang-ti's realm: extending west to the desert, south to where the houses face north, east to the ocean there, north to beyond Ta-hsia. Wherever life is found, all acknowledge his suzerainty...'
Inscription of Ch'in Shih Huang-ti

The rise of Ch'in

As far back as the reign of Ch'ung-erh of Tsin, the activities of the state of Ch'in had begun to impinge on the central region of Chinese civilisation. On several occasions during the following centuries, Ch'in armies marched from their stronghold in the remote west to terrorise their neighbours. And eventually it was to be Ch'in which succeeded in reuniting the Warring States, and created China's first true imperial government. Even today the name of 'China', in most Western languages, derives from that of Ch'in. So before proceeding to recount the career of the man who was to become Ch'in Shih Huang-ti, the last king and first emperor of Ch'in, it may be of interest to summarise the earlier history of this extraordinary nation.

Ch'in was founded in 897BC by Fei-tzu, a minor member of the Chou royal family, who had turned out to be an expert at breeding livestock. So the Chou king presented Fei-tzu with a fief on the north-western frontier of the kingdom, in what is now the province of Kansu, and charged him with the duty of raising horses for the royal army. This remote region really was China's 'Wild West' at the time. It was subject to drought, bitterly cold in winter, and was already partly occupied by the Jung 'barbarians', who were generally hostile to the colonists. However, the climate and extensive grasslands proved to be particularly suitable for horse-breeding, and Fei-tzu's clan prospered. They first participated in the affairs of China proper in 770, when

the Jung drove the Chou king east to Lo-yang, and Ch'in troops provided him with an escort. Although the barbarians were defeated, the king and his court never returned to the region of the old capital. Soon afterwards, the people of Ch'in moved in and occupied the deserted city.

This placed Fei-tzu's descendants in control of the 'Land Within the Passes' – the great natural stronghold of the west, of which it was later said: 'He who commands an army of a million lances commands a hundred times that number if he holds the land of Ch'in.' Here, in the upper reaches of the Wei and Yellow Rivers, was a fertile plain, almost completely cut off from the rest of China by encircling mountains. This barrier was broken only by a handful of easily defensible passes. As a strategic base, the area was almost invulnerable to invasion from the east. Safe from retaliation, the rulers of Ch'in could build up their strength before sweeping down, at a time of their own choosing, into the plains below.

Ch'ung-erh's great rival, Duke Mu, led armies into the lower Yellow River valley on several occasions, but after his defeat by Tsin, Ch'in lost ground and subsided once again to the second rank among the states. Meanwhile, in 623BC, the Ch'in people inflicted a decisive defeat on the Jung, and by about 400, they had largely absorbed them.

Ch'in's growing power, however, did not bring it immediate acceptance among the other states. It was regarded with contempt by its eastern neighbours as a still semi-barbarian marcher lordship, and its pretensions to Chinese culture were often mocked. This attitude was partly justified, as the Ch'in rulers themselves sometimes admitted. Jung influence remained strong, and the state was a long way from the great cultural centres of the Yellow River plain. As late as 237BC, King Cheng was graphically reminded by his minister Li Ssu of his ancestors' homespun cultural life: 'the beating of earthen jugs, knocking on jars ... and striking on thigh bones, the while singing and crying "Wu! Wu!"... such was the music of Ch'in'.

Yet this rough-hewn frontier background brought its own advantages. Ch'in was admired for its ferocity in war, and also for its pragmatism, unhampered by too much tradition. Lacking its own scholar class, it was

The Ch'in army

Thanks to the famous 'terracotta army' which was buried outside the First Emperor's tomb at Mount Li in Shensi Province, the appearance of the élite Ch'in soldiers of the imperial period is well known. We should bear in mind, however, that the figures probably represent a unit of household troops or palace guards, and that many warriors must have been less lavishly equipped. As in the case of other forces of the Warring States era, the core of the army was its infantry. Many of the life-sized terracotta figures are modelled with armour made from plates of leather or metal laced together – a fact that contradicts the impression gained from the passage from *Chan-kuo Ts'e* quoted above, that Ch'in troops did not wear armour. It seems likely, however, that as Ch'in extended its conquests and became wealthier, its lightly equipped soldiery gradually adopted better equipment, and came to resemble more closely the warriors of the other states. In one respect the *Chan-kuo Ts'e* account is supported by the evidence of the figures: they do not wear helmets, even though metal head protection was in use elsewhere in China.

The pottery warriors do not carry shields, and this has given rise to speculation that these items were not known in Ch'in. In fact there are several textual and artistic references to shields in Ch'in times, and in view of the fact that their rivals all used them, it would seem to make no sense for Ch'in soldiers to have had to do without such protection. The explanation for the omission may be that the figures were originally provided with real shields, which were commandeered when rebels broke into the pits during the civil wars following the fall of the dynasty. Certainly this is what happened to many of the weapons which were also interred there.

A theory that was once popular was that Ch'in owed much of its military superiority to its use of iron weapons against the bronze which was still in general use, but modern archaeological discoveries have tended to undermine this idea. Iron was gradually coming into use for armour and weapons around this time, but was more closely associated with states such as Han and Yen than with Ch'in. In any case, the cast iron of the period was not necessarily superior to bronze, the use of which had by this time been developed to an extremely sophisticated level. Various alloys were employed to improve its properties, and a technique for chromium plating was also known, as excavated weapons from the Mount Li site have shown.

To judge from the formations in which the tomb figures were buried, the standard infantry deployment was probably in dense, deep blocks of spearmen and halberdiers, flanked and screened by archers and crossbowmen in more open order. A deployment which is hinted at in some earlier Warring States texts, and was occasionally used in the Han period, involved drawing up the crossbows in close order, behind a front rank of

also happy to employ men of ability from elsewhere in China, whatever their origin. It was in fact a native of Wei, who came to be known as Lord Shang, who introduced the reforms which were to turn Ch'in into a great power.

Lord Shang

Lord Shang was the chief minister of Duke Hsiao, who reigned from 361 to 338BC.

Under their regime, Ch'in was radically reorganised along the lines proposed by the Legalist school of philosophers (discussed in Chapter 3). The Legalist philosophy was intended to produce a totalitarian society, which was completely dedicated to increasing the power of the state. In this scheme of things, nothing mattered except agriculture and war. The people were organised into small groups, which were

men with spears or halberds, but there is no evidence of this practice here.

Other formations suggested by the groups of terracotta figures include smaller, mixed units of chariots, cavalry, and sometimes also infantry. One group consists of sixty-four four-horse chariots and may represent a shock unit or mobile reserve, but in general chariots seem to be confined to high-ranking officers, who used them as

command posts, rather than as the skirmishing vehicles of the Springs and Autumns period. By this date, some cavalrymen had begun to wear armour and carry weapons for hand-to-hand combat, but many light horse-archers remained in service. It is also known that Ch'in, like the rival northern states of Wei and Yen, supplemented its own cavalry with mercenary Hu barbarians.

A close-up of a copy of one of the terracotta warriors from Shih Huang-ti's tomb at Mount Li. This figure shows the characteristic style of armour of the Ch'in and Han dynasties. The question of what these riveted plates were made of is still debated. In most cases they were probably leather, but may sometimes have been bronze, or even iron. (Royal Armouries)

responsible for the activities of all their
members, and were encouraged to spy and
inform on one another. The old nobility was
abolished, and replaced by a system of
ranks based solely on prowess in battle. The
populace was mobilised for huge irrigation
projects, which increased the amount of
grain available to feed the armies. Land
tenure was reformed, and the old system of
standard-sized fields was replaced with a
more flexible arrangement to make the
maximum use of the available arable land.
And Shang crushed all dissent with a
system of unbending laws and brutal
punishments.[1]

Lord Shang naturally made himself very
unpopular, and after the death of Duke Hsiao
in 338, he was put to death by his opponents
with appropriate cruelty. It is said that he fled
in disguise and tried to take refuge in an inn,
but the innkeeper turned him away because
he lacked a permit to travel. To take in a guest
without such a permit, the desperate fugitive
was told, was forbidden under the laws of
Lord Shang, which no one dared to defy!
Shang eventually managed to reach his old
home in Wei, but the authorities there sent
him back to Ch'in, where according to one
account, he was executed by being torn apart
by chariots.

The campaigns of conquest

The legacy of Lord Shang's reforms nevertheless remained. As more land was made
available for farming, the population grew.
Numbers were further augmented by peasants who migrated from farther east, drawn
by tax incentives. In 316 the semi-barbarian
nations of Shu and Pa, which were located in
the Szechwan Plain south of Ch'in, were
annexed, bringing thousands of ferocious
tribal warriors under the state's control. And
the Ch'in people themselves became wholeheartedly dedicated to war, as the only means
of achieving advancement.

A passage in the *Chan-kuo Ts'e* paints a
vivid picture of Ch'in's military power
around the beginning of the third century
BC. Chang Yi, a Ch'in spokesman who had

been sent to intimidate the king of Han,
told him:

'Ch'in has a million armoured troops, and
one thousand chariots. She has ten thousand cavalrymen and savage soldiers
beyond counting who will rush against
the enemy helmetless and barefoot, bran-
dishing their halberds... Troops east of the
mountains don helmets and put on
armour to meet their enemies. Ch'in
troops snatch off all protective clothes
and race barehanded after the foe. They
can grasp an enemy's head in the left
hand while holding a live prisoner with
their right.'[2]

Ch'in's enemies also acknowledged the
almost berserk ferocity of its soldiers.
Advising the marquis of Wei on how to deal
with his numerous enemies, the great strategist Wu Ch'i explained:

'The character of the Ch'in state is strong;
its country precipitous; its government
strict. Its rewards and punishments are to
be trusted. Its people are unyielding and
all individuals are determined to fight.
Therefore its formations are dispersed
and each fights for itself. The way to
attack Ch'in is first to offer them some
apparent advantage and entice them by
retiring. The officers will covet the bait
and will become separated from the
generals.'[3]

In practice, this was not so easily done. In the
century after Lord Shang's reforms the Ch'in
armies were seldom defeated. Instead, they
repeatedly crushed the armies of the other
states in at least fifteen major campaigns.
The total number of enemy soldiers who lost
their lives in these campaigns in the 130
years between 364 and 234BC has been
calculated from the accounts given by Ssu-
ma Ch'ien. His figures for the major battles
may well be exaggerated, but it seems
reasonable to assume that this might be
counterbalanced by losses in minor clashes,
which he does not mention. So as a rough
guide to the scale of the fighting, this casu-

alty list may not be too far from the truth. The total comes to nearly one and a half million men.[4]

The *Chan-kuo Ts'e* chronicles the increasingly desperate efforts of the victims to block this inexorable expansion. They tried to counter Ch'in's 'horizontal' strategy, of west-to-east advance down the Yellow River valley, with a 'vertical' one of their own, establishing a defensive north-south axis to block it. But they could never agree among themselves for long enough to make this plan effective, and they continued with short-sighted local feuds almost until the moment that the menace from the west overwhelmed them. As Ch'en Chen of Wei remarked bitterly, 'Our states boil one another alive, and Ch'in need not even supply the faggots.'

King Cheng

Prince Cheng, the future First Emperor, was born in 259BC. The name 'Cheng' means

No contemporary pictures of Shih Huang-ti are known. The accuracy of this seventeenth-century portrait of the First Emperor is therefore debatable, but it is probably a copy of an earlier original. The historian Ssu-ma Ch'ien described its subject in these words: 'The king of Ch'in is a man with a prominent nose, large eyes, a chest like a bird of prey; with the voice of a jackal; a man of little kindness; the heart of a tiger, or that of a wolf. He finds it easy to act humbly toward people: as soon as he obtains what he wants, he finds it just as easy to devour them.'

'Upright', or 'Correct'. His father – at least according to the official records – was King Chuang-hsiang, a prince whose accession to the throne had been assisted by the scheming of a minister named Lu Pu-wei. Lu was a merchant, allegedly the richest man of his age, and had apparently set out deliberately to use his wealth to buy himself a high office in the state – a thing otherwise unheard-of in ancient China, and surely only possible in pragmatic Ch'in.

Prince Cheng's mother had once been one of Lu's concubines before he donated her to the royal harem, and it was known that she resumed sexual relations with her old master after Chuang-hsiang's death. It is not surprising, therefore, that the rumour spread that Cheng's real father was in fact Lu Pu-wei – a story which is repeated in Ssu-ma Ch'ien's biography of Lu. In view of the low esteem in which merchants were usually held, and the stigma attached to female infidelity, this was a serious slur on Cheng's ancestry, and modern scholars have tended to dismiss it as a later fabrication designed to discredit him.[5] On the other hand, the circumstances are suspicious, and we should not be surprised that no other near-contemporary source records the claim. Whatever the facts, it would certainly have been unwise to cast doubt on Cheng's legitimacy during his lifetime.

However that may be, when Chuang-hsiang died in 247 and Cheng – still only thirteen years old – ascended the throne, Lu Pu-wei became the effective ruler of the Ch'in state. It was not until 238 that Cheng seized power for himself and, following another scandal, dismissed the minister. According to Ssu-ma Ch'ien, Lu was having an affair with Cheng's mother, but became worried that the king would find out. He wished to end the affair, but was afraid of antagonising the lady. He therefore introduced her to a commoner named Lao Ai, with whom she became infatuated. She gave birth to two children by this man, who subsequently hatched a clumsy plot to replace the royal dynasty with his own.

King Cheng soon discovered the details, and acted swiftly. Lao Ai and all his family were put to death. The queen mother was placed under house arrest, and Lu Pu-wei was thrown into prison. The law, which was normally paramount in Ch'in, called for the death penalty for Lu, but Cheng commuted it to banishment. Allegedly this was because of his past services to the state, but one is entitled to wonder. Did the king perhaps draw back from the awful act of killing his own father? In the event, it made little difference. Only two years later, the exiled Lu Pu-wei put an end to any hopes of solving the riddle by committing suicide.

One of Lu's protégés, Li Ssu, was also threatened with exile, but he so impressed the king with his persuasive arguments that he was retained. Li was later promoted to the position of chancellor, the highest office in the state. He was a hard-line Legalist, and an advocate of single-minded militarism and harsh punishments – teachings that Cheng espoused with enthusiasm. Another advocate of this approach to government was Han Fei-tzu, who in a famous essay dismissed scholars and intellectuals as useless 'vermin', and condemned as subversive the ideas of compassion and universal love. Cheng is also recorded as having commented favourably on Han's amoral doctrine.

It is pleasant to record that the appalling Han Fei-tzu met a fitting end, and at the hands of the very people who had put his theories into practice. Sent to the Ch'in court as an ambassador from the state of Han in 233, he fell foul of his fellow Legalist Li Ssu. Li, who perhaps regarded Han as a potential rival, persuaded Cheng that his visitor was probably a spy, and then contrived to have him poisoned while he was in prison awaiting investigation. Perhaps one should not expect such men to feel any affection for each other, however similar their views.

Under the ruthless direction of King Cheng and Li Ssu, the Ch'in armies resumed their march towards the sea. Already, in 260BC, the state of Chao had been permanently weakened by its defeat at Ch'ang-p'ing, where 400,000 of its soldiers are alleged to have been massacred. In 256 Ch'in troops had entered the feeble rump of Chou territory around Lo-yang and deposed the last Chou king, Nan, thus bringing the dynasty officially to an end. In 234, Chao was defeated again, losing another 100,000 men. Ch'in numerical superiority, not to mention military skill, was by now overwhelming. In 230, Cheng's forces began the final push. In that year the state of Han was eliminated, followed in quick succession by the rest of central China: Chao in 228, and then Wei three years later.

Ch'u, which for the past century had been Ch'in's most implacable foe, was next. Ch'u was still a great power, which had been left relatively unscathed by the preceding decades of war. In fact as recently as the fourth century BC, it had itself been aggressively expanding, annexing the lower Yangtze state of Yueh in 333. The soldiers of Ch'u were numerous and well-equipped, and their country was famous for its crossbows and razor-sharp, steel-tipped spears. The experienced Ch'in commander Wang Chien requested 600,000 men for the planned invasion, but Cheng had grown over-confident. A rival general promised to do the job with a third of that number, and his offer was accepted.

When the survivors staggered back home, having been cut to pieces by the Ch'u armies, Cheng was forced to beg Wang Chien to assume the command. Wang first insisted on receiving the 600,000 men he had originally requested. Then he took the opportunity to extort promises of lavish gifts for himself and his family. At last, he moved cautiously southwards to the borders of Ch'u. Despite the huge size of his army he was reluctant to engage in a pitched battle, but decided instead to employ a stratagem in the Sun Tzu tradition.

Wang built a fortified camp and entrenched himself there as if for a long stay, deliberately giving the enemy the impression that he was afraid. The Ch'u forces encamped nearby, but as the days passed they gradually became careless, and men began to drift off homewards. Probably Wang was also waiting for his enemies to run short of supplies, which must have had to be brought laboriously upstream against the current of the Yangtze, from the Ch'u heartland to the frontier. The river routes from Ch'in-held Shu and Pa, by contrast, were all downstream, making the going easier for heavily laden boats.

When he was sure that the enemy had been weakened sufficiently, Wang suddenly attacked. The Ch'u army was taken by surprise, and quickly disintegrated. King Hu-ch'u was captured, and Ch'in proceeded to extinguish the state. Ch'u was a large mouthful to swallow, however, and the task of pacification was probably never completed. As will be seen in Chapter 8, it was in Ch'u, only a few years later, that the revolt began which was to sweep away Ch'in in its turn.

First emperor

Once Ch'u had fallen to Cheng's armies, only the state of Ch'i remained free. Although once a great power, Ch'i had been fatally weakened by a century of warfare with its neighbours, and it could put up little resistance. Before the end of 221BC, Cheng was the undisputed master of 'All Under Heaven' – the whole realm of Chinese civilisation. The period of division which had begun in the eighth century BC was over at last. But this was by no means simply a restoration of the Chou kingdom. The nation which was now unified was immeasurably larger, richer and more populous than the possessions of the early Chou had ever been. The establishment of the Ch'in dynasty, even from the perspective of the time, marked a real turning point in China's history.

King Cheng certainly recognised this fact. His first public act after the fall of Ch'i was to call together his ministers and ask them for suggestions for a new title. *Wang*, or 'king', was felt to be inadequate for a man who had conquered half a dozen rival kings, and who now ruled a united empire for the first time in over 500 years. The formula eventually decided upon was *Huang-ti*. There was already a precedent for the use of the term *ti*. In Shang times it had signified a god, but more recently it had been downgraded to denote the overlord of a particular region. In 288, for example, the kings of Ch'i and Ch'in had agreed to call themselves *ti* of the east and west respectively. But Cheng was now to be *Ch'in Shih Huang-ti* or 'First August Emperor of Ch'in' – a man without equals anywhere. *Huang-ti* is the title which has been used ever since for Chinese emperors.

Another issue that needed to be resolved was the administration of the empire. The Chancellor Wang Kuan suggested that the emperor should revive the ancient Chou system by granting fiefs throughout the country to the imperial relatives and other members of the nobility. Li Ssu, however, objected to this, pointing out that the arrangement had not served the Chou at all well. So the emperor decided to centralise the government as far as possible. The empire was divided into thirty-six 'commanderies'. Each of these was controlled by a military and a civil governor, with an imperial inspector charged with overseeing them and reporting back to the Ch'in capital at Hsienyang.

Most of the dispossessed provincial nobility were forced to leave their own localities and take up residence in Hsienyang, where they would be isolated from their supporters, and hence less likely to be able to make trouble. Unfortunately, this system too had its weaknesses. Communications were too slow for proper central control over such a huge area, and even when deprived of their leaders, the people in many areas disliked Ch'in rule and resisted it whenever they got the opportunity. As a result, much of the army had to be split up into a multitude of small garrisons in order to protect the officials.

Ch'in, of course, was a state designed for war. It was not to be expected that Cheng would settle down easily to a peaceful career administering his new possessions. Almost as soon as the war in Ch'i was over, his armies

were on the move again. On the northern and north-western frontiers, another new power had recently arisen. This was the nomad confederation of the Hsiung-nu, who were now dominated by their own great unifier – a chief named Mao-dun. Shih Huang-ti's general Meng T'ien was entrusted with the task of establishing once and for all the superiority of the Ch'in over the Hsiung-nu.

Meng Tien and the Great Wall

Soon after the conclusion of the campaign against Ch'i, Meng T'ien invaded the Ordos region, which the Hsiung-nu were using as a base for incursions into China. Our main source for this campaign is Ssu-ma Ch'ien, but he provides few details, and even these are inconsistent. At one point he attributes the entire campaign to the year 215BC, but elsewhere he states that Meng T'ien was operating in the north for ten years. As Meng died soon after his master, in 209, this means that he must have spent most of the reign on the frontier, fighting the Hsiung-nu. Ssu-ma Ch'ien also contradicts himself about the numbers of troops involved. In one chapter he refers to 100,000 men; in another, to 300,000. Both figures, of course, may mean nothing more than 'a large number'. We do know, however, that Meng T'ien eventually inflicted a severe defeat on the nomads, and pushed the frontier as far north as the eastward-flowing section of the Yellow River which marks the northern boundary of the Ordos steppe. Following his victory, a road was built, leading north from Hsienyang as far as Chiu-yuan on the Yellow River.

It is the next phase of operations on the northern frontier which has captured the imagination of the world. What we actually know of it, however, appears to be derived entirely from a couple of brief notices in Ssu-ma Ch'ien's *Shih Chih*. Here are the relevant passages:

After Ch'in had unified the world Meng T'ien was sent to command a host of three hundred thousand to drive out the Jung and Ti (a classical allusion, referring here to the Hsiung-nu) along the north. He took from them the territory to the south of the river, and built a Great Wall, constructing its defiles and passes in accordance with the configurations of the terrain. It started at Lin-t'ao, and extended to Liao-tung (i.e. on the China Sea in the east), reaching a distance of more than ten thousand *li* (a *li* being about a third of a mile). After crossing the (Yellow) river, it wound northward, touching Mount Yang.[6]

And in a later chapter:

(Meng T'ien) seized control of all the lands south of the Yellow River and established defences along the river, constructing forty-four walled district

The name of Shih Huang-ti is often associated with the present Great Wall, seen here in a rebuilt section north of Beijing. In fact the Ch'in wall followed a different route, and few if any traces of it survive. (Duncan Head)

cities overlooking the river and manning them with conscript labourers transported to the border for garrison duty...Thus he utilised the natural mountain barriers to establish the border defences, scooping out the valleys and constructing ramparts and building installations at other points where they were needed. The whole line of defences stretched over ten thousand *li* from Lin-t'ao to Liao-tung and even extended across the Yellow River and through Mount Yang and Pei-chia.[7]

It is worth noting that the historian nowhere states that the wall was continuous. Indeed in the second passage, referring to fortifications 'where they were needed', he implies that it was not. This, then, is the evidence for the Ch'in 'Great Wall', and hence for the popular assertion – still made even today – that the current wall is over 2000 years old. In fact the Ch'in works had fallen into disrepair as early as the Han dynasty, and while some subsequent regimes built or rebuilt various frontier walls, at other times no such barrier was

Battlements along the modern wall. Reliefs of the Han period show that this style of construction was already known at that time, so it may also have been a feature of the original Ch'in defences. (Duncan Head)

maintained.[8] The present system, which dates mainly from the sixteenth century, in the period of the Ming dynasty, is not even in the same place as the Ch'in wall. Reflecting the less favourable situation vis-à-vis the steppe nomads at the time it was built, the Ming wall generally runs many miles to the south of the Ch'in line.

Lasting achievements

Other campaigns of Shih Huang-ti's reign saw Ch'in armies penetrate the far south, adding to the empire regions which had until then been scarcely touched by Chinese civilisation. Beyond the former state of Ch'u, the people known as the Yueh, who had been conquered by the kings of Ch'u during the

fourth century BC, had regained their independence. Beginning in 219, a series of campaigns was mounted to bring them under Ch'in control. Still farther south, the peoples of Nan-hai ('Southern Sea'), along the coast of what is now the province of Kwangtung, had never been subject to Chinese authority, but the emperor's ambitions did not spare them. With the conquest of these distant lands, Shih Huang-ti began the gradual process of colonisation of the south which was to be a major theme of Chinese history for many generations to come. In fact on several occasions in later centuries, when waves of barbarian invasions overran the north, this region would provide a refuge which could be said to have saved Chinese civilisation from destruction.

In 213 the Ch'in troops reached the sea not far from present-day Canton, where it seems that a permanent military presence was quickly established. At Canton, archaeologists have uncovered the remains of an immense naval dockyard, which is believed

HSIUNG-NU

"GREAT WALL"

MT. T'AI

HSIENYANG

YUEH

NAN-HAI

The boundaries of the Ch'in empire at the time of the death of Shih Huang-ti, c.210BC.

hsi.[10] It has been calculated that he spent half his reign on the road. His first trip, in 220, went to the western frontier, and his second, in the following year, east to Ch'i, where he ascended the sacred Mount T'ai, and performed the *feng* sacrifice – a precedent which many later emperors followed as a powerful means of legitimising their authority. In 218 and 215, Shih Huang-ti returned to the east coast, which, for reasons which will be discussed below, especially fascinated him.

Other non-military achievements of the reign were also of great significance for the future development of the empire. For example, the First Emperor presided over the standardisation of coinage, weights and measures throughout his dominions. Even the axle-widths of carts and chariots were fixed, so that the ruts made by the wheels were a standard distance apart, and vehicles were able to travel easily on the roads anywhere within the country. A further reform was the standardisation and simplification of the Chinese script, which has retained roughly the same form ever since.

The emperor's capacity for hard work was legendary. According to Ssu-ma Ch'ien, he read one *shih* (i.e. about sixty pounds in weight) of documents every day. This, of course, is not as improbable as it may sound to us, because these documents would have been written on strips of wood or bamboo. Paper did not come into use until some time in the Han era. Although Shih Huang-ti's many critics have always regarded his great energy as a manifestation of his megalomania, it is possible that he was motivated by

to date from the Ch'in period. In order to improve communications with the far south, the rivers Hsiang and Li were connected by a canal, known as the Magic Canal, which was constructed on the emperor's orders by the engineer Shih Lu. This is, so far as is known, the world's first contour canal, which follows the contours of the ground so carefully that it traverses a range of hills without requiring locks. It is still in use today, and enables waterborne transport to pass from the Yangtze river system to that of the River Hsi, which leads to the south coast.[9]

Parts of what is now Manchuria, in the far north-east, were also brought under Ch'in control. An extensive road system was constructed to join the far-flung regions of the empire to Hsienyang. Not content with presiding over all this activity from his palace, Shih Huang-ti embarked on a series of grand tours, in the course of which he probably covered more ground than any of the emperors who came after him, except perhaps the indefatigable Manchu, K'ang-a genuine sense of duty. An inscription which he left to commemorate one of his tours suggests that he at least wished to be remembered as a social reformer, albeit a somewhat heavy-handed one: 'The powerful and overbearing he boiled and exterminated; the ordinary folk he lifted and saved.' The 'ordinary folk', however, would not have agreed with him. Oppressed by forced labour, threatened with terrifying punishments, they were submissive only through fear. The miseries of the labourers on the Great Wall, for example, have passed into folklore. Ch'in Shih Huang-ti may have established the basis of the imperial Chinese state, but he did it on the sufferings of hundreds of thousands of his own subjects.

The mind of a tyrant

For a man of such immense historical importance, however, the First Emperor has come down to us in tradition as an oddly two-dimensional figure. Of his real personality we learn little from our sources, and what we have is obscured by propaganda. He is an archetype; or perhaps even two archetypes at once – a hero and a villain; both the founder and the 'bad last ruler' of his dynasty. Many of Ssu-ma Ch'ien's anecdotes portray him as a megalomaniac, increasingly divorced from reality – and not only in his last years. In 219, we are told, the emperor's progress through Ch'u was halted by a sudden storm as he passed beneath a mountain. Blaming the local spirits, he ordered 3000 labourers to cut down every tree on the mountain and paint the slopes red, which was the colour of convicts' clothing.

Eight years later, a meteorite fell to earth not far from Hsienyang. Some anonymous propagandist, taking it for an omen, carved on it the words 'The First Emperor will die and his land will be divided'. When he learned of this, Shih Huang-ti had everyone in the area put to death, and ordered the meteorite to be burned. Modern scholars naturally cast doubt on these accounts, pointing out not just their physical impossibility (How much paint would be needed to cover an entire mountain? How can you burn a meteorite?), but inconsistencies in the language, which suggest that these episodes may be later additions to Ssu-ma Ch'ien's text.[11] The point about such tales, however, is surely that not too long after Cheng's reign, there were plenty of people who were willing to believe them.

The best known of all the stories about Shih Huang-ti concern the 'burning of the books' and the 'burial of the scholars'. At a banquet held in Hsienyang in 213, a Confucian scholar named Shun-yu Yueh is said to have made a speech in which he advocated a return to the Chou feudal system. 'At present,' he pointed out, 'Your Majesty possesses all within the Four Seas, and still his sons and younger brothers are common men.' If anything should happen to the emperor, Shun-yu asked, what provision was there for the succession? New-fangled arrangements not based on the practice of antiquity, he said, never lasted long. Li Ssu spoke up in response. He not only condemned Shun-yu Yueh personally, but argued that the entire corpus of classical literature was dangerous because it encouraged such ideas. At Li's suggestion, therefore, the emperor ordered the destruction of all ancient books, making exceptions only for those practical works that dealt with medicine, farming and divination. 'The use of the past to discredit the present' was thus to be made impossible.

This measure has passed into popular consciousness as the very epitome of tyranny, but it is only fair to point out that modern commentators have cast doubt on the authenticity of the relevant passage in Ssu-ma Ch'ien. Certainly much pre-Ch'in literature did survive – including the works of philosophers like Confucius, whom the Legalists had singled out for particular disapproval. If the book-burning was ever carried out, it cannot have been particularly effective. Probably more serious were the losses caused by the burning of the imperial library in 206BC, when rebels sacked Hsienyang.

Similarly, the famous story that Shih Huang-ti ordered 460 Confucian scholars who had criticised his government to be buried alive is somewhat questionable. Even if Ssu-ma Ch'ien's narrative derives from a contemporary account – which cannot be confirmed from independent sources – he only says that the victims were 'buried'. This term was often used as a euphemism for 'put to death', and so need not necessarily imply the use of such a barbarous method of execution. Once again, however, we cannot avoid the conclusion that people were prepared to believe Shih Huang-ti capable of anything.

Immortality and death

The emperor himself certainly came to believe that nothing was beyond his grasp. Increasingly, towards the end of his life, the man who had conquered the world became more and more preoccupied with the possibility of defeating even death. This obsession had two facets: the prospect of warding off old age and illness by magical means; and the more prosaic desire to avoid premature death at the hands of the many enemies which his conquests had produced. Shih Huang-ti's attitude to the latter problem was clearly coloured by some of his own experiences.

Although one of the greatest conquerors in world history, he was personally no warrior. As far as we know, he never took the field himself, and was happy to leave the command of his troops to his generals. In the great campaign of 223 against Ch'u, for example, he accompanied the army as far as the border, but no farther. His great tours may be proof of his enormous energy, but they seem never to have taken him to the scene of any actual fighting.

On only one occasion do our sources reveal Cheng striking a blow in anger. The episode is not to his credit. One day in 227BC, an assassin from Yen succeeded in gaining an audience with the Ch'in king. This man, a famous swordsman named Ching K'o, brought with him a map of the country of Yen as a token of submission, and the severed head of a Ch'in renegade as a sign of good faith. But inside the rolled-up map he had concealed a dagger, and when the king reached out for the document, he

This Han period relief depicts the assassination attempt of 227BC, when Ching K'o nearly succeeded in stabbing the future First Emperor. Here the frustrated assassin throws his dagger in a despairing gesture at his target (shown on the left holding a jade pi, or symbol of his rank), while Ch'in guards and courtiers mill around in confusion. The head of an officer from Yen, which Ching K'o had brought to Ch'in to show his good intentions, can be seen in its box in the centre foreground.

grabbed his sleeve with his left hand and tried to stab him. Cheng panicked, tore the sleeve of his robe in his haste to get away, and then dodged behind a pillar. Ching K'o lunged after him.

None of the king's attendants were allowed to carry weapons, and although Cheng himself was wearing a long sword, he lacked the presence of mind to draw it. The court doctor hit the assassin with his medicine bag, but to no effect. The other courtiers were paralysed with shock. No one even thought to call for the guards. Pursued by Ching K'o, the king ran several times around the pillar, trying to ward off the dagger blows with his hands. Then at last one of the attendants called to him, pointing out that if he moved the long scabbard behind him, he would be able to draw his sword. Somehow, Cheng accomplished this and wounded his assailant. The latter threw his dagger in a last despairing gesture, but missed. The king then closed in on the unarmed and wounded man, and struck him seven times. Even then, he failed to finish him off. Ching K'o still had the strength to laugh at his enemy, explaining, 'I failed because I wanted to capture you alive.' Wounded and helpless, he was finally despatched by the Ch'in guards.

After this narrow escape, Cheng became increasingly insecure. His paranoia was accentuated by two more assassination attempts in 218. The first of these was carried out by a friend of Ching K'o. This man had been blinded for his complicity in the affair of 227, but had been allowed to live, and even to remain at court, because he was an exceptionally skilled musician. He was overpowered while trying to cosh Shih Huang-ti with a lead-filled harp. After that, none of the former followers of the feudal lords were ever allowed anywhere near the emperor. Soon afterwards, a certain Chang Liang from Han set an ambush for Shih Huang-ti while he was on tour. Chang Liang attacked the wrong carriage, but managed to escape before the emperor's guards arrived. He was never caught – a fact that naturally made his intended victim even more uneasy.

By 212, the emperor's paranoia had reached such a pitch that he was constantly on the move among the 270 buildings and pavilions of the Hsienyang palace complex, making use of a system of concealed walkways which he had built so that no one could observe his movements. For anyone within the palace to disclose information on his whereabouts was made a capital offence. Inside this sanctuary, musicians were employed to sing songs about the immortals and other spiritual beings, in a vain attempt to calm their master's fears.

Not content with thwarting earthly enemies, the emperor also determined to evade even a natural death. Taoist philosophers believed that by consuming secret potions and following a series of rituals, it might be possible to live forever. Those who had achieved this were thought to reside on islands in the eastern sea, and it was a logical conclusion that if the emperor could only make contact with these immortals, he would be able to learn their secrets. This, we can be sure, was a principal reason for his repeated visits to the east coast.

Expeditions were periodically sent across the sea in search of the mysterious islands, but none ever came back to report success. The emperor, obviously, concluded that some power – either natural or supernatural – was deliberately obstructing his quest. The most likely explanation, of course, is far simpler. The lands of the immortals did not exist. The myth probably has its origins in mirages, still seen today along the coast, which produce the illusion of strange mushroom-shaped land formations a few miles offshore. Sailors sent out to investigate would have found nothing, and would probably have been reluctant to return and face the wrath of their frustrated emperor. It has been suggested that the largest of these expeditions, which comprised hundreds of men and women, may have sailed onwards and colonised part of Korea, or even Japan. But that is speculation. What is certain is that Shih Huang-ti's failure to make contact with the immortals added to the troubles that were preying on his mind.

The fifth and last of the emperor's tours of inspection began in 211, and took him once again in the direction of the sea – this time south-eastwards, to what is now the Chekiang area, not far from the mouth of the Yangtze. While there, he had a dream, which his sycophantic advisers told him meant that a malignant sea monster was frustrating his attempts to locate the secret of eternal life. So, armed with a crossbow, the emperor set out in search of this monster. He eventually found and killed it – most likely his victim was a small whale which had unwittingly swum close inshore – but soon afterwards he fell ill. As is so often the case, we cannot be sure of the nature of his illness, but the south-eastern coastal zone was notoriously unhealthy, and malignant malaria has always been a particular problem there. It would be ironic if the most powerful man on earth, who struck down monsters in his quest for immortality, should have succumbed in the process to the unnoticed bite of a mosquito. Shih Huang-ti died on his way back to Hsienyang, in July or August of 210BC. All the skills and resources of the empire had failed to prolong his life beyond his fiftieth year.

Aftermath

His unexpected death left immediate authority in the hands of two ministers who had accompanied him – Li Ssu, and the unprincipled eunuch Chao Kao. Their first reaction was to leave the emperor's body in his covered carriage, and to pretend that nothing had happened. The two conspirators continued to enter the vehicle as usual to receive their 'orders'. Because the weather was hot, they arranged for a wagon-load of fish to follow the carriage, so that no one would notice the smell of decomposition. Then they forged a letter to Shih Huang-ti's eldest son, the Crown Prince Fu-su, announcing that the succession had been changed in favour of another son – the ineffectual Hu-hai. The missive concluded by ordering Fu-su to commit suicide.

This was not as implausible as it might seem. Fu-su had criticised his father's poli-cies, and was genuinely out of favour. It is perhaps a measure of the terror that Shih Huang-ti still inspired that the prince, seeing the imperial seal on the letter, obeyed its instructions without question. Meng T'ien, who apparently became suspicious, was then arrested and thrown into prison, where he too killed himself. (The great general is said to have confessed that he deserved to die in any case, as in the course of building the Great Wall he must have 'cut through the veins of the earth', and so offended its guardian spirits.) Then, with all obvious rivals eliminated, the emperor's death was at last made public, and Hu-hai was installed as the second ruler of Ch'in. Behind the scenes, however, Li Ssu and Chao Kao remained in control, running the empire with the apparent sole aim of enriching themselves, and increasing still further their own power.

This situation was perhaps an inevitable consequence of the First Emperor's still unsophisticated and over-centralised system of governmment, with its total lack of any check on unruly ministers apart from the personality of the individual ruler. But in any case, the Ch'in regime was already deeply unpopular. In many of the provinces, the broad idea of a unified empire had not yet taken root. The nobility had few ambitions beyond being able to resume their independent lives in their old localities; while among the common people, whose only contact with the new dynasty had been as victims of its brutal punishments, enduring military conscription or forced labour, even the chaos of the Warring States had begun to be remembered with nostalgia.

So as soon as Shih Huang-ti's firm hand was removed, the whole apparatus of government fell apart. The Han scholar Chia I, whose work on *The Faults of Ch'in* was the first to list the reasons for the dynasty's rise and fall, put the blame on the characteristic over-centralisation, and on the rigidity and brutality of the Legalist code. The empire could not be run on a sustainable basis as an armed camp. 'The power to conquer and the power to hold what has been won,' Chia I remarked, 'are not the same'. The course of the civil wars which erupted in 209 is explored in Chapter 8. It was not until 207 that the Ch'in dynasty was finally extinguished, but its effective authority outside the 'Land Within the Passes' had died with its founder.

Conclusion: the memorial at Mount Li

It is all the more remarkable in these circumstances that his successors managed to complete the extraordinary tomb complex at Mount Li, not far from Hsienyang, which Cheng had begun soon after his accession as king of Ch'in in 246. Ssu-ma Ch'ien provides us with a description of the work, which went on for nearly forty years. At one point, after the establishment of the empire, 700,000 forced labourers were gathered to work on the site. It was customary for the tombs of high-ranking persons to be elaborately furnished, including models of the servants and possessions which they had owned in life, and notwithstanding his evident hope that his own tomb would never be needed, Shih Huang-ti's provision for his afterlife was on an unprecedentedly lavish scale.

Not content with models of palaces and official buildings, he installed a mechanical device which caused mercury to flow along channels in a simulation of the sea and the Yellow and Yangtze Rivers, while a multitude of whale-oil lamps burned overhead to represent the constellations. The emperor obviously intended to have numbered among his possessions the whole of heaven and earth. The complex was booby-trapped with automatic crossbows, and in order that the defence system should remain a secret, the men who installed these devices were locked in the tomb with their master's body and buried alive. Accompanying them – though mercifully strangled beforehand – were the emperor's childless concubines. And at the foot of the artificial hill which was erected over the grave were buried his spirit bodyguards, in the form of the warriors of the terracotta army.

Nothing like this terracotta army has been found from any other period of China's history – nor, for that matter, from anywhere else in the ancient world. Miniature tomb guardians, sometimes numbering several hundred, were a common feature of noble interments, but the First Emperor's burial army remains unequalled, not only for its size – perhaps 10,000 life-sized figures, in four separate pits – but also for its artistic and technical quality. This burial army alone must have required the mobilisation of thousands of skilled craftsmen over a period of years. And yet our written sources make no mention of it. Ssu-ma Ch'ien's description refers only to the emperor's actual tomb, which has not yet been excavated. The staggering collection of pottery soldiers seems to have faded from people's memory not long after it was buried. The explanation, in all probability, is that the customary ruthless methods were used to keep it secret at the time. Just as the men who worked in the tomb were sealed up inside as soon as the job was finished, it seems only too likely that the splendid artists who sculpted the terracotta figures met a similar fate. Probably the secrets of their craft died with them, for the tomb figures of the Han emperors who followed Shih Huang-ti are both smaller and less well made.[12]

Ch'in Shih Huang-ti continues to fascinate historians and the general public alike. His terracotta army, which was rediscovered as recently as 1974, is now one of the world's great tourist attractions, and perhaps the best-known image in the whole of China's history, surpassing even the Great Wall. When the tumulus itself is finally opened, we can expect further revelations of equal impact. And in the late twentieth century, the First Emperor's public image has undergone a transformation. The Chinese people today, it appears, see him more as venerated founder than as archetypal tyrant – a symbol, in fact, of growing national strength and pride. Perhaps, after all, the man who met his death in the quest for eternal life has come as close to immortality as is possible in this world.

PRACTITIONERS AND THEORISTS OF THE ART OF WAR

Manuals on the 'art of war' have long been a part of Chinese tradition. Although the work of Sun Tzu is by far the best known, both in its country of origin and in the West, it is by no means unique. A catalogue of the early Han dynasty lists 182 books on the subject. By the Sung period, there were no fewer than 347 such works, although of this number only two are known to have survived to the present day.

There were books available on the military art even earlier than the fourth century BC. According to the *Tso Chuan*, a Ch'u commander quoted from such a manual before the battle of Pi, in 595BC: 'The *Art of War* says, "Anticipate your enemy, and you take away his heart."'[1] It should be pointed out, however, that these were not volumes which could be slipped into a pocket and taken into the field. Before paper came into use during the Han dynasty, books were painted on to strips of wood or bamboo, which were tied into bundles with leather thongs. The *Sun Pin Ping Fa*, for example, consisted of some 400 of these strips. It is hard to imagine that such an unwieldy item could ever have been carried on campaign, although officers might certainly have memorised key passages beforehand.

By the Sung period, seven of the oldest of these works had become accepted as the 'military classics'.[2] From a dispassionate modern viewpoint these are of variable usefulness, and seem to have been selected mainly on the basis of their alleged chronological seniority. The true dates of many of them, at least in their present form, are doubtful, and it may be that none actually predates Sun Tzu.

Ostensibly the oldest is the *Liu t'ao*, or *Six Secret Teachings*, which is traditionally attributed to the T'ai-kung, who was a contemporary of the founder of the Chou dynasty, King Wu. This would imply a date of around 1050BC, but most modern scholars consider it to be a work of the Warring States era. Some passages – for example those dealing with cavalry – are certainly very much later than the early Chou. The text goes into considerable detail about military administration, organisation and tactics, but the value of this information is reduced by the uncertainty of its context. It may reflect a real or theoretical system of one of the Warring States – possibly Ch'i, which was said to have been founded by the T'ai-kung, and where he was especially venerated.

Another of the seven classics, popularly believed to represent the teachings of the T'ai-kung, was the *Three Strategies of Huang Shih-kung*. (Huang Shih-kung is a pseudonym or nickname – 'The Duke of Yellow Rock'). An interesting tale associated with this book is recorded by Ssu-ma Ch'ien. It had apparently been kept secret in Ch'i for centuries, but during the civil wars at the end of the Ch'in dynasty it was presented to Chang Liang by a mysterious old man, who first set him a series of tests to see if he was worthy. The stranger then told him: 'If you read this you can become a teacher of kings...' Chang Liang looked at the book and discovered it to be the T'ai-kung's military strategy. He thereafter regarded it as something exceptional and constantly studied and worked over the book.[3]

The story may or may not be true, but it suggests that such a work might have been regarded as a state secret, something too powerful to be made available to all and sundry. In fact the *Three Strategies*, with its emphasis on administration and the selection of personnel, appears more characteristic of the Han period than of any earlier time.

Also included in the seven classics are the better known books of Sun Tzu and Wu Ch'i, and two more works which may date from the fourth century BC – the *Ssu-ma Fa*, or *Methods of the Horse Master*, and the *Wei Liao-tzu*. The former contains, as well as a discussion of benevolence and proper conduct in rulers, some interesting remarks on drill, and a remarkably lenient code of discipline, rather reminiscent of Hsun Tzu's appeal to men's better nature:

> In cases of great defeat do not punish anyone, for then both the upper and lower ranks will assume the disgrace falls on them.[4]

And elsewhere:

> Within the Three Armies disciplinary action is not imposed on anyone for more than half a day. Confinement does not go beyond a rest period, nor is their food reduced by more than half.[5]

The *Wei Liao-tzu,* like most of the classics, is of mysterious origin. Its author, Wei Liao, is associated in different traditions with both Lord Shang and Ch'in Shih Huang-ti – although, given the century or so which separates those two figures, both versions cannot be correct. The book is rather theoretical, and as might be expected from someone connected with the state of Ch'in, emphasises rigid hierarchies and an inflexible system of rewards and punishments:

> If a drummer misses a beat he is executed. Those that set up a clamour are executed. Those that do not obey the gongs, drums, bells, and flags but move by themselves are executed.[6]

The last of the seven classics is the *Questions and Replies Between T'ang T'ai-tsung and Li Wei-kung,* which purports to be a dialogue between the great T'ang emperor T'ai-tsung (see Chapter 12) and his general Li Ching. Like all the other books, however, it is of uncertain provenance, and is believed by some authorities to date from the Sung period.

In some cases, the commentaries on the classics provided by later experts are as interesting as the original works themselves. Useful details on T'ang fortification and Sung infantry organisation, for example, are found in the notes on Sun Tzu made by Tu Mu and Chang Yu. An even more eminent commentator on Sun Tzu's *Art of War* was Ts'ao Ts'ao, who founded the Wei dynasty after the collapse of the Han. He was recognised as one of the greatest generals of his age, and according to his biography in the *Wei Official History*, 'followed in the main the tactics laid down in the Sun-tzu and Wu-tzu (i.e. Wu Ch'i's *Art of War*) ... by deceiving the enemy, he won victory; he varied his tactics in demonic fashion.'[7] Ts'ao also wrote a book of his own on warfare, which has unfortunately been lost. It was said that whenever his generals followed his instructions they were successful, but when they did not, they were defeated. Another legendary figure of the Three Kingdoms, Chu-ko Liang, also wrote a commentary on Sun Tzu, as did Liu Chi, an advisor to Chu Yuan-chang, the founder of the Ming dynasty.

A separate tradition is represented by the military encyclopaedias or manuals, which began to appear from the late T'ang period onwards. These tend to be much more practical than the classical works. They concentrate on details of weaponry, organisation and tactics, and are generally illustrated with naive but informative diagrams. Most of them are also attributable to known authors, and hence to definite dates. Thus they are of enormous value to the historian, but unfortunately only a few passages from the best known of them have so far been translated into Western languages.

The earliest of these books which survives is the *T'ai Pai Yin Ching*, which was published in AD759. Other outstanding examples of the genre include: the *Hu Ch'ien Ching* of 1004; the *Wu Ching Tsung Yao* of 1044, and its updated 1510 edition; the *Huo Lung Ching*, a treatise on gunpowder weapons dating from 1412; and the *Wu Pei Chih* of 1621.

LIU PANG AND HSIANG YU: RIVALS FOR AN EMPIRE

'The Empire slipped from the House of Ch'in like a fleeing deer,
and all the world joined in its pursuit.'
Ssu-ma Ch'ien

The end of the Ch'in

The First Emperor of Ch'in had intended his dynasty to last for 10,000 generations. In the event, it collapsed within three years of his death. His successor Hu-hai, the Second Emperor, was firmly under the control of the conspirators who had put him on the throne – Li Ssu and Chao Kao. Under their rule, the people were exhausted with forced labour projects, and oppressed with the full force of the Legalist code. As one later scholar put it: 'Those clothed in red (i.e. convicts) filled half the road.' It was not long before the victims began to fight back.

The first targets of popular unrest were the Ch'in magistrates, who had been appointed to oversee local government in towns throughout the empire. Many of these men were murdered, while the tiny garrisons established to protect them looked on helplessly. In an attempt to maintain a presence everywhere, the Ch'in army had been spread too thinly. Often the only achievement of these isolated garrisons was to make a present of their arms and equipment to the first group of rebels strong enough to overwhelm them.

Early in 209BC, a group of 900 men set out from the former state of Ch'u in the Yangtze valley, having received orders to report for forced labour at the Ch'in capital, Hsienyang. A former labourer named Chen She was placed in charge of the men. The party was held up en route by heavy rain, so Chen – knowing that he would be blamed for the delay, and so would probably be executed – killed the small escort of Ch'in soldiers which was accompanying them, and led the men into hiding. He then made an astonishing announcement. He was, he said, actually the rightful emperor, Fu-su. He had not committed suicide after all, but had escaped and disguised himself as a common labourer. It seems unlikely that anyone really believed this story, but to the disaffected peasantry of Ch'u, any excuse to rebel was welcome. The people flocked to join him.

In some respects, Ch'u is reminiscent of the Deep South in the American Civil War. It covered a vast area and was potentially very rich, although sparsely settled. Its people were individualists, with a fiercely independent frontier mentality, and a sense of being culturally very different from the more progressive north. They were loyal to their local aristocracy, and bitterly opposed to unification. They believed that this had been achieved through trickery, rather than by conquest in a fair fight, and remained convinced that they were more than a match in battle for the troops of the hated Ch'in.

Inspired by the slogan, 'Great Ch'u shall rise again!', the people of the south set upon the Ch'in occupiers with hoes and staves. They captured the city of Ch'en, and then embarked on a reckless march into the Ch'in stronghold, the 'Land Within the Passes'. Inevitably, they were crushed. The Ch'in general Chang Han hastily armed a force of labourers who were working on the First Emperor's tomb at Mount Li, drove the rebels back in disorder, and recaptured Ch'en. Chen She was murdered by his own carriage driver after a 'reign' of less than six months.

However, even before his death, others had begun to follow his example. In Chao, Ch'i, Wei, Yen, and others of the former states which made up the Ch'in empire, the people arose to reclaim their independence. Chen She had begun a process which was not to end until Ch'in power had been swept away.

Hsiang Yu

It was amid this chaos that Hsiang Yu first came to prominence. He was a member of the old aristocracy of Ch'u, and a great nephew of a famous general of the Ch'u state, Hsiang Yen, who had been forced by the Ch'in conquerors to commit suicide. As a boy Hsiang Yu had first wanted to be a scholar, but he found the art of writing too difficult, and quickly gave it up. Instead he took up swordsmanship, at which he also failed. Ssu-ma Ch'ien records that his uncle, Hsiang Liang, became angry with him, but Hsiang Yu replied:

'Writing is good only for keeping records of people's names. Swordsmanship is useful only for attacking a single enemy... What I want to learn is the art of attacking 10,000 enemies!'

So Hsiang Liang took him under his wing, and began to instruct him in the art of generalship, knowledge of which had been handed down in the family through generations of military service in Ch'u. Predictably, Hsiang Yu quickly became bored with this too, and never pursued the subject in any depth – an omission that he must one day have come to regret.

As a young man, he was hot-tempered, and had a reputation as a bully. He grew up very tall and muscular, and we are told that all his contemporaries were afraid of him. Ssu-ma Ch'ien relates how one day Hsiang Yu and his uncle watched the First Emperor pass by on a tour of his domains. Stubbornly unimpressed, the youth suddenly blurted out: 'This fellow could be deposed and replaced!' Hsiang Liang quickly put his hand over his mouth to shut him up, but it seems that he secretly took note of his nephew's opinion. When the Chen She revolt broke

An alleged likeness of Hsiang Yu, from a seventeenth-century drawing.

out, Hsiang Liang was summoned by the local Ch'in governor and asked to raise an army to fight for the dynasty. He requested permission to invite Hsiang Yu to the discussions, and this was granted.

What followed must have been planned in advance. As the three men conferred in the governor's office, Hsiang Liang turned and winked at his nephew. Hsiang Yu immediately pulled out his sword, and struck off the governor's head. Then, as the dead man's attendants responded to the commotion and rushed into the room, he stationed himself at the door and cut them down, one after the other. Clearly he had remembered something from his sword-fighting lessons, because he is alleged to have killed several dozen men before the rest submitted. Having taken control of the building, Hsiang Liang fixed the governor's seals of office to his own belt.

Now irrevocably committed to rebellion, Hsiang Liang attached himself to Chen She's movement. He attracted considerable support in Ch'u because of his family's reputation. Rather surprisingly, he then entrusted the unreliable Hsiang Yu with a detached force to take the city of Hsiang-ch'eng, which was still held by the Ch'in. Ch'in resistance was strong, but Hsiang Yu eventually succeeded in his first independent mission, whereupon – apparently in a fit of temper – he had all the inhabitants of Hsiang-ch'eng massacred. This was to become a pattern which would be all too common throughout his subsequent career.

Soon after this, news came of Chen She's death. Hsiang Liang then found a member of the old Ch'u royal family who was in hiding, working as a shepherd. He had him crowned as King Huai, and in the name of this puppet ruler he continued the war against Ch'in. Once again Hsiang Yu was sent off with an independent command, and again he was successful, as well as unnecessarily bloodthirsty. He captured the city of Ch'eng-yang, killed everyone he could find within the walls, then went on to capture and decapitate a Ch'in general at the battle of Yung-ch'iu. But while he was away, his uncle, growing

over-confident, was surprised at Ting-t'ao by Chen She's old nemesis, Chang Han. Hsiang Liang was killed, and his army dispersed.

Hsiang Yu and the other Ch'u commanders retreated in confusion, but Chang Han was prevented from following them up by the emergence of another threat, from rebels in the northern state of Chao. With the death of his protector, King Huai attempted to assert his authority. He appointed a certain Sung I as overall military commander of Ch'u, with Hsiang Yu as second-in-command. It is difficult to see what Hsiang Yu had achieved to justify this. It is tempting to suppose that he had his family connections to thank for his promotion, rather than any outstanding ability. But humility, of course, was foreign to his nature. He immediately started to argue with his superior about strategy.

Ch'u triumphant

Early in 207BC, Chang Han was besieging the Chao rebels in the city of Chu-lu, north of the Yellow River, when the Ch'u army arrived on the opposite bank. Sung I wanted to wait and let Ch'in and Chao weaken each other, but Hsiang Yu was eager to cross the river and attack. Sung went ahead and issued the order to hold the current position, adding that anyone who disobeyed would be executed. That day – while Sung I held a drinking party to see off his son, who was returning home – Hsiang Yu toured the camp, putting his case to the officers. The weather was cold and wet, and food and other supplies were running short. No doubt the men were miserable and unwilling to prolong the campaign, and thus their commanders gave Hsiang the assurances of support that he was seeking. The next morning he went as usual to the commander's tent to make his report, drew his sword and decapitated the unsuspecting Sung I. Emerging from the tent, he announced that he had caught Sung in the act of communicating with the enemy, and so had executed him on the spot. The troops accepted this explanation – or pretended to – and proclaimed Hsiang Yu commander-in-chief. When King Huai received his report, he had no option but to confirm the appointment.

Hsiang Yu had progressed within a few months from hired muscle to supreme commander of the Ch'u army, but his military record was still nothing exceptional. He had come to power over the bodies of more colleagues and innocent civilians than enemy soldiers. The next few days, however, were to more than make up for the past. Free to pursue his own plan, he immediately crossed the river. Presumably he had pursued his military studies long enough to have read Sun Tzu, for what followed was a classic example of what the master meant by placing an army in 'death ground'. Hsiang Yu sank his boats, smashed his cooking pots – leaving his men with only three days' rations – and led them into battle knowing that they had no choice but to conquer or die.

Ten of the other rebel states' armies had also come to help Chao, but had not dared to engage the Ch'in in battle. Instead they had constructed fortified camps outside Chu-lu city, and taken refuge within them. Now they stood on their ramparts and watched in awe as Hsiang Yu's men advanced to the attack. Ssu-ma Ch'ien describes the scene:

Of the fighting men of Ch'u there was not one who was not a match for ten of the enemy; the war cry of Ch'u shook the heavens, and the men of the other armies all trembled with fear.

Nine savage battles ensued, the Ch'in struggling with desperate valour to avoid encirclement. But the Ch'u warriors were in just as perilous a position. As Hsiang Yu had calculated, the knowledge that there could be no retreat drove them on to incredible feats of arms. At the end of the fighting, three Ch'in generals and tens of thousands of their troops lay dead on the field. The survivors, finding themselves surrounded, at last laid down their arms. When the leaders of the other rebel armies arrived in the Ch'u camp to congratulate him, the triumphant Hsiang Yu made them crawl on their knees between two lines of his chariots, drawn up in battle formation.

Chang Han, the best of the generals still loyal to Ch'in, had somehow managed to avoid the débâcle, but was worried about political developments at the Ch'in court. The eunuch Chao Kao had turned against his fellow dictator Li Ssu, and had him executed. The brutal and vindictive Chao dominated the weak-minded Ch'in emperor, and was now effectively in control of the state. So, fearing that Chao Kao would punish him for his failure to defeat Ch'u, Chang Han arranged a meeting with Hsiang Yu, at which he offered his submission. Hsiang, blithely exceeding his authority, awarded Chang the title of 'King of Yung', and put one of his subordinates, Ssu-ma Hsin, in command of the Ch'in army. Hsiang's new allies were ordered to march with the rest of his army to Hsin-an.

On the way, however, rumours reached him of murmurings in the Ch'in camp. The other contingents still had unhappy memories of the arrogant way in which Ch'in troops had treated them in the First Emperor's day, and they now retaliated by insulting their former masters, and treating them as no better than prisoners of war. Furthermore, the Ch'in were worried by the possibility of reprisals against their families at home. When their dissatisfaction was reported to Hsiang Yu, his response was typical. 'In their hearts,' he decreed, 'they have not surrendered.' He ordered his Ch'u soldiers to attack their unsuspecting allies in their camp. The mission was carefully planned, and was carried out with complete surprise. In a single ghastly night, over 200,000 Ch'in soldiers were murdered in their beds.

Ch'in was clearly finished. Its manpower losses had been enormous, and its population was demoralised. Late in 207BC, Chao Kao murdered the Second Emperor. Chao seems to have intended to take the throne himself, but quickly realised that the people would not tolerate this. He therefore found a grandson of the First Emperor, Tzu-ying, and installed him as 'king' of Ch'in. On this occasion the title of *huang-ti* or 'emperor' was deliberately avoided – perhaps in the vain hope of placating the rebels. Tzu-ying, however, was no puppet. One of his first acts was to summon Chao Kao to court and have him killed. But it was too late. Tzu-ying was to survive as king for only forty-six days.

For the campaigning season of 206BC, King Huai deployed several separate armies to finish the job. They were ordered to break through the mountain passes into the Wei valley, where the Ch'in capital was situated. Whichever commander got there first, Huai promised, would be permitted to keep this productive region as his personal fief.

Hsiang Yu battered his way in from the east through fiercely defended mountain passes, squandering the lives of his men in an attempt to reach the city before his rivals. But when he finally arrived, he discovered that he was too late. Another general, Liu Pang, had come the long way round – from the west. In stark contrast to Hsiang Yu, Liu had forbidden plunder and massacre, and worked hard to reassure the people of Ch'in that he would treat them humanely. Consequently his approach had been welcomed, and he had been able to enter Hsienyang unopposed.

Liu Pang

This was not the first time that Hsiang Yu and Liu Pang had met. The latter had been a village headman in the district of P'ei, which lay between the Huai and Yellow Rivers. He was something of an eccentric, and was known for a peculiar bamboo hat of his own design, which he insisted on wearing. In his biography, Ssu-ma Ch'ien describes him thus:

> a prominent nose and a dragon-like face, with beautiful whiskers on his chin and cheeks... He always had great ideas and paid little attention to the business the rest of his family was engaged in... He was fond of wine and women and often used to go to Dame Wang's or Old Lady Wu's and drink on credit.

This does not sound much of a character reference, but Liu had already made an impression in his locality. The *Han Shu* or *History of the Former Han Dynasty*, which describes him in almost the same words as Ssu-ma Ch'ien, adds: 'He was kindly disposed to others, benevolent and liked people. His mind was vast.' There were stories that he had seventy-two moles on his left thigh – a mystical sign of heaven's favour – and that 'wonderful sights' were seen above him when he slept. Other accounts suggest that the kindly disposition was more a matter of policy than of personal inclination, but it seems to have had the desired effect.

A man of noble rank, a Master Lu, who once came to visit the local magistrate in P'ei, was so taken with Liu Pang that he offered him his daughter in marriage. This was despite the protests of Lu's wife, who thought that Liu was not good enough. Liu did, in fact, marry the girl, who fared better than her mother had perhaps expected. Under the name of Empress Lu, she was one day to rule the whole empire.

When the rebellions broke out in 209, Liu Pang at last found his role in life. The Ch'in magistrate had barricaded himself within the city of P'ei, so Liu shot an arrow over the walls which bore a message urging the populace to kill the magistrate and choose themselves a new leader. They did so, and inevitably chose Liu Pang – allegedly over his own protests. Liu improvised an army, which he distinguished by providing it with red flags, and led it to two minor victories over Ch'in armies. He then marched to join the army of King Huai. He subsequently fought alongside Hsiang Yu in several of the early campaigns, and then in 207 was given command of a Ch'u army in his own right.

It was later said of Liu Pang that, while no military genius himself, he knew how to pick and retain able subordinates. He was careful to maintain discipline, and never to alienate the people by permitting plunder and massacre. He was just as ruthless as Hsiang Yu, but in a very different way – calm and calculating, with boundless ambition. Hsiang would have done well to treat him with respect, and had, in fact, been forewarned. En route to Hsienyang, an officer named Fan Tseng had observed:

'When the governor of P'ei (i.e. Liu Pang) was living east of the mountains, he was greedy for possessions and delighted in beautiful girls. But now that he has entered the Pass he has not taken a single thing, nor has he dallied with any of the wives or maidens. This proves that his mind is not set on minor joys.'

Whatever King Huai may have promised, Hsiang Yu was by now beyond his control. When Liu reached Hsienyang there was an unpleasant stand-off which lasted for several days, but as Hsiang had 400,000 men with him and Liu Pang only a quarter of that number, the latter had no choice but to withdraw and allow his rival to take the prize. In fact Hsiang was only dissuaded from launching an unprovoked attack on Liu by the intervention of one of his uncles, Hsiang Po, who had a close friend who was an officer in Liu's army.

Hsiang Yu then resorted to what, for him, were subtler tactics. He sent an invitation to Liu to dine with him in his tent. During the meal one of Hsiang's cousins performed a traditional dance with a drawn sword, during which he was supposed to approach Liu and kill him. But Hsiang Po thwarted him, joining in the dance himself in such a way as to shield Liu every time the assassin approached. Seeing what was happening, one of Liu's entourage sneaked away and went to the gate of the camp, where Liu's carriage attendant – a tough character called Fan K'uai – was waiting. Fan took up his sword and shield, and strode towards Hsiang Yu's tent.

Two sentries tried to bar his way with crossed spears, but Fan knocked them both down with his shield and pushed his way inside. It must have been a dramatic scene. Ssu-ma Ch'ien, probably drawing on an eyewitness account which is now lost, describes it for us. The prospective assassin broke off the dance and stood at the ready

with drawn sword. Hsiang Yu's own hand went to his sword hilt. Fan K'uai loomed on the threshold, grasping his own weapon. Then Fan began to speak, telling the most powerful warlord in China, in the bluntest of terms, exactly what he thought of him.

The fall of Ch'in, Fan pointed out, was due to the dissatisfaction caused by its excessive punishments. Liu Pang deserved to be rewarded for the capture of Hsienyang, but instead Hsiang Yu had obviously listened to 'some worthless talk', and was about to have him killed. 'If I may be so bold,' he added, 'I advise you not to go through with it!'

Hsiang Yu was silent for a moment. 'Sit down,' he said at last. He ordered Fan to be served with meat and wine. Everyone relaxed a little, but the atmosphere was still tense. Realising that he would still be lucky to get away alive, Liu waited until the wine had been flowing for a while, then asked to be excused in order to relieve himself. Fan drifted outside with him, and the two men ran for the carriage, then drove off quickly to their own camp. Still maintaining the pretence of friendly relations, Liu sent a message to Hsiang apologising for his rudeness, and explaining that he had been too drunk to take his leave properly.

The outcome was predictable: a fuming Hsiang Yu took out his rage on Hsienyang. The city was thoroughly looted, set on fire, and its population slaughtered. It was said to have burned for three months, while Ch'u soldiers ran wild in the ruins. Tzu-ying, whose submission Liu Pang had accepted, was seized by Hsiang Yu and beheaded. Meanwhile Hsiao Ho, one of Liu Pang's most trusted officers, braved the chaos to locate and salvage the Ch'in emperors' magnificent map collection, which Hsiang Yu had ignored and left to burn. These maps were to prove invaluable to Liu in his later campaigns. Also rescued were large quantities of land registers and other legal documents, which would eventually provide the basis for the administration of a new dynasty. Already the pattern of future events was becoming clear. Reckless violence was to be opposed by careful planning.

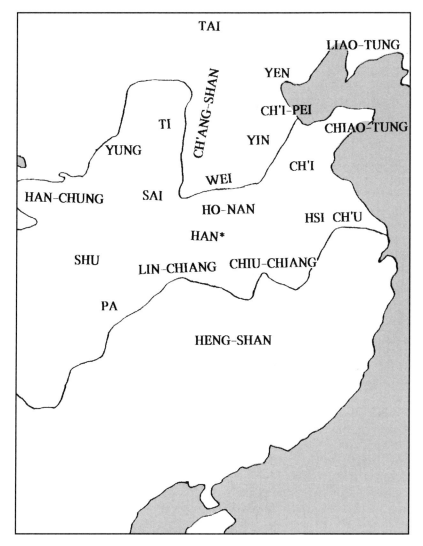

TAI

LIAO-TUNG

YEN

CH'I-PEI

CHIAO-TUNG

TI

CH'ANG-SHAN

YIN

YUNG

CH'I

WEI

HAN-CHUNG   SAI

HO-NAN

HSI CH'U

HAN*

SHU

LIN-CHIANG   CHIU-CHIANG

PA

HENG-SHAN

The abortive settlement of 206BC, showing the artificial principalities established by Hsiang Yu. This arrangement lasted only a few months before the various rulers were once again at war with each other. (*Note: The state of 'Han' should not be confused with Liu Pang's fief of Han-chung. It was from the latter that the imperial Han dynasty arose.)

Settlement and conflict

Hsiang Yu was now in a position to dictate terms to the whole of China. The last obstacle to his ambitions, King Huai, was dealt with in Hsiang's usual style. Tricked into moving his court into the city of Ch'en, which was occupied by Hsiang's troops, Huai was there set upon and murdered. Hsiang Yu then began to establish his own followers as subordinate 'kings', in the various provinces of the empire. He himself was to be 'Lord of Ch'u', and supreme ruler.

This arrangement, which seems to have been a crude attempt to re-establish the conditions of the Warring States, was doomed to failure from the start. Most of the 'kings' were unhappy with their allocations, and they did not command the loyalty of their new subjects. When Tsang Yu arrived in Yen, in the north-east, to take control of his new kingdom, he found it occupied by another warlord, who had already taken to styling himself 'King of Yen', and who flatly refused to move to the land assigned to him on the remote Liao-tung Peninsula. Tsang Yu therefore killed him, and kept both Yen and Liao-tung for himself. Meanwhile, the people of Chao kicked out their new overlord in favour of a member of their old royal family, who became known as King Hsieh.

Shortly afterwards, in the east of the country, a rebel leader named T'ien Jung, who had done nothing to help Hsiang Yu and so had received no allocation, used his private army to drive out three of the new 'kings' and establish himself in the former state of Ch'i. This was too much for Hsiang, who, in 205BC, marched into Ch'i and tried to bring it to heel with the usual campaign of pillage and mass slaughter. The populace rose against him, and he spent most of the year bogged down in the east, unable to restore order.

Liu Pang, the original captor of Hsienyang in 206, was fobbed off with the remote western outpost of Han-chung – on account of which his regime was henceforth known as the Han. But the Ch'in people hated the generals who had been placed in charge of them, as they were defectors from the Ch'in army and were regarded as traitors. So as soon as Hsiang Yu's back was turned, they invited Liu to come and rule them. Ssu-ma Ch'ien suggests, in fact, that the Ch'i war had been deliberately stirred up by Liu as a distraction. He had somehow acquired or forged letters proving that T'ien Jung was planning an attack on Ch'u, and forwarded them to Hsiang Yu. As might be expected with clandestine operations of this type, the truth is impossible to establish. But it would certainly have been in character – both for Liu to devise such a plan, and for Hsiang to fall for it so unthinkingly.

Liu at first claimed that he had only taken what was rightfully his, and that he had no further ambitions. But by now Hsiang Yu's settlement had collapsed, and it must have been obvious to everyone that the whole empire was ripe for the taking. Liu suddenly appeared without warning far to the east, at the new Ch'u capital of P'eng-ch'eng, north of the Huai River. He captured the city, but Hsiang Yu returned from Ch'i by forced marches and in turn surprised Liu, who appears to have grown careless.

Ssu-ma Ch'ien gives the respective strengths of Ch'u and Han in the ensuing battle as 30,000 and 560,000, though the outcome must cast doubt on these figures. It does seem, however, that Hsiang was considerably outnumbered. Nevertheless the ferocity of his attack threw back the Han to the Sui River, where they tried in vain to reform their line of battle. Hsiang charged again, driving his enemies into the river. It was said that so many died that the flow of the stream was blocked. Liu Pang found

himself surrounded, but at that moment a storm broke, blowing sand from the river bank into the faces of the Ch'u troops. Seizing the opportunity, Liu cut his way out and escaped with just thirty horsemen. His father and wife were left behind to be taken as hostages.

This – his first defeat – seems to have unnerved Liu Pang. He fled back to his old home district of P'ei, hoping to find shelter with his relatives, but most of them were in hiding. He collected his young son and daughter, took them into his carriage and drove west. But the Ch'u cavalry were in hot pursuit, and the heavily burdened vehicle was making slow progress. Ssu-ma Ch'ien – who, it must be remembered, was writing under the dynasty founded by Liu, and so had a strong motive for showing him in the best possible light – relates that on several occasions Liu tried to lighten the load by kicking his own children out of the carriage. Each time, a certain Lord T'eng, who was riding with him, had to pull them back.

The panic-stricken flight eventually ended when Liu met a relief army sent from Ch'in. This force was composed of old men and under-aged boys, but it was enough to seize and hold a fortified camp at Jung-yang, on the south bank of the Yellow River. There the Ch'u pursuit was halted, and the two armies faced each other once again. On the advice of his second-in-command, Fan Tseng, Hsiang Yu rejected an offer of negotiation, and settled down to a long blockade.

The strategic situation here was interesting. West of the Han camp was an immense storehouse known as the Ao Granary, which had been built by the Ch'in government to stockpile a reserve supply of grain. Liu had a walled road built along the riverbank so that the grain could be brought in safety to Jung-yang. With the walls and palisades to the south, and the Yellow River to the north, Liu seemed fairly secure. However, on the north bank of the river lay the newly independent state of Chao, whose ruler was believed to be inclining towards Ch'u.

Early in 204, therefore, Liu sent Han Hsin, one of his best officers, to deal with Chao. The army which Han Hsin led was another hastily gathered collection of conscripts – recruited 'from the market-place', as their commander later put it. This makes the ensuing campaign all the more remarkable. Its two principal battles were to become classics of Chinese military history, studied by aspiring generals for the next 2000 years. Although neither Hsiang Yu nor Liu Pang was involved directly in these battles, they are worth examining here.

H'an Hsin's northern campaign

King Hsieh of Chao fortified the Ching-hsing Pass against the approaching Han army, and occupied it with a large force of his own. Knowing that his raw troops were not equal to the task of storming this position, Han Hsin hatched a plan. He advanced to within ten miles of the pass, then halted his army for the night. Under cover of darkness, he detached 2000 cavalrymen and sent them on a wide flank march, which would bring them to a point overlooking the Chao defences. Every man of this detachment was issued with a red flag – the distinguishing emblem of the Han armies. Han Hsin then embarked on an elaborate ploy to lure the Chao out of their positions.

As dawn broke, a division of 10,000 Han troops could be seen drawn up in a line in full view of the pass, with its back to the River Ti. The Chao defenders were amused by the apparent ineptitude of this deployment, and were eager to rush forward and wipe out the enemy force, which had so rashly cut off its own retreat. Hsieh managed to keep them under control, but when Han Hsin himself appeared in an exposed position well in front of his own line, accompanied by the flags and drums which identified a commander-in-chief, the sight proved too tempting to resist. The Chao commander ordered an immediate charge, and his men poured out of the pass, leaving the defences almost deserted.

Abandoning his flags and drums, Han Hsin retreated to the shelter of the division on the riverbank. Some of his pursuers stopped to pick up the trophies, while others rushed ahead. They struck the Han battle line with an almost overwhelming shock, but Han Hsin's conscripts, with nowhere to run to, were now fighting for their lives. The point of the unorthodox deployment now became apparent; men who could not otherwise have been relied upon to face a charge resisted the onslaught with the courage of desperation. As Hsiang Yu had done against the Ch'in, Han Hsin had placed them in 'death ground'. They held on just long enough for their commander's trap to be sprung.

When they saw the pass denuded of its defenders, the 2000 Han cavalry charged down from the hills and occupied the fortifications. Then they set up a host of red flags along the ramparts. Some of the Chao soldiers, returning to their base with the captured trophies, looked up and saw what must have looked like the banners of an immense Han army which had suddenly appeared in their rear. The news spread quickly through the Chao ranks, and produced an almost immediate panic. As their enemies broke and fled in terror, the Han rallied and followed up. The entire Chao army is said to have been either killed or captured. Among the prisoners was King Hsieh himself.

The effect of this victory was to bring Chao firmly into the Han camp, but there was more fighting to be done before the north was fully pacified. In the next year, 203, Han Hsin found himself facing a combined Ch'u and Ch'i army across the Wei River. He had learned that the Ch'u commander, Lung Wu, was contemptuous of him, so he used this weakness as the basis of a yet more ingenious plan. One night, Han sent a contingent of troops upstream with thousands of sand-bags, with which they dammed the river at a point out of sight of both armies, reducing the flow to a trickle. In the morning the Han army crossed to the west bank and made a half-hearted attack on Lung Wu's division. As soon as the Ch'u forces counter-attacked, the

The theatre of the civil wars of 209 to 202BC, and of Liu Pang's later campaigns as Han emperor, showing principal battles.

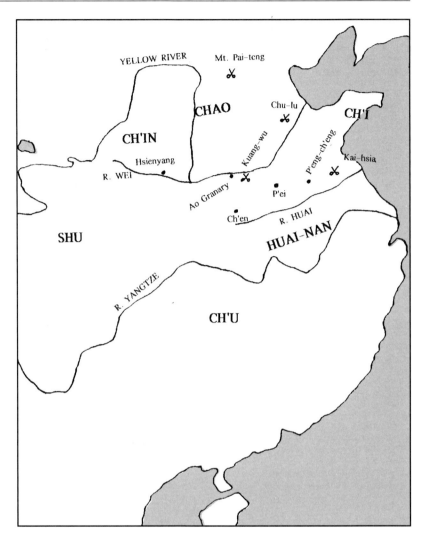

Han pretended to flee back across the river, which was now no obstacle to their movements. Lung Wu, exclaiming, 'I always knew Han Hsin was a coward!', led his men in a hasty pursuit. At this point, Han Hsin gave the prearranged signal to break open the dam.

Lung Wu got across to the far side with a few followers, but the rest of his army was checked by the suddenly rising waters. Helplessly, they watched as Lung was overwhelmed by the Han conscripts, and killed. The Ch'i contingent – reluctant allies in any case – promptly turned and marched off home, and the leaderless Ch'u troops followed them in disorder. Han Hsin then recrossed the river at leisure and harried the retreating enemy for miles, capturing many of them.

The struggle along the Yellow River

Meanwhile, Liu Pang's position at Jung-yang had become increasingly difficult. The Ch'u troops had stormed the walled road along the river, and cut off the Han camp from its source of supply at the Ao Granary. So once again Liu decided to abandon his army – they were only replaceable conscripts, after all – and break out with just a small bodyguard. On this occasion, he had time to prepare the ground properly. When a messenger from Hsiang Yu arrived to propose surrender terms, Liu pretended to jump to the conclusion that the man had come from Fan Tseng, Hsiang's second-in-command. Naturally Fan was not supposed to communicate with the enemy on his own initiative, so when this was reported to Hsiang, he interrogated his deputy about it. Fan was offended at the insinuation that he might be engaged in treacherous correspondence, and resigned his command in protest.

While the Ch'u were still preoccupied with the confusion caused by Fan's resignation, Liu sent out one of his generals, Chi Hsin, in a yellow-canopied carriage to parley with Hsiang Yu. Yellow was the colour used for royal vehicles, and Hsiang assumed that Liu Pang himself was coming out to surrender. While the enemy was thus further distracted, Liu and a handful of cavalry broke out and escaped. In a fit of rage, Hsiang Yu had the unfortunate Chi Hsin burned alive.

By this time, however, Han Hsin had secured the north bank of the Yellow River, and Liu was able to evade pursuit and join him there. What was more, the state of Ch'i had also been detached from the Ch'u alliance by the victory at the Wei River. Liu therefore sent an army under an officer named P'eng Yueh to co-operate with the Ch'i forces, and cause trouble for Ch'u. Normally, to divide one's forces in this way would be a recipe for disaster, but by now Liu had the measure of Hsiang Yu, who was easily provoked into action but lacked the patience to finish what he had started.

Sure enough, Hsiang raced off eastwards to deal with P'eng Yueh. Liu Pang and Han Hsin recrossed the Yellow River, and replenished their supplies from the Ao Granary. This time they were able to choose a better position for their camp, at a spot called Kuang-wu. Here their perimeter was protected by a maze of creeks and ravines, and they were able to strengthen it further with field fortifications. Hsiang Yu soon drove off P'eng Yueh, but after chasing him for a while he lost interest, and returned to face his main enemy. As the Kuang-wu position was so difficult to

attack, and as Liu Pang had no intention of facing the formidable Ch'u soldiers in open battle, the two armies sat and watched each other for several months. But soon P'eng Yueh was back on the scene, hovering in Hsiang's rear, and threatening his supply lines from the east.

So Hsiang resorted to what, for him, passed for diplomacy. He was still holding Liu Pang's father, whom he had captured at the Sui River, and now he threatened to boil him alive if Liu did not surrender. In his reply to this message, Liu explained that when the two rivals had both sworn allegiance to King Huai, this had technically made them brothers. 'If you insist now upon boiling your own father,' he concluded, 'I hope you will be good enough to send me a cup of the soup!' In the face of this callous *sang froid*, even Hsiang Yu was nonplussed. He yielded to the advice of his staff that the threatened murder would damage his own reputation without in the least diverting Liu Pang from his purpose, and so the victim was spared.

A mounted archer or lou-fan, depicted on a pot from a Han tomb. (British Museum)

Hsiang's next idea was to challenge his rival to single combat. Liu turned down the invitation with the comment, 'Since I am no match for you in strength, I prefer to fight you with brains.' So a champion was sent out between the lines to insult the Han, and perhaps to provoke them into attacking. In the Han army there was a famous archer, who was especially skilled at shooting from horseback; he galloped out of the camp, shot the Ch'u champion dead, then rode back before anyone could catch him. Two more of Hsiang's best fighters repeated the performance, only to suffer the same fate.

At this point, Hsiang Yu's temper finally got the better of him. He strapped on his armour, seized a spear, and went storming out himself into no-man's-land. The Han champion was about to shoot, but Hsiang – in Ssu-ma Ch'ien's words – 'shouted and glared so fiercely at him' that the archer fled in terror. By this time, Liu Pang had come out to watch. He was standing safely behind a ravine where Hsiang could not get at him, and the two of them exchanged insults for a while. Liu launched into a long list of Hsiang's crimes, to which the latter replied by once more demanding satisfaction in single combat. When Liu again refused, Hsiang pulled out a crossbow which he had somehow concealed under his clothing – it may have been one of the one-handed 'pistol' crossbows which are occasionally excavated from Warring States tombs – and shot him in the chest.

The wound was not fatal, and Liu managed to conceal it from his men for a while, walking around the camp as usual until the pain became too great. He was nevertheless effectively out of action for some time. Typically, Hsiang Yu did not take advantage of this. Instead, he decided to settle accounts once and for all with P'eng Yueh. Taking with him a detachment of his best troops, he left the main Ch'u army under the command of three of his generals: Ts'ao Chiu, Tung I and Ssu-ma Hsin. His instructions to them were clear: they were not to attack the Han camp, but simply to hold their present positions for fifteen days, until Hsiang returned to take over.

Hsiang Yu went off on his usual rampage, failing to pin down P'eng, but venting his frustrations on captured civilians. When he took the town of Wai-huang, he assembled all the adult male citizens, planning as usual to massacre them. He was dissuaded by a boy of thirteen, who was the only person who dared to speak out. The boy told Hsiang that the people of Wai-huang district had always been his supporters, and when he first arrived had regarded him as a liberator. If he lived up to that image now, the whole region would willingly submit to him. Surprisingly, Hsiang took this advice and spared the men, with the predicted result: several neighbouring cities, on hearing the news, opened their gates without a fight. Hsiang Yu had learned a vital lesson, but for him it was already too late.

The tide turns

When he returned to the front at Kuang-wu, it was to find his army gone. Liu Pang had discovered his absence, and sent messengers out to taunt and insult the three Ch'u generals. In a blind rage, they had launched an attack with their depleted forces across the Ssu River, which protected part of the Han line. Liu had waited until they were halfway across, and then counter-attacked, cutting the Ch'u army to pieces. Tung I and Ssu-ma Hsin had committed suicide in disgrace. Hsiang Yu realised at once that his losses were so great that he would be unable to continue the blockade.

Even now, however, Liu would not risk a general engagement against Hsiang in the open field. Instead he merely demanded the return of his family, and proposed that they should divide the empire between themselves, forming two independent states – Ch'u in the east, and Han in the west. Hsiang had no choice but to agree. It can have surprised neither man, however, that the resulting peace lasted only a few months.

The victory of Han

By the spring of 202BC, Liu Pang had made his final plans. His enemy's portion of the country had been ravaged by years of war, and despite his brief change of heart at Wai-huang, Hsiang's increasingly erratic behaviour was alienating many of his supporters. On the other hand, the few months' respite allowed Liu to receive massive reinforcements. Ch'in and Chao both sent every man they could spare. The former especially remained staunchly loyal to the Han, and had been left largely undamaged by the previous three years of fighting. From farther west, the frontier regions of Shu and Pa provided supplies of grain, as well as large contingents of their renowned warriors.

The intention was for three Han armies – under Liu Pang, Han Hsin and P'eng Yueh – to link up at Ku-ling on the border with Ch'u. However, although even Ssu-ma Ch'ien is unsure of the details, something went wrong. Liu's two subordinates were delayed, and he had to face a sharp counter-attack by the Ch'u army without their support. Once again, Liu proved no match for Hsiang Yu in a stand-up fight on equal terms, and he was driven back in some disorder. He sent frantic messages to Han Hsin and P'eng Yueh – this time not giving orders, but promising them large grants of land in return for their help.

Liu obviously assumed that their slowness had been deliberate – an attempt, perhaps, to wring some concessions out of him. Much later, his suspicions were to lead to tragic results, but it is not certain that this was actually what had happened. Han Hsin had until recently been campaigning hard in the north against Lung Wu, and had then been expected to march his weary and inexperienced troops hundreds of miles in the early spring, when the rivers were swollen and the roads muddy. P'eng Yueh had not needed to travel so far, but recently he had been carrying out a guerrilla campaign in the face of Hsiang Yu's powerful offensive. His forces must have been dispersed, and would have taken some time to reassemble. Whatever the true facts, soon afterwards both

generals were reunited with Liu at Kai-hsia. What was more, they were also joined by the troops of Chou Yin, the Grand Marshal of Ch'u, who had decided to change sides. The combined Han army is claimed to have numbered 400,000: this may be an exaggeration, but it seems certain that it outnumbered the Ch'u by roughly four to one. Han Hsin was put in command of the centre, with three-quarters of the available troops. Liu Pang commanded from a position in the rear.

When Hsiang Yu arrived, following up his earlier success, he immediately launched his customary headlong charge. This time, however, superior numbers told, and he found himself encircled. Even so he managed to hold off his enemies for an entire day, and at night retired battered but undefeated into his fortified camp. There, during the night, Hsiang heard a sound which must have made his blood run cold. Drifting over from the Han camp came the sound of singing – the unmistakable southern tunes beloved of his own Ch'u soldiery.

There are several possible explanations for this. One source says that many of Liu's western troops had campaigned in the south, and had learnt the Ch'u songs there. Chou Yin had brought Ch'u soldiers with him, although it is not known how many. But to the impetuous Hsiang Yu there could be only one explanation: his own men were deserting to the enemy under cover of darkness. He mounted Dapple, his favourite horse, hurriedly assembled 800 cavalry on whose loyalty he knew he could rely, and led them in a sword-swinging charge at the Han lines, leaving the rest of his army to its fate.

Breaking through the astonished Han troops, Hsiang galloped south for the safety of the Yangtze River, pursued by the Han general Kuan Ying with 5000 horsemen. One by one Hsiang's followers were left behind, and when he reached Tung-ch'eng, on the far bank of the Huai River, only twenty-eight of them were still with him. Here the fugitives were overtaken and surrounded on a small hill. But it was at this sort of man-to-man fighting that Hsiang Yu excelled. He led charge after charge down the hill into the encircling Han cavalry, each time striking down his opponents and then wheeling away out of reach. At last he managed to break through and escape, leaving behind two of his own men dead. But – according to Ssu-ma Ch'ien's account – a Han general and a hundred of his troopers had also been killed.[1]

Kuan Ying, nevertheless, pressed on after him. Hsiang reached the Yangtze at Wu-chiang, where boats were available to ferry him across. But he seems to have realised that his cause was lost, and decided that there was no further point in running. He and his last handful of companions dismounted, turned their horses loose, and waited with swords in their hands for their enemies to arrive. They fought desperately until all hope was gone, and then Hsiang Yu retired and cut his own throat to avoid capture.

His head was brought back to Liu Pang, who ordered it to be taken around the few remaining cities still loyal to Ch'u, and displayed to the garrisons there. Realising that there was no hope of relief, all these cities soon surrendered. By the end of 202, Liu Pang was the undisputed ruler of the entire empire. He took for himself the title of Emperor Kao-ti, the first emperor of the Han dynasty.

Emperor of Han
It is obvious from Hsiang Yu's attempt to turn back

the clock in 206 that the concept of a unified empire was by no means universally accepted prior to Liu Pang's accession. Yet from Han times onwards it was seldom seriously questioned. The dynasty which Liu Pang founded was to last for four centuries, and set the pattern of China's system of government for two millennia.

In its early days, however, it was still a rather rough-and-ready arrangement. The new emperor originally decided on Lo-yang

A later portrait of Liu Pang as the emperor Han Kao-ti.

as his capital, but he was soon persuaded to move it 'within the passes' to Ch'ang-an, not far from the Ch'in site at Hsienyang. In many other respects, he followed the precedents set by the Ch'in, including the Legalist system of specific rewards and punishments. Even the Ch'in religious ceremonies, with their veneration of the element water, were retained.[2]

The civil service manned by scholars would not be introduced until the seventh century AD, and Kao-ti was only following the normal procedure when he filled the leading posts in his government with long-time friends and supporters, and with members of his own family. He seems to have regarded over-centralisation as having been one of the fatal weaknesses of the Ch'in, and thus preferred to leave power as much as possible in the hands of local magnates. The empire was therefore divided into fourteen commanderies, located in the west, and ten 'kingdoms', which comprised the eastern half of the country, and included most of the population. These semi-independent kingdoms were originally left under the control of men who had established their power bases in those regions during the civil wars, but gradually the local warlords were replaced by brothers or sons of the emperor.

One of Liu Pang's preoccupations in the years after his victory was to establish exactly why he had been so successful. One day he asked two of his officers this question. Ssu-ma Ch'ien has preserved their frank reply:

'Your Majesty is arrogant and insulting to others, while Hsiang Yu was kind and loving (!) But when you send someone to attack a city or seize a region, you award him the spoils of the victory, sharing your gains with the whole world. Hsiang Yu was jealous of worth and ability... No matter what victories were achieved in battle, he gave his men no reward... This is why he lost possession of the world.'

The emperor's own opinion is also worth quoting. He gave the credit in part to three of his most outstanding followers:

'When it comes to sitting within the tents of command and devising strategies that will assure us victory a thousand miles away, I am no match for Chang Liang. In ordering the state and caring for the people, in providing rations for the troops and seeing to it that the lines of supply are not cut off, I cannot compare to Hsiao Ho. In leading an army of a million men... I cannot come up to Han Hsin. These three are all men of extraordinary ability, and it is because I was able to make use of them that I gained possession of the world.'

Kao-ti seems to have felt guilty about the way in which he had risked his father's life when the latter was a prisoner of Hsiang Yu. After he came to the throne, he bestowed on him the title of 'Grand Supreme Emperor', and always treated him with great respect. But on one occasion he made his true feelings known. Ssu-ma Ch'ien quotes him as saying to his father:

'You always used to consider me a worthless fellow who could never look after the family fortunes and had not half the industry of my older brother Chung. Now that my labours are completed, which of us has accomplished more, Chung or I?'

But if Kao-ti really considered that his labours were completed, he was soon proved wrong. In 200BC war broke out with the Hsiung-nu, who had taken advantage of the civil wars in China to rebuild their power after their defeat at the hands of Meng T'ien. The emperor himself led the expedition on to the steppes, and it was a disaster. First came blizzards and freezing weather, in which two or three men in every ten lost fingers to frostbite. Then at Mount Pai-teng, near the town of P'ing-ch'eng in what is now Shansi Province, a huge horde of Hsiung-nu surrounded the Han army. The emperor and his troops were besieged for seven days, and Kao-ti was able to extricate himself only by agreeing to significant concessions. There-

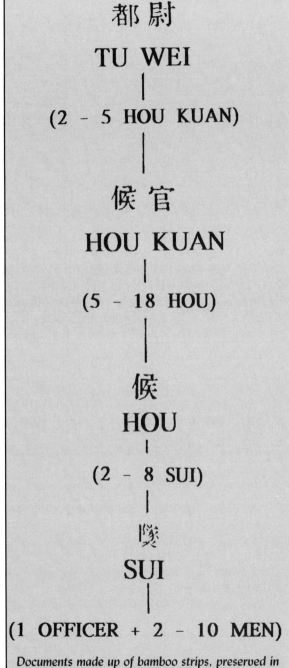

都 尉

TU WEI

|

(2 - 5 HOU KUAN)

|

候 官

HOU KUAN

|

(5 - 18 HOU)

|

候

HOU

|

(2 - 8 SUI)

|

隧

SUI

|

(1 OFFICER + 2 - 10 MEN)

Documents made up of bamboo strips, preserved in the forts along the northern frontier, have enabled scholars to piece together the organisational details of early Han armies – information which is seldom available for forces of this period. This order of battle of a Tu Wei, or 'battalion', is based on the work of Michael Loewe.

after, he dealt with the Hsiung-nu through a policy of paying tribute and arranging diplomatic marriages, rather than attempting to fight them again. For other troubles within the empire were now claiming his attention.

By 196, several of the kingdoms which he had set up were beginning to demand full independence. P'eng Yueh, who had been made king of Liang, was caught plotting a revolt, and was put to death. An additional tragedy of this affair was the execution of Han Hsin, who had done as much as anyone to ensure the victory of the Han. It is not clear whether the great general was also guilty of treason, or whether the emperor was becoming excessively suspicious, per-haps recalling the delay in reinforcing him at Ku-ling. Either way, the loss of Han Hsin was a severe blow. Soon after this purge, the king of Huai-nan, Ch'ing Pu, came out in revolt, and in 195 Lu Wan, king of Yen, defected to the Hsiung-nu. These two men seem to have believed that Kao-ti was old and tired of war, and that with his best generals now dead, he would have no stomach for a fight. How wrong they were, Ch'ing Pu was quickly to discover.

Kao-ti's last campaign

Kao-ti knew that drastic measures would be needed to prevent his empire disinte-grating even faster than had the Ch'in. In the autumn of 196, he led an army south to Huai-nan. On the way there was a touching scene when he passed through his old home town of P'ei. The emperor held a great feast for all his old friends, and he personally entertained their chil-dren by singing and playing the lute. He taught 120 of the children to sing some of his favourite songs. Then, overcome with nostalgia, he announced that he was exempting the people of P'ei from all taxes in recognition of their friendship.

Ch'ing Pu had already won two great victories over the local Han armies. But at

Kuei-chui, the emperor himself brought him to battle. As the armies faced each other, Kao-ti noticed to his fury that his adversary was using a method of deployment which Hsiang Yu had favoured. Our sources are silent on the details of the fighting, but it was a long and bitter struggle. At the end of the day Ch'ing Pu fled, only to be murdered soon afterwards. Huai-nan was restored to its allegiance. Kao-ti, however, had been wounded by a stray arrow. He returned home, but the wound would not heal. On 1 June 195, in the Palace of Lasting Joy in Ch'ang-an, he died. He was probably between fifty and sixty years old.

The emperor was succeeded by his fifteen-year-old son, who took the throne as the Emperor Hui-ti. He left seven other sons by various wives. One of these boys was allegedly murdered by Hui-ti's mother, the Empress Lu, in order to secure the succession. In 188 Hui-ti himself died, and the empress ruled as regent for eight years. The situation seemed ripe for further civil war, but the Han dynasty survived. After another generation of growing prosperity, the Emperor Wu-ti was strong enough to initiate a series of campaigns which made the Han the first of the great conquering dynasties.[3] The Hsiung-nu were beaten and subdued, the Silk Route to the west brought under Chinese control, and Han armies penetrated the deserts of Central Asia as far as what is now Uzbekistan. All this was part of Kao-ti's legacy.

It was the tradition for a son to establish temples in memory of an illustrious father. Hui-ti built the customary shrines to the great founding emperor in his capital, Ch'ang-an. But he also set up a more personal memorial, in P'ei, where 120 children were employed in perpetuity to sing in his memory the songs which Liu Pang had taught them.

THE HEYDAY OF THE ARMOURED 'KNIGHT'

Just as cavalry had first appeared in China much later than in the West, so the development of mounted shock tactics also lagged behind. The heavily armoured 'cataphract', armed with a lance and riding a fully armoured horse, had been a feature of warfare in western Asia since the early third century BC. Such warriors had helped to smash the Roman legions at the famous Parthian victory of Carrhae in 53BC. Chinese horsemen, however, remained for a long time basically skirmishers, protected by at most a light corselet, wielding bows, halberds and swords, and riding unarmoured horses. A Han period relief from Hsiao-t'ang-shan illustrates these skirmishing tactics in action: some horsemen are seen shooting their bows at the gallop, while another hooks his opponent off his horse with the transverse blade of his halberd.

Only in the Three Kingdoms period, after the fall of the Han dynasty, did things begin to change. This is surprising, because the Han had already come into contact, in the Bactrian region of Central Asia, with peoples who employed the Parthian type of 'cataphract'. Three Kingdoms cavalry, it seems, were fewer in numbers than their Han predecessors, but actually become more prominent in battle accounts, especially in the armies of the northern kingdom of Wei. Horse armour now makes its appearance. Ts'ao Ts'ao of Wei claimed that at one point he possessed ten such panoplies, while his opponents had three hundred. A memorial dated to AD226 mentions an item of equipment called *ma-k'ai i-ling*, which must refer to some sort of horse armour. But it is highly unlikely that these references are to full metal protection of the 'cataphract' type. The earliest archae-ological evidence for horse armour is a tomb model of AD302, and this shows no more than a simple quilted band around the animal's chest.

During the fourth century, however, a revolution took place in cavalry warfare. The Western Ts'in dynasty, which replaced the Wei in 265, suffered badly from civil unrest, and proved unable to defend the northern frontier against the Hsiung-nu and Hsien-pi barbarians, who had been infiltrating into the area since the late Han. The leaders of the Hsiung-nu, who had for centuries been in the habit of marrying into the Han royal family, took this opportunity to claim the empire as their own inheritance. In 311 a Hsiung-nu chief named Liu Ts'ung sacked Lo-yang, and five years later Ch'ang-an suffered the same fate. The shattered Ts'in retreated south of the Huai River, and the Yellow River valley fell into the hands of the barbarians. Despite their grandiose claims, none of their leaders were able to exert control over the whole area, and North China was shared out among a collection of unstable and continually warring regimes.

For the native Chinese of the region, this was a disaster. But in some respects it brought unexpected progress. So many people fled to the safety of the Yangtze valley region that the demographic map of the country was permanently changed, and the long, slow process of Chinese colonisation of the south received a significant boost. The invasions also marked an important step forward in the Chinese art of warfare. For the barbarians brought with them the concept of the heavily armoured cavalryman, equipped with stirrups, and riding a fully armoured horse.

Representations of early 'cataphract' cavalry from Oriental tombs 1) From the tomb of Tung Shou in Korea, AD357. 2) Relief carving on a brick from Teng-hsien in south China, c.AD500. 3) From Mai-chi-shan, north-west China, early sixth century AD. The spectacular plumes attached to the horses' rumps in these last two pictures are also known from contemporary Korea. They must have been made of some light material, such as cloth streamers, or perhaps the long tail feathers of tropical birds. A traditional title for mounted guard units, revived under the Northern Wei, was 'Forest of Feathers'.

The exact details of the introduction are uncertain. We know that the Hsiung-nu first acquired examples of this type of equipment in 312, when they captured 5000 armoured horses from the Hsien-pi. Thirty years later the Hsiung-nu were still acquiring many of their heavy horses from the Hsien-pi. It is a reasonable assumption, therefore, that the latter were the first to introduce the technology into China. Whether it was actually invented in the Hsien-pi homeland, in what

is now Manchuria, is not known. Another possible source is Korea, where the earliest known depiction of oriental 'cataphract' cavalry in art has been found. This is a wall painting from the tomb of a Chinese officer, Tung Shou, which has been dated to AD357.[1]

The second development which affected cavalry warfare at around the same time was the widespread adoption of the stirrup. Unlike horse armour, it is possible that this was an indigenous Chinese invention. Single stirrups, used only for mounting, were certainly in use in the Three Kingdoms period. A relief from the Eastern Han has been construed as showing true stirrups, but this interpretation is controversial. In any case, it appears that it was not until the fourth century AD that they became commonplace.

Scholars are divided over the question of the value of stirrups in mounted combat, and the argument that they were a crucial factor in the rise of the medieval knight in the West has been largely discredited. The early cataphracts of the Mediterranean and Western Asia operated effectively without them. But in China, the spread of the stirrup does seem to have been closely associated with the adoption of heavier armour. This may be connected with the method of using the lance and other weapons – a topic that will be discussed below.

Once introduced into China, horse armour spread rapidly. It was adopted enthusiastically, not only by the barbarian horsemen, but also by the Chinese themselves. By the end of the fourth century, illustrations of 'cataphract' equipment are found as far away from its point of origin as Yunnan, in the extreme south-west. It was some time, however, before there was general agreement on the tactics and weapons best suited to the new type of horseman.

The fourth century in particular witnessed some odd experiments. In one battle against their Hsiung-nu rivals, the Mu-jung clan of the Hsien-pi chained 5000 of their cavalry together in a huge square block to resist an enemy charge. Rather surprisingly, this unusual tactic was successful. The Hsiung-nu commander led a charge against the square, but was unable to break it, and was subsequently captured. On this occasion the Hsien-pi fought with bows, and the Hsiung-nu – if their leader's equipment was typical – with spears and halberds.

It appears to have been quite commonplace for generals at least to fight with two weapons simultaneously – a sword in the left hand and a lance in the right, or a lance in the left and a halberd in the right, for example. Even the most heavily armoured cavalrymen also habitually carried bows – a fifth-century relief from Tan-yang shows such a warrior with a strung bow slung around his neck. Contemporary paintings and carvings suggest that lances were often wielded overhead in both hands – a method that was also characteristic of the Parthians and other Western 'cataphracts'.

The Mu-jung experiment with chained horsemen, however successful, seems not to have been repeated. To judge from both pictorial and textual evidence, the usual style of fighting was far more energetic, involving rapid charges and retreats, and also a considerable amount of individual combat between rival leaders. At the same time, the weapons in use could be very heavy, and must have required exceptional strength to wield. Some halberds are said to have weighed up to ninety pounds. Ch'en An, who was killed in a battle in 323, carried not only a bow and a lance, but a sword which is supposed to have been seven feet long.

With the additional weight of their armour, the burden on the troopers would have been considerable. In these circumstances, stirrups must have been a very useful aid to stability. In contrast, the style of fighting of the early Western 'cataphracts' seems to have been rather more sedate, and their formations more solid and slow-moving – a sort of mounted pike phalanx, rather than a horde of charging heroes.

Where the stirrup really comes into its own, however, is as support for a rider who uses the momentum of his horse, rather than the strength of his arms, to deliver his blows. The Norman knights, who at some time in the eleventh century began to couch their lances securely under their arms and train their horses to run at the enemy, could allegedly 'make a hole in the walls of Babylon'. There is tantalising evidence from Chinese sources, however, that a similar method may have been adopted in the East as early as the sixth century.

At around this time, the emphasis of battle accounts seems to undergo a change. In earlier wars, the accent had been on the feats of individual heroes. When massed formations of cavalry are mentioned, they are basically static, like the chained square of the Mu-jung. But a series of battles in the 520s and 530s involved massed charges by thousands of heavy cavalry, which punched great holes in the opposing lines and threw entire armies into confusion. The first of these – at Yeh in 528 – is examined in detail in Chapter 10. Another spectacular example was at Sha-yuan in 537. In a campaign against their Western Wei enemies, 200,000 troops of the Eastern Wei attacked through the T'ong Pass. They drove the westerners ahead of them until they emerged on the far side of the pass, at which point 10,000 western cavalry under Yu-wen T'ai charged them in the flank. About 6000 easterners were killed, and another 70,000 were captured in the collapse which followed.

Clearly, some new and effective method of employing the heavy cavalry been introduced. Whether or not this involved the use of the couched lance as known in medieval Europe, it must have entailed a doctrine of closing with the enemy en masse, using the combined force of thousands of disciplined cavalrymen and their horses to shatter his formations. It does not seem to be inappropriate, therefore, to compare the warriors of this period to the armoured knights of the West.

EHRCHU JUNG:
THE BARBARIAN KINGMAKER

'He saved the people and served the country with a true heart. The gods know this...'
Ehrchu Shih-lung

The empire of the Northern Wei

By the fifth century AD, a new order was beginning to emerge from the chaos of the barbarian invasions. A Hsien-pi clan from Mongolia – the Toba – succeeded in harnessing the very different skills of nomadic warriors and Chinese farmers, and created a new imperial dynasty. This regime became known as the Northern or 'Toba' Wei. Originally based at P'ing-ch'eng in northern Shansi, by the fourth decade of the century it had extended its control over the whole of North China. The south, however, remained in the hands of a series of native dynasties: notably the Liu Sung (420–79), the Southern Ch'i (479–502), and the Liang (502–52). The region was militarily weak compared to the north, as its population base was still much smaller, and it lacked suitable conditions for breeding cavalry horses. The warlike Toba made fun of the southerners, laughing at the way they 'rode facing backwards on water buffaloes', and caricaturing their rulers as fussy old men, obsessed – in the words of the Wei general Yu-wen T'ai[1] – 'with clothes and caps, with rites and liturgical music'.

The southern regimes nevertheless clung to the ambitious dream of driving out the barbarians and reunifying the empire under a native dynasty. Although this was beyond their powers, they did manage to frustrate repeated attempts by the Northern Wei to conquer the rest of the country. The resulting stalemate dragged on for more than a century, punctuated by frequent costly but indecisive campaigns.

The Northern Wei, threatened both from the south and by its nomadic cousins who had remained on the Mongolian steppe, was forced to become more and more of a traditional Chinese state. It gradually came to rely on walls, fortified towns and infantry garrisons to supplement its Toba cavalry. Under the 'Three Leaders' system, native Chinese heads of hamlets, villages and districts were made responsible for collecting taxes and conscripting troops for the army. The Toba themselves were forced to give up their nomadic ways and settle on the land. However, the nobility continued to serve as armoured cavalry, supplied with remounts from immense herds which grazed on the government pasturelands along the Yellow River.

A number of formerly nomadic groups remained outside this system, providing auxiliary troops and furnishing supplies when required. Foremost among these was a clan known as the Ehrchu. The origin of the Ehrchu is something of a mystery, but they are described in contemporary writings as belonging to the race of the 'Chieh Hu'. The term 'Chieh' referred to a nomadic steppe tribe, and 'Hu' in this period had come to denote westerners, from Central Asia or India. The Ehrchu may have been descended from the Yueh-chih, who had originally inhabited the Kansu region of north-western China – the original Chou homeland – but had been driven west by the Hsiung-nu in about 170BC. Explorers of the Han period had discovered the Yueh-chih living in Bactria.[2] The Ehrchu had subsequently migrated eastwards again, and entered China at some time during the period of the barbarian invasions. They had been firm allies of the Toba since before the founding of the Northern Wei.

Eventually the clan had come to enjoy a privileged position in the empire. It occupied extensive lands in Shansi, which it held under a sort of feudal arrangement. Its leaders were expected to supply horses and fodder to the Wei armies in time of war, but they were independent of the military and civil bureaucracies, and seem to have maintained their hereditary chiefs and their autonomy in internal affairs. In effect, they were answerable only to the Wei emperor himself. Over the years, the Ehrchu had become very rich. Their herds of horses, cattle, sheep, goats and camels were so huge that – so the story went – they themselves had no idea how many they possessed, having given up trying to count them, and simply reckoning them by the valleyful. But as the Ehrchu prospered, things had begun to go wrong for the Northern Wei dynasty.

The turning point came in 493, when Emperor Hsiao-wen-ti decided to move his capital south from P'ing-ch'eng to Lo-yang. P'ing-ch'eng had always been a rather rough and ready frontier town, situated on the northern edge of the cultivated lands of China, and looking out across the Gobi Desert towards Mongolia. Lo-yang, on the other hand, was an ancient capital city on the edge of the Chinese heartland on the Yellow River plain. It had been founded by the Western Chou around 1000BC, and had been a place of immense cultural and strategic significance ever since. The symbolism of the move was obvious. Hsiao-wen-ti was determined to make his regime into a true Chinese dynasty, and to bring his still half-wild horsemen into an environment where they could not help but absorb some of the ancient culture of the land which they had conquered.

From a practical point of view, however, Lo-yang was far from an ideal site for an imperial capital. It had once been a vast metropolis of half a million or more inhabitants, which at the beginning of the fourth century had served as the capital of the Ts'in dynasty. When the Ts'in lost control of the northern frontier, Lo-yang took the brunt of the barbarian invasions which followed. When he captured the city in 311, the Hsiung-nu chief Liu Ts'ung had sacked it so thoroughly that it had never recovered.

In the subsequent chaos, barbarian armies rampaged across the Yellow River plain, looting and burning as they went. Most of the surviving inhabitants of the Lo-yang fled south to safety. By the time the Toba arrived, the only occupied part of the city was the little fort of Chin-yung, where a small garrison watched over the strategic route between the Wei and Yellow River valleys. Outside the fort lay a vast expanse of deserted ruins – all that was left of the Ts'in capital.

Hsiao-wen-ti was not deterred. He ordered the entire population of P'ing-ch'eng to relocate southwards – an operation which took two years to complete. Then he set about building a capital worthy of his empire. The process was a long one. The forced move, carried out simultaneously with an ambitious and quite unnecessary attack on the Southern Ch'i, caused immense disruption to the economy. But by 515, when the boy emperor Hsiao-ming-ti succeeded to the throne, Lo-yang was once again a thriving city.

According to the nostalgic reminiscences of Yang Hsuan-chih, whose *Record of the Monasteries of Lo-yang* is our main source for this period:

> The state was rich and its treasuries and storehouses filled to overflowing ... historical records were all full of good events, and there were no natural disasters ... widows and unmarried men did not have to know the taste of dogs' and pigs' food.

At the other end of the social scale, the princes and courtiers became famous for their extravagance. The architecture of the new city was equally spectacular. Countless

beautiful Buddhist monasteries and nunneries were endowed within the walls. The towers beside the main gate, the Ta-hsia Gate on the western side, were 200 feet high, and, in Yang Hsuan-chih's words, 'reached into the clouds'. The most celebrated building of all was the Yung-ning Pagoda, which according to even the most restrained of contemporary descriptions must have towered over 400 feet above the bustling city. Yang, who had climbed it, vouched for the truth of the tale that from the top, just as the locals had claimed, 'one could look down on clouds and rain'.

But all this splendour hid serious problems within the state. Many of the more traditionalist Toba had bitterly resented the policy of sinicisation and the enforced migration which went with it, and government corruption and intrigue added to the contempt in which they had come to hold the capital. Hsiao-ming-ti was only four years old when he came to the throne, and for the first five years of his reign power remained in the hands of his mother, the Dowager Empress Hu. In 520 a coup led by Yuan Yi overthrew the empress. She was imprisoned, while Yuan took over as regent. Unfortunately, his regime was even more corrupt than that of his predecessor. Especially ominous was the way in which officials enriched themselves by appropriating funds intended for the garrisons on the northern frontier. Deprived of pay and rations, the troops inevitably grew resentful.

Early in 523 the Juan-juan – a steppe people whom some have thought to be the ancestors of the Avars – launched a massive raid on the frontier. They broke through the

This pottery tomb-guardian figure from the sixth century AD is characteristic of a genre well known from the sixth and seventh centuries. The beard, round eyes and prominent nose have led archaeologists to speculate that they are intended to represent non-Chinese – possibly warriors from Central Asia, such as the Ehrchu and their relatives. (British Museum)

line of garrisons and ravaged the northern districts of the empire, carrying off horses and captives by the thousand. At the fort of Huai-huang-chen, the Wei commander called out his men to beat off the raiders. They protested that they were starving, but he refused to release the supply of grain which they knew he was holding. No doubt he hoped to sell it later at a huge profit – a practice which had become all too common under Yuan Yi's government. But this time the commander had miscal-culated. The infuriated soldiers killed him, seized the grain, and raised the standard of revolt against the Wei. The news spread quickly, and soon the entire frontier was in arms against the capital and its self-serving officials.

This uprising, which became known as the 'Revolt of the Six Garrisons', shook the Northern Wei dynasty to its core. Under the leadership of a man called P'o-lu-han Pa-ling, a descendant of ancient Hsiung-nu royalty, the battle-hardened rebels routed the first two loyalist armies sent against them. The government temporarily damped down the flames by the drastic expedient of bribing the Juan-juan to inter-vene on its behalf, but by 526 the revolt had broken out again. Soon, almost the whole region

north of the Yellow River was under the control of one or other of the rebel bands.

The rise of Ehrchu Jung

It was amidst this turmoil that Ehrchu Jung began his brief career in the limelight of history. His date of birth is unknown, and almost nothing has been recorded of his early

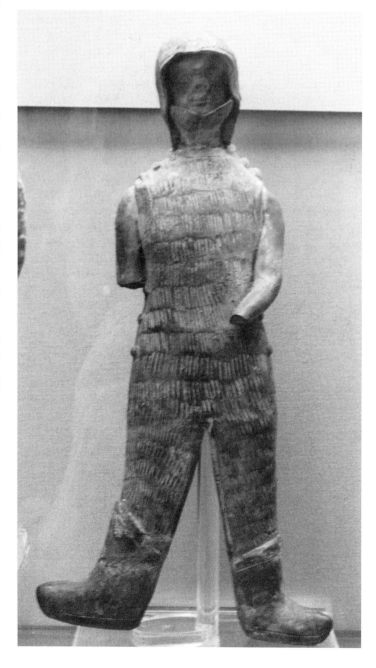

Another figurine from the same period shows a warrior in what appears to be a split coat of lamellar armour, with heavy boots obviously designed for a horseman. His appear-ance fits written descriptions of the 'iron-clad' Ehrchu cavalry, and it may be that this figure is the closest we possess to a likeness of Ehrchu Jung. (British Museum)

life. His family were hereditary chiefs of the Ehrchu, and his father, Hsin-hsing, enjoyed the official title of Duke of Po-ling-chun. Jung succeeded to the chieftainship not long before the Six Garrisons revolt broke out. The first campaign in which he is known to have commanded was the Juan-juan invasion of 523, when he led 4000 cavalrymen in a vain pursuit of the raiders. He is described as white-skinned, which would not be unusual given his Central Asian ancestry. No portrait of him exists, but the art of the period often depicts men of similar origin, who are distinguished from the Chinese by their large eyes and noses, and sometimes by their long beards. A statuette in the British Museum, depicting an armoured cavalryman with such non-Chinese features, may well be intended to represent an Ehrchu nobleman.

It might be supposed that Jung would have had more in common with the nomad traditionalists among the Six Garrison rebels than with the court in Lo-yang, but he decided early on to maintain his people's tradition of loyalty to the Wei. Although at first he declined to launch a large-scale offensive against the rebels, his people proved strong enough to preserve their independence, even when the rest of the north was in enemy hands. Between 524 and 526 they made limited attacks on neighbouring rebel bands, and also provided sanctuary for numerous Wei officials who fled into their territory.

By 527, Jung was in control of most of northern and central Shansi – the only significant area north of the Yellow River which the rebels had not overrun. And with the destruction of most of the imperial forces in the south, the Ehrchu cavalry now constituted the largest battle-worthy force still loyal to the emperor. Their leader seems already to have been planning to take a more active part in the war – perhaps by invading the rebel-held Hopei plain – when an urgent message arrived from Hsiao-ming-ti.

The young emperor was now eighteen, but was still as far as ever from wielding real power. In 525 his mother had reappeared on the scene, and was now ruling with the aid of two unprincipled henchmen named Hsu Ho and Cheng Yen. These men had proved to be utterly incapable of dealing with the revolt, and Hsiao-ming-ti was desperate to be rid of them. Would Jung bring his forces to Lo-yang and help him?

Before the Ehrchu leader could respond, another message arrived hard on the heels of the first. Hsiao-ming-ti had died suddenly, in highly suspicious circumstances. There seems to be little doubt that as soon as he showed signs of wanting to assume power in his own right, the Empress Hu had had him poisoned. He left as his heir a nine-month-old child, and the dowager immediately proclaimed this 'boy' emperor, with herself as regent. The embarrassing fact soon came to light that the child was in fact a girl. Unabashed, Hu quietly got rid of her and found another candidate, a two-year-old boy with a tenuous connection to the royal line. Obviously, she intended at all costs to keep hold of the reins of government for herself.

It is difficult to say how Jung was affected by the murder of Hsiao-ming-ti. It is unlikely, in fact, that he had ever met him; but as a personal vassal of the emperor, the legitimacy of the succession must obviously have concerned him. Other men in similar circumstances might have considered seizing the throne for themselves, but at least at this stage, this does not seem to have occurred to Jung. Instead, he conferred with Yuan T'ien-mu, a member of the Wei imperial family who had taken refuge with the Ehrchu during the rebellion. 'My family has benefited from the grace of the dynasty for generations,' he told Yuan. 'So I cannot sit idly by... I shall take 5000 iron-clad horsemen to mourn at the burial mound, and ask the ministers in attendance the cause of His Majesty's decease.'

This sounds rather naive, but it appears that Yuan explained to him the realities of court politics. If he was going to become involved, he told Jung, he would have to intervene decisively, and take along with him a new ruler who could legitimately replace Hu's child emperor. So the two men set to work. Their first move was to cast a bronze statue to represent each of the imperial princes. This was an ancient method of divination, traditionally used by the northern tribes to find out which of a number of candidates to the throne enjoyed the approval of Heaven.

Of course, this need not be seen as evidence that Jung was genuinely in need of divine guidance. The process would be easy enough to manipulate secretly, and it is not surprising that only one of the castings came out without a flaw – in Yang Hsuan-chih's words, 'a wonderfully majestic statue, perfect in both likeness and lustre'. This was the figure of one Yuan Tzu-yu, the popular Prince of Ch'ang-lo. The prince, in fact, turned out to be the ideal choice – as Yuan T'ien-mu had no doubt realised all along. He was immediately contacted with an offer of the throne, and just as quickly accepted. With appearances satisfied, Jung was ready to move.

Confrontation at Lo-yang

Ten thousand Ehrchu heavy cavalry, wearing white robes over their armour as a sign of mourning for the murdered Hsiao-ming-ti, rode south towards Lo-yang. In the palace of the Dowager Empress, the courtiers dismissed the threat: Jung's men, they pointed out, had no boats. To reach the capital, they would have to cross the only bridge over the Yellow River, at the Meng Ford. And this was securely held by 5000 picked troops under Li Shen-kuei, an officer who was rumoured to be the empress's lover. Hsu Ho explained:

'Ehrchu Jung is a petty barbarian ... a man of mediocre talents... He is like a mantis trying to stop a cart wheel... His unsupported army, a thousand *li* from its base, will be exhausted and weary, so if we meet his tired troops with our fresh ones his defeat is inevitable.'

But now the wisdom of Yuan T'ien-mu's diplomacy became apparent. Li Shen-kuei was less attached to the empress than she had supposed. When he learned that the Prince of Ch'ang-lo was with the enemy, he defected, taking his men with him. Jung and his horsemen rode across the bridge without a hand being raised against them, and on the thirteenth day of the fourth month of 527, they set up camp on the plain of Ho-yin, outside the walls of Lo-yang.

With their most reliable troops gone, the Empress Hu's lackeys decided that the only chance of avoiding a brutal sack of the city lay in prompt submission. When Jung ordered all the aristocrats and officials to come to his camp and pay homage to the new emperor, they obeyed without a murmur. A procession of 2000–3000 people, led by Hu herself, streamed out of the city gates and across the open plain towards the Ehrchu tents.

We have no detailed eyewitness description of the ensuing events, but the scene can be imagined. The host of ministers and officials in their gorgeous court costumes, looking ill-at-ease on the bleak plain outside their familiar city walls, the wind snatching at their robes and silk headgear. Facing them, drawn up in line of battle, were three times their number of grim-faced, armoured horsemen, perhaps with their hands already gripping sword-hilts, bows and lances. How much warning the victims had, we cannot tell. There appears to have been time for Jung to make a brief speech, telling them that they deserved punishment for their cruel and selfish misrule. What he did not say was that he had no way of knowing which individuals were responsible for the death of Hsiao-ming-ti, but that he and the new emperor would never be safe as long as a single one of the Empress Hu's supporters was left in power. Indeed, one of the officers who had already defected to him had told him as much. There is also the suspicion that, despite his loyalty to the Wei dynasty, Jung must surely have shared something of the traditionalists' resentment of everything that Lo-yang stood for.

Possibly some of the victims realised what was going to happen and started to run back towards the city, but they can have stood little chance. At Jung's signal, the Ehrchu cavalry charged, rode down the officials, and slaughtered them. Unarmed, and with nowhere to hide, the ministers and courtiers died almost to a man. The Dowager Empress was taken alive, but remained unrepentant. She bitterly denounced Jung, whose reply was to order her and her child emperor to be slung unceremoniously into the Yellow River.

The massacre deprived the empire at a stroke of its Toba ruling class, and most of its native Chinese intelligentsia. Even the Prince of Ch'ang-lo was horrified. He now tried to decline the throne, but Jung gave him no choice. He was hurriedly enthroned as Emperor Hsiao-chuang-ti, but the occasion was not auspicious. When he made his ceremonial entry into the palace, only one surviving official of the court could be found to greet the new ruler.

Jung seems quickly to have realised that, unpopular though the previous government had been, his brutal method of dealing with it had undermined his own reputation. He had especially alienated the Chinese ruling classes, whose collaboration in governing a great empire was essential. He now made a clumsy attempt to avoid the blame. His statement ascribed the deaths to what we would nowadays call 'collateral damage', claiming that there had been a battle on the Ho-yin plain, and that the civilians had been somehow caught up in the middle. Jung then went on to bestow a series of posthumous awards on his victims.

This hypocrisy convinced no one. Thousands of frightened citizens fled from Lo-yang, which never fully recovered from the shock. New building stopped, and the palaces of the nobility lay deserted, their owners either dead or in hiding. The Buddhist religious community, however, was made of sterner stuff, and moved in to convert the abandoned buildings into monasteries and nunneries. Jung apparently considered relinquishing the city altogether and moving the capital back to the north – perhaps to his own base at Chin-yang. But, so the story goes, someone persuaded him to climb to the top of one of the high towers, and see for himself the famous panoramic view of the city. As expected, he was so impressed that he could not bring himself to leave.

Victory at Yeh

There was still much to be done before the splendours of Lo-yang could be enjoyed in safety. The rebels from the Six Garrisons had taken advantage of the respite provided by the troubles at court to reorganise and unite. Under their new leader, Ko Jung, they had amassed a force which the chroniclers claimed was a million strong. This must be an exaggeration, but their army was certainly very large. It had already consumed all the resources of the rich province of Hopei, leaving its people starving. Now the rebels were threatening the great eastern city of Yeh, and even sending patrols to probe the vicinity of Lo-yang itself.

Ehrchu Jung was now in control of the surviving Wei forces around the capital, but he decided not to rely on them. Instead, he marched out with only 7000 of his own Ehrchu warriors, intending to seek out the vast rebel host and bring it to battle. The clash came in the Yellow River valley north of Yeh. The rebels deployed in a great crescent, extending for several miles from tip to tip across the open plain. Like the Ehrchu, these northerners favoured heavily armoured cavalry, and a majority would probably have been mounted, armed with lances, swords and bows. Many of them were hardened warriors, veterans of years of campaigning. It is understandable, therefore, that Ko Jung repeated Hsu Ho's mistake, and regarded the tiny band of Ehrchu with scorn. He had even issued ropes to his men, for tying up the prisoners after the battle.[3]

But Ehrchu Jung was confident in the abilities of his men. His tactics also show that he was able to keep them under tight control – a remarkable feat with such an army of aristocratic horsemen. He had provided each trooper with a mysterious weapon called a *shen-pang*, which they were ordered to hold alongside their horses, and to use in the mêlée instead of their swords. They were then divided into units of a few hundred men each, which were instructed to gallop about in front of the rebel host, kicking up dust and making as much noise as possible. The fine, wind-blown soil of the North China Plain has always been notorious, and if the weather was dry, it could not have taken long before the Ehrchu army was hidden behind a huge yellow pall of dust.

For a brief but decisive moment Ko and his men, uncertain of what was happening, seem to have reined in and surrendered the initiative. We have no way of knowing whether Jung had read Sun Tzu, but his tactics are a perfect example of the master's precepts:

> ... against those skilled in attack, an enemy does not know where to defend; against the experts in defence, the enemy does not know where to attack... The ultimate in disposing one's troops is to be without ascertainable shape.[4]

Then, out of sight of the enemy, Jung rallied his men and led them in a massed charge at a single point of the extended enemy line. The selected spot was near a feature known as the Fu-k'ou Pass. Unfortunately, there is no record of the methods Jung used to exert control over the scattered troopers in the swirling dust and deafening din. Neither is it certain what the *shen-pang* was, although the reason for the prohibition of swords is clear enough. Jung was afraid that his men would throw away their initial advantage by stopping to cut off the heads of their enemies. Taking heads was a time-honoured practice in Chinese warfare, and many armies based their systems of promotion and rewards on this tangible evidence of a warrior's prowess. But for a small group of men in the midst of overwhelming numbers, such a distraction could have been disastrous. So Jung had to ensure that swords were sheathed, and that the Ehrchu relied on a weapon which could not be used for cutting.

The term *shen-pang* has been translated as 'miraculous cudgel', but if it was a mace or similar weapon, it is hard to see what would be gained by holding it down along the horse's body – unless the idea was to conceal it from the enemy until the last moment. Some commentators have speculated that what we have here is the first recorded use of the couched lance. Lances had been popular in the East for centuries, but as discussed in Chapter 9, they were usually used in conjunction with other weapons, or thrust overhead, using both hands.

On the other hand, there would have been nothing 'mysterious' about a lance, whatever the method of using it. On balance, it seems likely that the secret of the *shen-pang* was that it enabled the outnumbered Ehrchu to recover quickly after striking a blow, ready to defend themselves, or to take on the next opponent. Just as a sword would have encouraged them to waste time cutting off heads, a deeply thrust lance might have been difficult to extract from an enemy's body. For such a purpose a concussive weapon such as a mace would obviously be most suitable. But perhaps the exact nature of the weapon was less important than the tactics which it prescribed. And these tactics worked spectacularly. Charging as a single mass and stopping for nothing, the Ehrchu rode straight through the astonished rebels and broke out into their rear. Then, rallying them again, Jung smashed into the reeling enemy from behind.

Under this impact, the unwieldy rebel host fell apart. In a situation like this, its huge numbers must have been a hindrance rather than an asset, since redeploying them to face an attack from an unexpected direction would have been a task beyond any commander of the time. Ko was captured, and most of his men threw down their arms and surrendered. Jung's leniency was in stark contrast to his treatment of the courtiers of Lo-yang. The best of the rebel troops were immediately enrolled into his own army, while the rest were permitted to choose a plot of land on the frontier and settle there in peace. There were of course far too many prisoners even for the Ehrchu to massacre, but it also seems that Jung was instinctively more in sympathy with these fellow northerners than with the sly bureaucrats of the capital. The former rebels, in their turn, respected him as a successful warrior, and so readily accepted him as their overlord. After the victory at Yeh, there would be no more trouble from the northern garrisons.

The power behind the throne

The threat which had hung over the city of Lo-yang for the past five years had been dramatically removed. But others were only just emerging. The new Wei emperor was a reluctant figurehead and, whether intentionally or not, Ehrchu Jung found himself burdened with the responsibility of ruling an empire. At the end of 528, a peasant rebellion broke out in Hopei. Jung and his colleague Yuan T'ien-mu were still occupied in trying to suppress the revolt when, early in 529, the Liang regime in the south decided to take advantage of the distraction.

The Liang Emperor Wu-ti sent his general Ch'en Ch'ing-chih northwards with an expeditionary force of around 7000 men. By now, Jung was leading the main Wei army, perhaps several hundreds of thousands strong, but he was unable to bring Ch'en to battle. The history of this period is full of instances of huge armies being outwitted by smaller, more mobile forces, and this time it was Jung who found himself in the position of the unwieldy Goliath.

Ch'en Ch'ing-chih was clearly a bold and skilful commander. The southern states were always short of horses, and most of their native Chinese troops fought as infantry, either with sword and shield, or with bows and arrows. It is likely, therefore, that the bulk of Ch'en's force was on foot. Nevertheless, he decisively outmanoeuvred

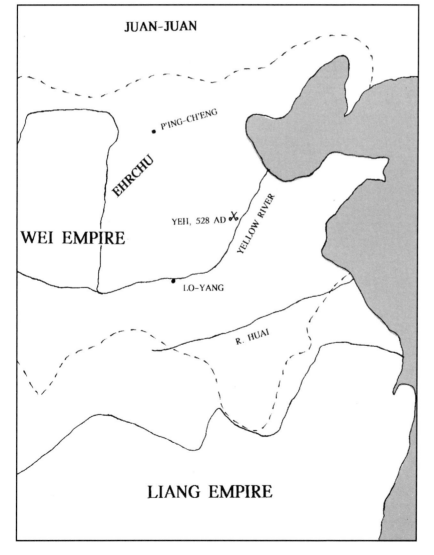

Northern China in the time of Ehrchu Jung, c.AD525, showing the rival empires of the Northern Wei and the Liang.

his opponents, took several provincial towns, and then marched on Lo-yang. Jung, attempting to pursue, was left floundering behind him.

Ch'en entered the city unopposed, and proclaimed a cousin of the Wei emperor, Prince Yuan Hao, as 'king of Wei', under the overlordship of Wu-ti. Yuan Hao attempted to justify his apparent treachery in a letter to emperor Hsiao-chuang-ti, in which he claimed that he was trying to save the dynasty from the man who represented the real threat to it – Ehrchu Jung. Yuan pointed out:

'As the empire is still in turmoil, he (Jung) cannot yet usurp the throne; this is why you and he are, for the time being, ruler and subject... He is building up his strength and biding his time: how long will he remain a loyal subject?'

Perhaps if the Liang ruler had reinforced Ch'en immediately, Jung and his puppet emperor would have been in serious trouble. Luckily, however, the crisis passed. Initially at least, Hsiao-chuang-ti ignored Yuan's attempt to sow dissension. Jung closed in on Lo-yang, bringing the full might of the Wei armies against Ch'en and his handful of warriors. The southerners resisted with great courage, but they were too few in numbers to hold Lo-yang against a determined attack. Two months after it had fallen, Jung retook the city. Ch'en's men broke out and retreated southwards, but this time the Wei cavalry overtook them and destroyed them. Among the many dead was the usurper, Yuan Hao.

After this final victory, Jung devoted the next year to leisurely campaigns in the provinces, bringing the last few rebel bands to heel, and to enjoying the riches and honours showered upon him by a grateful emperor. The year cycle of the new reign was aptly named *ch'ien-yi*, or 'Justice Established'. Hsiao-chuang-ti took Jung's daughter as his empress, and conferred on his new father-in-law a series of prestigious titles. Among these were: Prince of T'ai-yuan;

Senior General Controlling Domestic and Foreign Military Affairs; Commissioner for the Northern Circuit; Commander of the Imperial Bodyguard; Controller of the Chancellery; and 'Pillar of State General' – this last being a new position created specially for him. Along with the titles came immense wealth in goods, livestock, land and concubines.

But Yuan Hao, as it turned out, had been a good prophet. With unimaginable wealth and power already in his grasp, Jung's ambitions continued to soar. Yet at bottom he was still the politically unsophisticated semi-barbarian from the northern frontier. Whether or not he actually planned to overthrow Hsiao-chuang-ti and take the throne for himself, his increasing presumption gave many people that impression. He told his confidant Yuan T'ien-mu that he intended to conquer the whole of China; and he complained of the continuing 'insolence' of the emperor's new set of courtiers, some of whom had obviously failed to learn their lesson from the fate of their predecessors at Ho-yin. One of Jung's more interesting proposals – perhaps fortunately never carried out – was to tame these persistent critics by pitting them, unarmed, in gladiatorial combats against tigers.

By now, however, the emperor had begun to pay heed to the warnings of Jung's enemies. And in the prevailing climate, there was only one way to dispense with his services. One day, in the ninth month of the year 530, Jung and Yuan T'ien-mu received a summons to visit the palace. An heir to the throne had supposedly been born, and they were invited to come and pay their respects. They arrived accompanied by Jung's eldest son and twenty or so retainers. If they had any suspicions, or even thought to arm themselves merely as a precaution, we are not told of it. As they entered the Enlightenment Hall, concealed soldiers leapt out at them with drawn swords. Yuan T'ien-mu was cut down at once, as was Jung's son. Then Hsiao-chuang-ti himself rushed at Jung and stabbed him fatally.

Vengeance and commemoration

It was inevitable that the Ehrchu would take a terrible revenge. Their code of honour demanded it. When they learned of their leader's death, their first reaction was to appear in a body outside the walls, tears of grief streaming down their cheeks, and beg to be allowed to retrieve his corpse for an appropriate burial. It was said that the sound of their weeping could be heard throughout the city. In an emotional speech, one of their leaders, Shih-lung, delivered his verdict on their late chief: 'He saved the people and served the country with a true heart. The gods know this.'

Their request for Jung's body was dismissed out of hand, whereupon their mood changed, and they rampaged through Lo-yang in a mob. There was heavy fighting in some districts of the city for a while, but the disorganised and temporarily leaderless Ehrchu were eventually driven out. They then regrouped on the other side of the Yellow River. In what seems like growing panic, Hsiao-chuang-ti emptied his treasury and hired 10,000 mercenaries to protect him against their inevitable return. Then he ordered fireships to be used to destroy the bridge at the Meng Ford, in order to stop the Ehrchu recrossing the river.

The bridge was burned, but the unpredictable Yellow River once again proved no defence against the Ehrchu. Shortly afterwards the water level dropped suddenly, and the tribesmen found a shallow spot where they were able to cross on horseback. The hapless emperor discovered that his hastily raised mercenaries had no stomach for the fight. The Ehrchu stormed Lo-yang, sacked it and set it on fire. Hsiao-chuang-ti was captured and dragged back to Chin-yang, where he was strangled.

For a while Jung's nephew, Ehrchu Chao, took over the leadership of the clan, but soon they were quarrelling among themselves over the spoils of victory. They split into warring factions, each aligned with other forces, and when they did briefly reunite in

532, they suffered a disastrous defeat at the hands of the Wei commander Kao Huan. The Ehrchu quickly disappeared as a political or military force. The Northern Wei dynasty itself soon followed them into oblivion. In 534 the empire split into two warring successor states, and Lo-yang became a disputed no-man's-land. Kao Huan ordered the capital moved east to Yeh, and Lo-yang was once again abandoned. Within four decades, it had gone from an uninhabited ruin to a city of half a million people, and back again to ruins. The two new states – known as the Eastern and the Western Wei – were to remain locked in vicious conflict for another twenty years, until each was overthrown in its turn.

As for Ehrchu Jung, who had saved the Northern Wei in the moment of its greatest peril, his memory too was destined for oblivion. Within a generation his own people were scattered and absorbed, and the native Chinese, who as usual outlived all their conquerors, had no reason to love him. After Jung's death the Ehrchu built a temple to him on Mount Shou-yang, where once had stood the temple of Duke Wen of Chou. His people wanted Jung to receive sacrifices in the Chinese tradition, but the scholars refused to sanction this, arguing that a subject could only be so honoured in association with a deceased emperor. And none of the Wei emperors would be appropriate, as there was no one to whom Jung could be considered to have been truly loyal – not even Hsiao-ming-ti, whose mother he had killed.

The Ehrchu blustered and threatened, but the scholars remained obdurate. Then not long after its completion, Jung's temple burned down. Soon afterwards a single remaining column, which had been left standing after the fire, was struck by lightning. Yang Hsuan-chih, whose *Records of the Monasteries of Lo-yang* is our source for these events, reports them without comment, but others must have drawn their own conclusions about Heaven's verdict. Ehrchu Jung never did receive his sacrifices.

STRATEGY AND LOGISTICS IN CENTRAL ASIA

For nearly 2000 years after the appearance of the Hsiung-nu confederation in the late third century BC, the predominant theme of China's foreign policy was its relations with the nomadic powers which controlled the northern steppe. These relations were by no means always hostile. Both economies produced goods which the other wanted: for instance, grain, silk and tea from China, and horses, cattle, hides and furs from the steppe. So at some periods, when neither side was sufficiently strong or united to seriously threaten the other, peace was maintained through trade and diplomatic contacts, and the political frontier followed roughly the line dividing the cold, dry grasslands from the regions suitable for agriculture. The first part of the second century BC, and the latter part of the sixteenth century AD, provide examples of this type of situation.

At other times, when China was divided and the nomads were strong, the frontier could disintegrate altogether, and the 'barbarians' overran large areas of the settled country to the south. The worst of these episodes took place in the fourth century AD; in the eleventh century, under the Sung dynasty, when first the

Khitan and then the Jurchen peoples were able to set up their own empires in the north; and in the thirteenth century, when with much local assistance the Mongols actually managed to conquer the whole of China. The warlike nature of the steppe peoples, the mobility provided by their herds of horses, and a social and economic organisation which enabled them to put into the field almost their entire able-bodied male populations, often gave them a decisive advantage over their more numerous settled opponents.

In some periods, however, the boot was on the other foot. When they were blessed with a strong government and a thriving economy, it was often possible for the Chinese to take the offensive. The Han and T'ang dynasties, in particular, established extensive if temporary empires in Central Asia, breaking up the nomad confederations

A tomb model of a bullock cart from the sixth or seventh century AD. Vehicles like this provided much of the logistic support for the Chinese armies which penetrated the deserts and steppes of Central Asia. (British Museum)

which opposed them and seizing control of the trade routes to the west as far as the Pamir Mountains, and even beyond. In doing so, they were forced to campaign in country where water was often scarce, heat and cold were excessive, and neither crops nor trees could grow. Such alien regions presented enormous difficulties to the agricultural Chinese.

The Ordos region

The Ordos Loop of the Yellow River has often been described as the strategic key to the whole of the northern Chinese frontier. This is because of its defensible situation – the Yellow River surrounds it on three sides, while mountains and the Wei valley enclose the fourth – and the region's position on the very edge of the settled country, where arable land gives way to steppe. At various times, as climate and political fortunes have fluctuated, the Ordos has been used by both nomads and Chinese as an advanced base from which to launch attacks on their enemies.

The first imperial regime to control it was the Ch'in, whose complex of fortifications known as the 'Great Wall' ran along the Yellow River where it forms the region's northern boundary. The other great conquering dynasties, the Han and the T'ang, also brought the Ordos under their control at the peak of their success, but in Sung times it fell to the Tanguts of Hsi Hsia, who invaded it from the west. The Ming dynasty was able to occupy the region only temporarily. When their Great Wall was built in the sixteenth century, the Ordos steppe lay outside it, abandoned to the Mongolian tribes.

Two long-distance campaigners – Li Kuang-li and Kao Hsien-chih

Some of the imperial campaigns in Central Asian have become legendary examples of what Chinese armies could accomplish at their best. In the 'War of the Heavenly Horses', which broke out in 104BC, a Han expedition was sent as far as the Ferghana Valley, west of the Pamirs, in what is now Uzbekistan.[1] The Emperor Wu-ti had heard rumours that in this almost inconceivably remote region was a breed of 'heavenly horses', which possessed extraordinary speed and stamina, and were famous for sweating blood. The ruler of Ta-yuan, who owned these wonderful animals, had refused a request to send some of them to China as tribute, and so Wu-ti despatched his general Li Kuang-li to Ta-yuan with 20,000 Chinese and 6000 nomad troops to take them by force.

Li marched for 1000 miles through the great inland drainage basin known as the Tarim, from the border fortress at Tun-huang along the edge of the Takla Makan desert. Supplies soon began to run short. The area was not entirely uninhabited, but the city states in the oases along the route were unwilling to share their provisions with the Chinese, and so closed their gates when Li approached. With incredible courage, the starving Han troops struggled over the mighty mountain barrier of the Pamirs and arrived on the borders of Ta-yuan; but Li realised that they were too reduced in numbers, and the survivors too exhausted, to stand any chance in a battle. Bitterly disappointed, he ordered a retreat.

Normally, commanders who let Wu-ti down lived just long enough to regret it, but back at court Li managed to talk his way out of trouble. He explained that the supply difficulties had arisen because his force was too small. If he had had more men, he argued, he would have been able to force the cities of the Tarim Basin to provide him with food. The emperor was persuaded, and sent his general west a second time, with 60,000 men. Li turned out to have been correct. When they saw a force of that size approaching, most of the cities opened their gates and submitted. A few did not, but the Chinese were able to take these by storm.

Losses were still frightful: 30,000 men died on the westward march. But the survivors reached Ta-yuan in sufficient force to complete their task. Li defeated the king in battle, and established a compliant puppet king who quickly swore allegiance to the Han. Then, with 3000 of the 'heavenly horses' as tribute, he returned in triumph to China. The Tarim Basin cities were so impressed by Li's campaign that they also accepted Han overlordship, extending the boundaries of the empire westward by nearly 1000 miles.

Another result can be seen in the superb statuettes of horses which are such a well-known feature of the Han period. When compared with, for example, the stocky

The campaigns of Li Kuang-li (104–103BC) and Kao Hsien-chih (AD747–751) in Central Asia. On these and other occasions, Chinese expeditionary forces covered more than half the distance between the Yellow River and the Mediterranean Sea. However, their only clash with a major Middle Eastern power was a disaster for the Chinese.

beasts depicted in the Ch'in terracotta army, with their short legs and bristly manes, the later Han horses are clearly animals of superior breeding. It seems certain that a major influence on the new improved stock was Li Kuang-li's herd of Ferghanan 'heavenly horses'.

The Han dynasty eventually lost control of its conquests in Central Asia, and it was not until the T'ang that Chinese armies again occupied the Tarim Basin. Another classic campaign was that of Kao Hsien-chih between AD747 and 751, during the reign of the emperor T'ang Hsuan-tsung. At that time the T'ang empire was at war with the rival empire of Tibet, and Kao was sent west to outflank the Tibetans by occupying the little kingdoms of Wakhan and Balur, in what is today the northern part of Pakistan.[2]

Much of Kao's route lay through very difficult mountain terrain, and unlike Li Kuang-li, he was provided only with a small

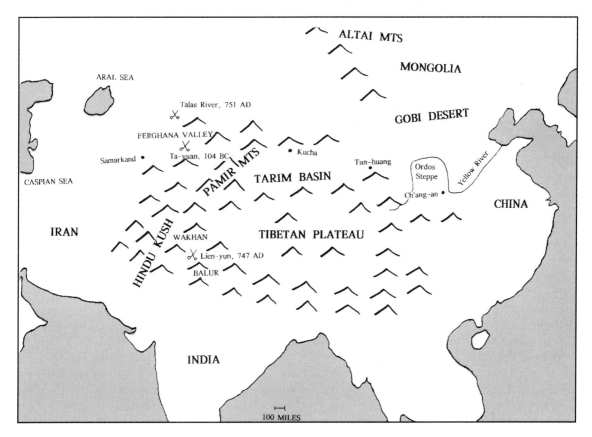

mobile force. This consisted of 10,000 cavalry and mounted infantry, who left the city of Kucha early in 747. Penetrating into the Pamirs, Kao split his army into three parts and ordered them to converge on the Tibetan fort at Lien-yun three days later. Despite the difficulty of the route – which required Kao's own detachment to ford the flooded Wakhan River – this risky manouevre was successful, with all three forces meeting up as instructed.

The Tibetan garrison of Lien-yun was defeated, and the fort taken. Then Kao moved on to the capital of Balur, which quickly surrendered to him. A Tibetan army was reported to be on its way to drive him out, but it had first to cross a bamboo bridge over a ravine east of the city. Kao dealt with the problem by cutting the cables that held the bridge, leaving the Tibetans stranded on the far side. Then he went on to add another Tibetan vassal state to the list of his conquests.

At this point, Kao Hsien-chih was the toast of the empire. He was honoured by Hsuan-tsung with the title of 'Lord of the Mountains of China'. Unfortunately, in 751 he found himself being dragged into another and more dangerous conflict. The state of Ferghana had asked for Chinese aid in a dispute with its rival, Tashkent, and so, on instructions from the court, Kao attacked and plundered Tashkent. The son of the king of that city, however, escaped to Samarkand and enlisted the aid of the Abbasid Caliph of the Muslim Arabs.

At this time, the Arabs were probably the world's most formidable military power. Both they and the Chinese were at the furthermost limits of their empires, so the clash was perhaps not a fair test of their respective abilities, but it was the only occasion in pre-modern history on which an army from China met an army of one of the major powers of the West, so it is worth examining here. Abu Muslim, the local Abbasid governor, advanced on Tashkent, while Kao Hsien-chih came west to meet him. Kao's army included a core of T'ang troops, but

consisted largely of Ferghanan and Qarluq Turkish allies, who probably fought mainly as mounted archers.

The battle was joined near the town of Atlakh on the Talas River, on 28 July 751. According to one account, it lasted five days. The combat appears to have been indecisive at first, until Kao's Qarluq allies decided to change sides, and the Chinese were left with no choice but to retreat. Their way east lay through a pass across the White Stone Mountains, but the panic-stricken Ferghanans got there first, and blocked the route with a mass of men and baggage animals. Kao and some of his men cut their way through and escaped, but many others were taken prisoner by the Arabs. The disaster marked the end of T'ang influence west of the Pamirs. Chinese armies would not return to the region for a thousand years.

The logistical dilemma

Li Kuang-li's experience had turned one of the most fundamental lessons of Central Asian strategy on its head. He followed an unusually well-populated route, and was not faced with concerted opposition. Under normal circumstances, as might be expected, supply difficulties increased as armies became larger. Nomad armies could live for extended periods off their horse herds, and they were experts at locating grass and water. The Chinese had to take with them grain, fodder for their animals, firewood and other necessities, and this often entailed a supply train of staggering dimensions. One Han army is recorded as taking with it 100,000 oxen, 30,000 horses, and tens of thousands of donkeys, mules and camels. A strategist of the Han period, Yen Yu, produced a study which suggested that no army could operate on the northern steppes for more than a hundred days. The main reason for this was that the oxen which pulled the carts could not transport enough food for themselves as well as their other loads. They were unaccustomed to subsisting on grass, and so tended to die on long marches.

LI SHIH-MIN: FOUNDER OR USURPER?

'An emperor receives Heaven's Mandate naturally. It cannot be sought, either by mere cleverness or strength. Yet how eagerly you are seeking it!'
Li Yuan to Li Shih-min

The rise and fall of the Sui

For almost five decades after the fall of the Northern Wei, North China remained divided. By 580, however, a new power, the Northern Chou, had arisen to dominate the region. Meanwhile, it was the turn of the native dynasties of the south to tear themselves apart in fratricidal struggles. In 552 the Liang state split into two parts, one of which – the Later Liang – fell under the domination of the northerners. So it was that when in 581 Yang Chien, an officer of the Northern Chou, came to power in that state following a *coup d'état*, he found himself by far the most powerful leader in the whole of China. With the defeat of Yang's last rival in 589, the empire was once more brought under the rule of a single man.

But Yang's new dynasty – which he named the Sui – failed to put down enduring roots. He and his successor, the emperor Yang-ti, squandered the empire's wealth on foreign wars and extravagant construction schemes. One of their projects, the Grand Canal connecting the Yangtze and Yellow River basins, was eventually to be of incalculable benefit to the country, but at the time the cost was ruinous, and the burden of forced labour which it imposed on the populace undermined the regime's popularity. Then in 612 Yang-ti launched a massive invasion of the Korean kingdom of Koguryo. A million men are said to have been enlisted for this expedition, but it quickly became bogged down among the Korean border fortresses.

For four years Yang-ti persisted with this war, although it brought only nominal gains, while a combination of bad weather, starvation and Korean resistance inflicted enormous losses. By 617 the Chinese – nobles and commoners alike – had had enough. Yang-ti returned home to a people no longer prepared to obey him. Rebellious nobles set up two of his grandsons as rival emperors, and the country relapsed into chaos. Among the men who joined the scramble to fill the power vacuum was a certain Li Yuan, the Duke of T'ang.

Li Yuan was born in the year 566, during the period when the successor states of the Northern Wei were contending for power in North China. He was of noble ancestry, which could be traced back at least to his grandfather Li Hu, who had been one of the 'Eight Pillars' of the Western Wei in the 550s. His mother was also from the aristocracy, being related to two of the recent dynastic families: the Northern Chou and the Sui. In later years, when Li Yuan had become famous as the founder of the T'ang dynasty, scholars claimed to be able to trace the origin of the Li clan much further back – to Li Ping, founder of the Western Liang dynasty in the early fifth century, and through him to Li Kuang, a distinguished general of the Han period. This genealogy, however, is nowadays generally assumed to be a work of historical fiction. It was probably constructed with the dual purpose of legitimising the T'ang, by deriving it from the illustrious Han, and of covering up the fact that Li Yuan's family was actually part-barbarian, being descended from Hsien-pi tribesmen who had intermarried with local Chinese.

The Li clan was certainly of major importance in its own locality, which was centred around the garrison town of Wu-ch'uan on the northern frontier. Li Yuan had inherited his title of Duke of T'ang at the age of six. At fifteen he joined the bodyguard of the first Sui emperor, and later rose to high rank at the Sui court. Early in 617, in recognition of his loyal support for the dynasty, he was appointed commander of the garrison of the Tai-yuan fu region, based at the nearby town of Chin-yang. Chin-yang, it will be remembered, had been the base from which Ehrchu Jung had set out on his career of conquest, ninety-four years earlier.

By the time the Sui started to crumble, Li Yuan had already built up a very strong power base in the north, founded on his position in the Sui government as well as his own local connections. Coincidentally, perhaps – it was a common name in China – a popular prophecy had been circulating that the Sui would be overthrown by a man called Li. It is at this point that we must take a very careful look at the orthodox account of the founding of the T'ang. This is derived mainly from the *T'ang Official History*, and from Ssu-ma Kuang's *Tzu Chih T'ung Chien*, or *Mirror of History*. The latter is a work of the Sung dynasty, which covers the main events of Chinese history from 403BC to AD951. It is one of the most important sources available to us for the events of that period, but of course the historian is only as good as his own sources.

Li Shih-min

According to the tradition which Ssu-ma Kuang repeats, the real impetus behind Li Yuan's actions came from his teenage son, Li Shih-min. As we shall see, Shih-min's own role in the compilation of the official T'ang records is enough to justify suspicion. Furthermore, recent research based on the narrative of Wen Ta-ya, an eyewitness of many of the events in question, who produced an independent account in his *Diary of the Founding of the Great T'ang*, has shed new light on the subject.[1] There are therefore two separate themes running through the story of Li Shih-min: his undoubted abilities as a military commander and later as an emperor; and on the other

hand, his attempts to rewrite history.

Li Yuan – a man in his early fifties, who had recently risen to the highest rank in the service of the Sui emperors, who certainly did not suffer fools gladly – is portrayed in the traditional version as a half-senile ditherer. Although it was obvious that the Sui regime was finished, and that someone would have to take over the throne in order to save the empire, he allegedly failed to recognise his opportunity. Shih-min, who was about seventeen at the time, suggested to his father that he throw off his allegiance to the Sui, but a horrified Li Yuan threatened to have him arrested.

The boy then set out to force his hand, and hatched a plot in conjunction with a disaffected Sui officer, Liu Wen-ching. In the city of Chin-yang was a subsidiary harem, maintained for the pleasure of the emperor Yang-ti, who had often passed that way on campaign. Li Shih-min and Liu Wen-ching bribed the official in charge of the harem to present some of the women to Li Yuan, without telling him where they came from. Only after Li Yuan had set them up in his own household was he informed of the truth. Since the penalty for stealing women from the imperial harem was death, and since Yang-ti could hardly be expected to believe that Li Yuan was innocent, the latter was faced with the realisation that a Sui resumption of power would no longer be in his own interests. Reluctantly, he agreed to lead the revolt.[2]

The young rebel

The whole story sounds like a fabrication, designed to give Shih-min the credit for beginning the enterprise which would lead to the founding of the T'ang. Li Shih-min was the second of Li Yuan's five children. Accounts differ slightly, but he was probably born in the year 600. He was clearly precocious, but not necessarily a prodigy. In that period it was not unusual for young noblemen to be given command of troops at a very early age. Fitzgerald, Shih-min's biographer, quotes the examples of Tu Fu-wei, who

Figure of a warrior from Mingoi in Central Asia, probably eighth century AD. During the early T'ang period, Turkish styles of armour such as this supplanted the earlier versions used by sixth-century horsemen. The heavy cavalry was the main striking arm of T'ang armies, and was instrumental in all of Li Shih-min's victories. (British Museum)

character of the t

In the far west, tl close contact with the Silk Route. Cu the Near East, ver thus were added t decorative styles o

was also seventeen when he led an army of rebels against the Sui, and Lo Shih-hsin, who was an officer of Sui cavalry at the tender age of thirteen.

Li Shih-min's alleged behaviour at this stage is remarkable mainly for its total lack of respect for his father. The Chinese have always regarded filial piety as the highest of virtues, and the converse as the very vilest of sins. By that standard, Shih-min's conduct was appalling. In the historical tradition, only one set of circumstances ever excuses such lack of regard for normal morality. This is the special case of the founders of great dynasties. With Heaven obviously behind them, the end might be considered to justify the means.

Shih-min, however, did not found the dynasty. He later made strenuous efforts to give the impression that he did, and commentators have often believed him, describing him in such terms as 'the true founder' of the T'ang. Wen Ta-ya, however, provides us with a very different perspective. In his version, Li Yuan appears as a bold, decisive leader, who took the initiative on his own account, and who in fact issued orders to

his sons to raise troops for him. By the fifth month of 617, Li Yuan had 10,000 loyal soldiers in Chin-yang, and was ready to take the field.

His first move, however, was to secure his rear by making peace with the Turks, who had replaced the Juan-juan to become the new nomadic power on the northern frontier. The man entrusted with this vital mission was Liu Wen-ching – a fact which strongly suggests that Liu had not really been involved in any sordid conspiracies with

Shih-min. Li Yuan's message addressed the Turkish ruler in obsequious terms, and asked for assistance in return for a share of the booty. The Turkish Qaghan agreed to supply 500 warriors and, even more importantly, thousands of horses as remounts for the T'ang cavalry.

With his strength increased to 30,000, Li Yuan marched south in the seventh month of 617. Assisting him as subordinate commanders were his eldest son, Li Chien-ch'eng, and his second son, Shih-min. Yuan's daughter, the Lady Li Che, was placed in command of a separate force, which became known as the 'Heroine's Legion'. A third brother, Li Yuan-chi, was left behind to guard Chin-yang.

The Sui regime may have been disintegrating, but many cities in the north were still held by troops loyal to it. Elsewhere, other rebel armies were in the field. One of these, led by Liu Wu-chou, was rumoured to be preparing to outflank the T'ang and attack Chin-yang. Ssu-ma Kuang's account has the cautious Li Yuan preparing to turn back, and being talked out of it by Shih-min. Whatever the truth of this, the T'ang army continued its advance southwards, and the threat from Liu Wu-chou did not materialise. First capturing the city of Fen-chou, Li Yuan's men next came to Huo-chou on the Fen River. Here the stage was set for Shih-min's first major battle.

The Ta-hsing Ch'eng campaign

Huo-chou was held for the Sui by Sung Lao-sheng, who was well known to the T'ang as a brave but rash commander. They therefore devised a plan to exploit his weakness. Li Yuan and Li Chien-ch'eng deployed their contingents openly in front of the city, while Shih-min was sent with a detachment of cavalry to a concealed position on the flank.

A T'ang saddle, as depicted on a tomb model of the eighth century. Note its modern appearance, in contrast to the earlier equipment in the photograph on page 52. (British Museum)

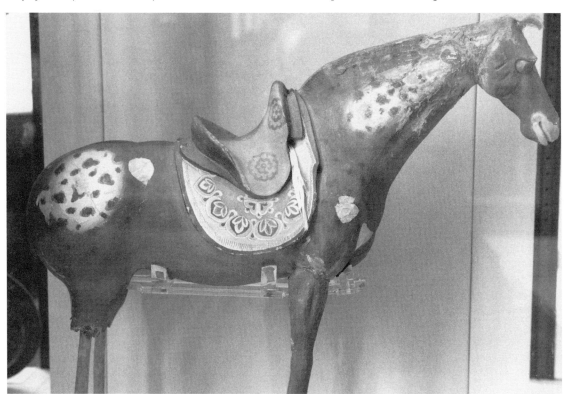

T'ang officers then pretended to start laying out siege works, as if preparing for a long operation.

As expected, Sung Lao-sheng led his troops out of Huo-chou in a headlong attack on the enemy units which were visible to him. It is not entirely clear what happened next. The T'ang army fell back, in what is usually interpreted as a deliberate manoeuvre to lure the Sui into a vulnerable position. There is, however, a passage in the 'Questions and Replies Between T'ang T'ai-tsung and Li Wei-kung' which preserves what purports to be the account of Li Shih-min (i.e. the future Emperor T'ai-tsung) himself. Here, Shih-min gives the impression that the retreat was unplanned. Chien-ch'eng, he says, was unhorsed in the fight, and 'our slight withdrawal almost defeated our great affair'.[3]

Shih-min would later have good reason to denigrate Chien-ch'eng, so this cannot be regarded as an unbiased account. But whatever happened, Shih-min's intervention was decisive. In his own words:

'I then personally led our elite cavalry to race down from the Southern plain, cutting across in a sudden attack on them. After Lao-heng's troops were cut off to the rear, we severely crushed them, and subsequently captured him.'

According to Ssu-ma Kuang's version, Shih-min fought in person 'till his sleeves were running with blood'. Sung Lao-sheng, in fact, fled as far as the gates of Huo-chou, but the people refused to let him in. The T'ang troops caught up with him, and cut off his head.

Huo-chou fell without further resistance, and many of its defenders defected to the T'ang, as did the garrisons of several other towns, together with numerous smaller bands of rebels. In a masterly campaign of manoeuvre, Li Yuan then bypassed the city of P'u-chou, which guarded the main crossing over the Yellow River, and slipped across farther upstream at Han-cheng. This placed him 'within the passes', in the strategic stronghold now known as Kuan-chung. It was in this natural redoubt that the Sui had established their capital, Ta-hsing ch'eng, but this time its defences were to be turned against them.

Armies loyal to Yang-ti were now hurrying up from the east. Their direct route back to Ta-hsing ch'eng ran through the T'ong Pass, where the Yellow River turns abruptly from its southward course to an eastward-flowing one. But Li Chien-ch'eng got there first, from the west, and occupied it with 10,000 men. Meanwhile Li Shih-min turned westwards, towards the Sui capital. On the way he linked up with his sister, Li Che, and was followed soon afterwards by their father with the T'ang main body. Soon, 200,000 troops were surrounding Ta-hsing ch'eng, while the Sui relief forces tried in vain to break through the pass.

In the eleventh month of 617, the city fell. At first Li Yuan maintained his façade of loyalty to the Sui, and placed Yang-ti's grandson, Yang Yu, on the throne. Six months later, however, Yang Yu was deposed, and Li Yuan proclaimed himself the first emperor of a new dynasty. The old Han dynasty name for the city of Ta-hsing ch'eng – Ch'ang-an – was revived, and under this name it became the capital of the T'ang. But the new ruler was careful to preserve continuity where possible, and he retained many of the civil and military officials who had served the Sui.

Consolidation

This humane and sensible policy won many more adherents for Li Yuan, but as yet the process of consolidating the new dynasty had scarcely begun. The T'ang, in fact, was but one power among many rebel groups which had replaced the authority of the Sui in their own areas. One of its rivals was the regime of Hsueh Chu in the far north-west, in what is now the province of Kansu. Early in 618, Hsueh advanced on Ch'ang-an from the west. Li Shih-min had proved himself in the campaign of the previous year, and so his father, who was now occupied by the demands of imperial administration, appointed him commander-in-chief of the army sent to face Hsueh. This was the young Shih-min's first independent command. He was still only eighteen years old.

Shih-min confronted Hsueh at Fu Feng and defeated him, but instead of pursuing him, he turned back to the east and pacified the P'u-chou area. Soon Hsueh was advancing again. A second battle was fought at Ch'ien Shui Yuan, in which Hsueh was victorious. The T'ang histories state that Shih-min was ill with a fever at the time, and that his deputy, Liu Wen-ching, was in command on that day. It is impossible to know the truth behind this, but it is noticeable that these sources always provide the young hero with a convenient alibi whenever things go wrong. What we are probably seeing in this confused and at times inept campaign may well be the process by which Shih-min taught himself the difficult art of strategy.

Hsueh Chu swept on towards Ch'ang-an, but died suddenly before he reached it. His death may have saved both the city and Shih-min's reputation. Hsueh's son attacked again in the autumn, but Shih-min had built a fortified camp, and was waiting for him. The Hsueh army attacked the camp, only to find that it was a decoy. Li Shih-min was learning quickly. He led his men into the enemy rear by a circuitous route through the mountains, then struck when they least expected it. This battle destroyed the Hsueh, and so secured the western frontier of the T'ang territories.

The next major threat came in the north, where the warlord Liu Wu-chou invaded Shansi, and threatened the base at Chin-yang, which was still being held by Li Yuan-chi. Early in 619, Yuan-chi was beaten and much of the region overrun by the enemy. Once again we are expected to believe that Li Yuan panicked and proposed to abandon the province, but was dissuaded by Shih-min. In fact, another anecdote from Ssu-ma Kuang, who is usually favourable to Shih-min, shows how much the young prince still had to learn.

Shih-min was put in charge of the army sent against Liu Wu-chou, and at first advanced cautiously into the northern steppe country. One day, he was leading a force of cavalry on a reconnaissance. He decided to ride ahead, accompanied by a single officer, to observe the area from the top of a nearby hill. Apparently, as soon as they reached the top, the two men lay down on the grass for a rest, without even bothering to look around them. But they had themselves been observed, and a hundred or so enemy cavalry emerged from a defile and surrounded the hill without their noticing. The pair were saved by a stroke of luck, when Shih-min's companion was startled by a snake and jumped to his feet. He spotted the enemy horsemen closing in, and shouted a warning to the prince.

Shih-min may not have been much use as a scout, but he was already gaining a reputation as a superlative archer. He took aim at the officer in charge of the enemy contingent, and brought him down with a single shot. As the dead man's followers recoiled in confusion, the prince and his comrade mounted their horses and broke through to safety.

The rest of the campaign went rather better. Towards the end of the year, the T'ang won a battle at An-yi and took the city of Hsia Hsien. The citizens refused to surrender when summoned to do so; thus, when the town was stormed, Shih-min ordered them to be massacred. This was in accordance with the normal practice of the time, but was out of character for Shih-min, who usually preferred to win conquered peoples over to his side with lenient treatment. He is said to have later expressed regret for his bloodthirsty impulse.

After this victory he settled down to wait for winter, knowing that Liu Wu-chou's men were operating at the end of a long supply line, and would have difficulty in feeding themselves. Early in 620, Liu was forced to order a retreat, and Li Shih-min seized his opportunity. The T'ang army followed up, and caught Liu's rearguard at a place known as Squirrel Pass. The surprised enemy broke and fled, and Shih-min's cavalry chased them through the pass for seventy miles, beating them in ten separate battles. The

The campaigns of AD617 to 624, showing Li Shih-min's principal battles, and (in large type) the power bases of the leading rival warlords.

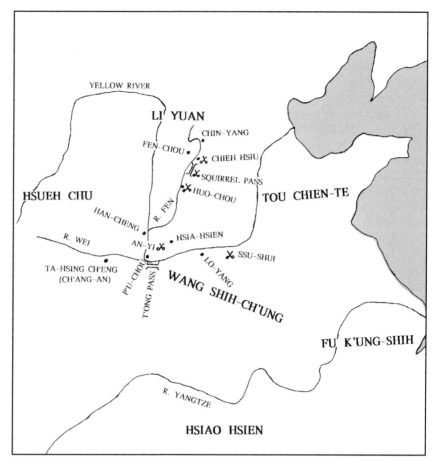

YELLOW RIVER

LI' YUAN

CHIN-YANG

FEN-CHOU

CHIEH HSIU

SQUIRREL PASS

HSUEH CHU

HUO-CHOU

TOU CHIEN-TE

HAN-CHENG

R. FEN

R. WEI

AN-YI

HSIA-HSIEN

SSU-SHUI

TA-HSING CH'ENG (CH'ANG-AN)

PU-CHOU

LO-YANG

WANG SHIH-CH'UNG

T'ONG PASS

FU' K'UNG-SHIH

R. YANGTZE

HSIAO HSIEN

young prince was at the head of his troopers all the way, on his white horse called T'e-lei-p'iao[4]: it is said that he did not stop to eat for two days, nor take off his armour for three.

The surviving enemy soldiers escaped into the city of Chieh Hsui, but decided to fight outside the walls rather than be starved into submission. They tried to frustrate the usual T'ang outflanking tactics by deploying with their backs against the city walls. Shih-min therefore sent in his infantry under Li Shi-chi, an able commander who had recently defected from the army of a rival warlord. Eventually the enemy began to tire, and Shih-min once more led one of his ferocious cavalry charges – this time straight through the enemy front line. Liu Wu-chou's troops were routed, and the city fell. On this occasion Shih-min was merciful, and most of the defeated enemy were incorporated into his own army. Liu Wu-chou himself fled into exile among the Turks. Another threat to the T'ang had been eliminated.

The Lo-yang campaign

Luckily for the infant T'ang dynasty, its numerous enemies never managed to coordinate their attacks. While Shih-min was recapturing Shansi, one of Sui Yang-ti's former generals, Wang Shih-ch'ung, advanced on Ch'ang-an from the east. However, Wang did not press his attack with much vigour, and soon retired into Lo-yang, farther east along the Yellow River. This long-suffering city had again begun to thrive after its vicissitudes under the Wei, and with its walls rebuilt it was once more a strategic base of major importance.

Early in 621, Li Shih-min marched eastwards and besieged Wang in Lo-yang. One day, he repeated his mistake of a couple of years earlier and rode up on to the grave mound of one of the Wei emperors, which was outside the walls, to overlook the city. This time he took an escort of 500 men, but the defenders spotted him and sallied out in force – 10,000 of them, according to one account. Shih-min was surrounded, and only

saved by the timely arrival of T'ang reinforcements.

For a while, little progress was made by
either side. There were numerous sorties and
skirmishes, and the T'ang managed to inter-
cept some food convoys destined for the city,
but still Lo-yang held out. Wang Shih-ch'ung
responded by making an alliance with the
other surviving major power in the north, a
commander named Tou Chien-te, who
controlled the rich farmlands along the banks
of the lower Yellow River, and who styled
himself emperor of the Hsia dynasty. Tou
recognised the danger which he would be
facing if the T'ang succeeded in defeating
Wang, but he took his time about raising an
army to relieve his new ally. Wang, therefore,
decided not to wait, but to come out from the
city and risk a battle.

The confrontation took place in the second
month of 621. The T'ang deployed along a
range of low hills north of the city known as the
Pei Mang Shan, after which the battle was
named. Wang had perhaps 20,000 men, Shih-
min probably somewhat more. Two T'ang
cavalry charges – the second led by Shih-min
himself – were beaten back. Once again the
prince was in the thick of the fighting; his
horse was killed under him, and he fought on
foot until rescued by one of his officers. Casu-
alties were very heavy on both sides, but eventually Wang retired into the city. The T'ang
pressed the siege with increased vigour, but
were still unable to take it. Then came the news
that Tou Chien-te was at last on the move.

Shih-min reacted decisively. Although, as
usual, we are told that his staff advised him
against it, this time there was no realistic
option but to take the boldest course. His
enemies could not be allowed to link up and
combine against him. Shih-min left the main
T'ang army under his younger brother, Li
Yuan-chi, to blockade Wang in Lo-yang, and
with only about 3500 picked troops, he rode
east to meet Tou Chien-te. He had already
selected the place where he would fight him
– the ford across the Ssu-shui River, soon to
become one of the most famous battlefields in
all of China's history.

Shih-min's masterpiece: the battle of Ssu-shui[5]

The Ssu-shui is a tributary of the Yellow River
which flows northwards along the edge of the
great eastern plain, about fifty miles east of
Lo-yang. It runs through a mile-wide valley
edged on either side by steep cliffs: above
them on the eastern side is the flat plain,
while on the west a series of narrow defiles
leads up into hilly country. A small T'ang
garrison already held the little town of Ssu-
shui, commanding the main ford across the
river of that name. This was the way that Tou
Chien-te would have to come to relieve his
ally, and it was here that Li Shih-min
proposed to stop him.

With the defensive advantages provided
by the terrain, Ssu-shui was the obvious
place to make a stand. Even so, the task
facing the T'ang was formidable. Allowing
for the addition of the garrison of Ssu-shui
town, they could still hardly have mustered
more than 7000 to 10,000 men. Ssu-ma
Kuang credits Tou Chien-te with a total of
300,000. This may be another exaggeration
designed to boost Shih-min's reputation, but
the eastern plain of the Yellow River, where
Tou recruited his troops, was densely settled
by a population with strong military traditions, and must have been able to supply
huge numbers for this supreme effort. Even if
we divide Ssu-ma Kuang's figure by three,
which seems reasonable, Tou's men must still
have outnumbered the T'ang by at least ten
to one. Shih-min knew that the enemy was
very numerous, and he did not bother to hide
the fact. Before the battle, he is said to have
remarked to one of his close companions, an
officer named Yu-ch'ih Ching-te, that 'you
with the spear and I with my bow are a match
for a million of them' – a figure of speech no
doubt, but perhaps a revealing one.

Despite the odds, the prince proposed to
take the offensive, with the aim of establishing from the outset a moral ascendancy
over the enemy. Tou Chien-te, en route to the
river crossing, had camped about seven miles
short of Ssu-shui, out on the eastern plain.
Shih-min rode out to reconnoitre his camp

with only a handful of followers, leaving 500 horsemen in ambush in a ravine a little farther back. The first enemy patrol they met at first took them for more of Tou's men, until Shih-min shot an arrow into their leader and announced his identity in a loud voice.

The rest of the patrol galloped back with the news, and soon a force of several thousand cavalry came out to try to capture the prince. The little party fell back, Shih-min and Yu-ch'ih Ching-te covering their retreat with their arrows, until they passed the

The battle of Ssu-shui, AD621. This was the victory which sealed Li Shih-min's reputation as a military genius, as well as securing T'ang control of the Yellow River valley.

mouth of the ravine where the T'ang cavalry were hidden. These suddenly dashed out into the flank of Tou's troops, who were thrown into confusion. Three hundred of them are said to have been captured or killed, while the survivors fled back to their camp.

This little stratagem succeeded beyond all reasonable expectation, because it appears that Tou Chien-te lost his nerve. He closed up to the Ssu-shui River, made a half-hearted and unsuccessful attack on the town, then set up camp on the east bank of the river and sat there for several weeks. What he was waiting for is unclear: the longer he hesitated, the more likely it was that Lo-yang would fall. Even Tou's own supply situation began to deteriorate, because his boats had to come up the Yellow River against the current,

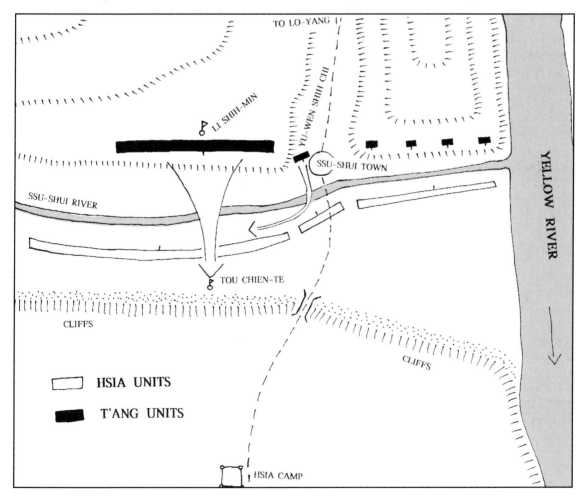

while the T'ang supply vessels, floating downstream when laden and going back empty, had a much faster turn-around time. So Tou's huge army slowly starved, while his enemy was if anything growing stronger.

The obvious solution was proposed by Tou's staff: leave a small decoy force in place, cross the river farther upstream, and ravage the T'ang territories there until his enemies were forced to raise the siege of Lo-yang, and march to stop him. But this would take months, and increasingly desperate emissaries from Wang Shih-ch'ung were assuring him that their master could not survive much longer. 'I came to save Lo-yang,' Tou concluded, 'which can scarcely hold out from dawn to dusk. If I abandon this purpose and go elsewhere, is it not a breach of faith?' But he was still afraid to venture into the hills beyond the river, where he would once again be vulnerable to ambush. He would have to lure Li Shih-min out to fight in the open.

Shih-min was happy to oblige. In fact he tried to encourage Tou to fight, by detaching 1000 remounts with their grooms to ride off ostentatiously northwards and then sneak back under cover of night, making it look as if the T'ang were dissi-pating their forces. One morning in the early summer of 621, Tou's army came out from its camp and deployed along the east bank of the river along a seven-mile front. The T'ang sat on the western hills, and watched them.

Tou sent out 300 cavalry to skirmish with the T'ang, in the hope of provoking them to charge. As they splashed across the river, the skirmishers were met by a similar number of Shih-min's horsemen. Both sides made a brave show, dashing about and exchanging missiles, but the fight was indecisive. At one point a Hsia cavalryman rode up close to the T'ang lines, and Shih-min noticed that he was mounted on a particularly splendid horse. He commented on this to Yu-ch'ih Ching-te. This brave officer, ignoring Shih-min's order to stop, charged out with two men, seized the horse, and brought it to his

commander with the dumbfounded rider still on its back.

The cavalry skirmish eventually petered out with the exhaustion of both sides. But the bulk of the T'ang troops were well supplied and rested, while the Hsia were standing under arms just short of the river, baking in the hot sun. With a front so long, it was impossible for Tou to keep them under proper control. By midday, having decided that the T'ang were not going to fight, the men had started to break ranks in search of food and water.

Shih-min sent Yu-wen Shih-chi[6] to cross the river near Ssu-shui town with a unit of cavalry, and make a probing attack on the enemy there to test their resolve. If they stand firm, Yu-wen was told, then retire; but if they waver, charge them. From the high ground, the prince could see the Hsia soldiers running in all directions as Yu-wen's horsemen approached, falling into disarray as they tried to form up. 'Now we can attack!' he shouted, and led the T'ang army down the slopes towards the river.

A complacent Tou Chien-te had chosen this moment to gather all his generals in his tent to discuss the next move. When he learned that the T'ang were attacking, he sent his officers running back to their units with orders for a counter-attack. It was too late: the leaderless Hsia troops were already falling back. But at the cliffs which marked the eastern edge of the valley they rallied, and a ferocious mêlée ensued.

Despite the disparity in numbers, the heavily armed T'ang cavalry continued to charge into the enemy formations. In one attack, Shih-min's eighteen-year-old cousin, Li Tao-hsuan, found a weak spot and cut his way right through the Hsia army, then wheeled his horse and rode back to join his comrades, with arrows sticking in his armour 'like the quills of a porcupine'. He then repeated his feat, returning safely a second time, although his horse was killed.

This seems to have given Shih-min an idea. Bringing the courageous youth another horse, the prince accompanied him back into the fray, with his own bodyguard following. The party broke through into the rear of the Hsia, yelling and waving the banners of the T'ang army. When Tou's men saw this, there was panic. The rumour quickly spread that the T'ang had circled behind them and cut off their line of retreat. Tens of thousands of the Hsia laid down their arms and surrendered; about 3000 of them were overtaken trying to scramble up the cliffs and killed by the exuberant T'ang. The rest fled. Shih-min's horsemen chased them for ten miles.

Tou Chien-te was swept away by the rout, and was captured after his horse threw him. Realising that the Hsia forces had dispersed beyond recovery, Li Shih-min immediately returned to Lo-yang, where Tou was displayed beneath the walls to prove to the defenders that the relief attempt had failed. Seeing his ally a prisoner, Wang Shih-ch'ung had no choice but to surrender. The whole of north China was now in the hands of the T'ang.

Over the next three years, the dynasty consolidated its power. With the defeat in 624 of Fu Kung-shih, a local warlord based on the lower Yangtze, Li Yuan became the unchallenged ruler of a reunited China. It was around this time that the organisational framework was established which would serve the T'ang for nearly three centuries. Notable among the institutions set up under Li Yuan were the examination system for civil servants, and a militia system, the *fu-ping*. Both were in fact derived principally from Sui antecedents.

T'ang military organisation

The army which served Li Shih-min so well was based on the *fu-ping* system, which had been inherited from the Sui. Although commonly described as a 'militia', the *fu-ping* was not a mass levy but a system of conscription which applied only to certain hereditary military families. Despite this apparent unfairness, it was not at first unpopular. The communities concerned were concentrated in the northern frontier areas – especially in Kuan-chung – and had a long tradition of military service, which they regarded as an honourable calling. Furthermore, they were exempted from the usual liability for forced labour. When not called up for a specific campaign, the *fu-ping* troops completed either short tours of duty at the capital – where they were engaged in training and guard duties – or longer ones in the frontier garrisons. Officers were usually drawn from the nobility and could find permanent employment in the *fu-ping*. Other ranks were required to serve on a rotational basis.

The advantages to the government were considerable: it saved money, since the troops could support themselves by farming when not actually on duty; it provided a large number of trained reservists in the vulnerable northern regions in case of invasion; and it prevented the generals from amassing private armies away from the scrutiny of the capital. (This, of course, was exactly what Li Yuan had done before he revolted against the Sui, and so the practice was naturally regarded with extreme suspicion.)

Under the early T'ang the *fu-ping* army comprised about 600 units, each with 800–1200 men – although on average only about one-sixth of these were under arms at any one time. Units were based in specific localities, but were kept separate from the local civil administration, reporting directly to the Ministry of the Army in Ch'ang-an. Not all troops, however, were recruited in this way. As emperor, Li Shih-min frequently supplemented the *fu-ping* for active service by nationwide calls for volunteers. Such was his prestige, and the lure of the plunder to be won in a successful war, that, in his own words: 'When we call for ten men we get a hundred; when we call for a hundred we get a thousand.'

The victors fall out

After the end of the civil wars in the north, Li Chien-ch'eng, the heir apparent, began to see Shih-min's brilliant reputation as a threat to his own position. The emperor appointed Shih-min to be commander of the whole eastern plain region, with his base at Lo-yang. In contrast to the normal T'ang practice, this post combined both military and civil command – a measure of the trust that Li Yuan placed in him. How far Shih-min's ambitions extended at this point is uncertain, but before long he had set up a rival power base at Lo-yang. He recruited his own staff, many of whom were formerly officers in Tou Chien-te's army, and even established a military academy, with eighteen scholars who acted as his advisers on matters of strategy.

Chien-ch'eng, supported by the third brother, Yuan-chi, began a similar process in Ch'ang-an. He raised a private army of 2000 young men of the city, which came to be known as the Ch'ang-lin Army, after the Ch'ang-lin Gate of Chien-ch'eng's Eastern Palace, where they were based. He also put some of the ladies of the imperial harem on his payroll, and used them to intercede on his behalf with his father.

Li Yuan must have known that his sons were plotting against one another, but in this matter at least, he lived up to the traditional view of his character. He seems to have been unable to bring himself to discipline any of them, even though their increasing rivalry threatened the stability of the empire. In 624, Chien-ch'eng was accused of planning a coup while the emperor was away at his summer palace. He was summoned to his father's presence, but denied the charges, and no action was taken against him.

When Li Yuan could tolerate the situation no longer, it was Shih-min who had to face his wrath. The emperor forced him to dismiss his two closest advisers – Tu Ju-hui and Fang Hsuan-ling – who were thought to be encouraging his ambitions. The young hero was also summoned to Ch'ang-an, where his father lectured him sternly:

'An emperor receives Heaven's Mandate naturally. It cannot be sought, either by mere cleverness or strength. Yet how eagerly you are seeking it!'

Just what Shih-min had done to merit this reprimand is not clear. The traditional account has him meekly enduring all the provocations of his brothers, while his officers tried in vain to stir him to defend himself. Obviously, Shih-min was not the wronged innocent that the T'ang histories like to portray. But Chien-ch'eng and Yuan-chi were becoming increasingly determined to get rid of him.

They sent assassins to kill Shih-min's loyal companion Yu-ch'ih Ching-te, then when that failed they tried to impeach Yu-ch'ih at court. Shih-min had to intercede personally with the emperor to save his officer from execution. Chien-ch'eng was even said to have tried to poison his brother. When, early in 626, the Turks once more invaded, Chien-ch'eng persuaded Li Yuan to second many of Shih-min's troops to an army which was being raised under Yuan-chi to combat the barbarians. While they were under his command, Yuan-chi tried to bribe their officers to turn against Shih-min, and join in a plot to murder him when he came to Ch'ang-an for the ceremony marking the departure of the army.

The coup at the Hsuan-wu Gate

When his spies reported this, Shih-min decided to strike first. He went to his father and accused his brothers of being involved with ladies of the imperial harem. The charge was at least partly true, but that did not matter in this instance. The long-suffering emperor wearily announced another investigation, and summoned the two princes to the imperial palace.

Chien-ch'eng and Yuan-chi arrived at the Hsuan-wu Gate of the palace without bodyguards, as protocol demanded. But Shih-min had bribed the commander of the guard on the gate, and was lying in wait there with a force variously described as comprising nine or twelve men. Among them was Yu-ch'ih Ching-te, who of course now had his own reasons for wanting vengeance. When the ambush was sprung, the two victims drew their weapons and attempted to fight, despite the odds. Yuan-chi shot three arrows at Shih-min, but missed each time. Though the range was short, his hands must have been trembling with shock and fear. Shih-min coolly ignored him, and let fly a single arrow at his elder brother, Chien-ch'eng. Once again Shih-min showed his skill at archery. Chien-ch'eng was struck in the chest, and died instantly.

Yuan-chi immediately turned and ran for Shih-min's horse, which was tethered not far away. He grabbed its bridle, but the animal was frightened by the shouts and screams of the battle. It reared and plunged wildly, making it impossible for the prince to mount. Then Yu-ch'ih Ching-te came up, and shot him dead. Too late, the two princes' attendants heard the noise and stormed up to the gate, but when they saw their leaders' severed heads displayed on the walls they broke and ran in confusion.

So far, Shih-min could be said to have acted in self-defence; but what followed puts the affair in a different light. He sent Yu-ch'ih Ching-te into the imperial palace, armed with a spear, to inform his father of what had happened. To carry weapons into the emperor's presence was itself an act of treason, but Li Yuan seems to have taken the hint. Three days later, while Shih-min's troops were consolidating their hold on the capital, he officially proclaimed his surviving son heir apparent. Chien-ch'eng and Yuan-chi each had five sons: none of them could have been more than children. Shih-min had them all killed, to remove any future source of dispute over the succession. Two months later, Li Yuan was quietly pushed aside. He abdicated, adopting the title of 'Retired Emperor'. On 4 September 626, Shih-min ascended the throne as the Emperor T'ang T'ai-tsung.

Emperor T'ai-Tsung

It is arguable that in this instance the end did justify the means. No one could deny that the reign of the new emperor was one of the most glorious periods in all China's history. Up until modern times, it has been looked back upon as a model of good government. Yet there remained a cloud over T'ai-tsung's reputation. His father lived for nine more years after his abdication, but his relations with his successor were always strained. In 632 the censor Ma Chou was bold enough to accuse the new emperor of unfilial conduct, pointing out that although his ageing father was living next door in the Ta-an Palace, he never visited him, and that when T'ai-tsung himself went off to his summer palace in the hills, he left the old man to swelter in the heat of Ch'ang-an. The embarrassed emperor accepted the criticism, and on his next trip invited his father to accompany him. Li Yuan stubbornly declined. His son then built a new, more comfortable palace for him, but the job was carried out at a leisurely pace, and the Retired Emperor died before it was finished.

Even then, the tomb which was constructed for him aroused unfavourable comment, as it was conspicuously smaller than the one that T'ai-tsung built for his own wife, who died in the following year. But Li Yuan was at least spared the ultimate insult, which did not occur until after his death. This was the manner in which the story of the founding of the T'ang was rewritten in order to diminish his true role, and to exaggerate beyond all reason the admittedly heroic deeds of his disloyal son.

Great men, however, are invariably complex characters. It is difficult to portray T'ang T'ai-tsung as a villain. As emperor he was a resounding success, remembered for his dignified and commanding appearance, his energy and his concern for the people. As he once said:

'The ruler depends on the state, and the state depends on its people. Oppressing the people to make them serve the ruler is like someone cutting off his own flesh to fill his stomach.'

During his early years, at least, he was concerned to lighten the burden of government, living frugally and cutting back on extravagant building projects, and even on the prodigious hunting expeditions so beloved by his father. Such an attitude must have been a welcome change indeed to those who recalled the excesses of Sui Yang-ti.

T'ai-tsung appears to have been a genuinely emotional man, and his rages were a sight never forgotten by those exposed to them: in anger, it was said, his face would literally turn purple. But he was also a showman. Like Louis XIV, he was conscious that, in an era when government was largely face-to-face, an important part of the job was the ability to put on a good performance. In 628 a plague of locusts struck the farming communities around Ch'ang-an, and the emperor rode out to visit the affected areas. He dismounted, picked up a handful of locusts and cried out, 'The people regard grain the same as life itself, yet you devour it! Better that you devour my own lungs and bowels!' His attendants, seeing what he was about to do, rushed to stop him, worried that he would make himself ill. But it was too late. T'ai-tsung stuffed the insects into his mouth and ate them. 'Since we will suffer this calamity for the sake of the people,' he explained, 'how can we try to avoid illness?'

The emperor suffered no ill effects. He was probably well aware that locusts were not harmful to eat, and that the common people often consumed them in times of famine. But the story spread widely as proof that he was happy to put the welfare of his subjects before his own. He often pretended to feel inadequate for his role, insisting that he was too ignorant to be a ruler. It was true that he relied heavily on a circle of advisers, men of proven ability, who were often allowed a surprising freedom to criticise him. As a man of action, he was impatient of courtly ritual and had no time for superstition. When his astrologers told him that the

date he had selected for the inauguration of his son Ch'eng-ch'ien as heir apparent was inauspicious, he refused to change it, explaining that it had been chosen so that the associated ceremonies would not interfere with the agricultural calendar.

Shih-min's accession to the throne did not curtail his military career. In fact, in the following years the T'ang armies went on to some of the most outstandingly successful campaigns in China's history. In the first of these they were aided by some good fortune, for in 627 the Turkish empire began to break up from within. Two years later, realising that its troubles gave him an opportunity to remove the Turkish threat once and for all, T'ai-tsung sent Li Ch'ing to attack them with 100,000 men. The Turks were defeated, and many of them settled within the empire as T'ang allies. Between 634 and 641 other Turkish tribes, which had remained hostile, were pursued far to the west and similarly crushed. Li Yuan, who had had to accept the Turkish Qaghan as his overlord, lived long enough to see the Turks in their turn become the vassals of his son.

These campaigns brought the T'ang armies into the Tarim Basin, where a group of independent city states controlled the lucrative trade routes to the west. These were gradually brought under Chinese authority, eventually forming what became known as the Protectorate of An-hsi, or the 'Pacified West'. The fame of the T'ang empire spread even farther afield, and before the end of T'ai-tsung's reign he was visited by embassies from Persia, Constantinople and the newly emerging power of the Muslim Arabs.

The 640s saw the rise of a new rival on the western frontier. This was the empire of Tibet, which under its ruler, Srong-btsan-sgam-po, had recently extended its power over a huge region bordering the Tibetan plateau. What Srong-btsan-sgam-po now sought was recognition by his neighbours of his great power status. He demanded that the T'ang send him a princess to be his wife. T'ai-tsung at first refused, but after a brief Tibetan invasion of Szechwan Province, he changed his mind and agreed to send the lady. She was instrumental in converting the Tibetans to Buddhism, and the Chinese and Tibetan rulers enjoyed good relations until the deaths of both men in 649.

As he grew older, however, T'ai-tsung began to lose the self-restraint of his earlier years. During the 630s he began building expensive palaces, only to have them knocked down as soon as they were finished because for some reason they displeased him. He even resumed his father's great hunts, although they were a burden on the people of the districts where they were held. He began to hark back constantly to the military glories of his youth, and to worry about the judgement of posterity. He repeatedly badgered the scholars of the court to let him see what they were writing about him in the

official histories, although by tradition an emperor was never allowed to do this. There can be no doubt that the T'ang histories, as they have come down to us, have been rewritten so as to show him in the best possible light.

One day in 637, T'ai-tsung asked Wei Cheng how his rule compared to that of his early years. Wei Cheng was a former follower of the emperor's elder brother, Chien-ch'eng, who had been employed by T'ai-tsung as an adviser because of his outspoken honesty. He appears to have been allowed to say things that few others would have dared. On this occasion he told his master:

> 'Before the empire was pacified, you always made righteousness and virtue your central concern. Now, thinking that the empire is without troubles, you have gradually become increasingly arrogant, wasteful and self-satisfied.'

The emperor sulked for a while, but no harm befell Wei Cheng. Neither was Liu Fan punished when he replied to T'ai-tsung's criticism of the tutor of one of his sons for allowing the prince to spend too much time

Li Shih-min was very fond of his horses, and arranged for them to be commemorated in a series of reliefs on his tomb. This charger, a chestnut named Shih-fa-ch'ih, was ridden at the battle of Ssu-shui, where he was wounded five times. (After Fitzgerald)

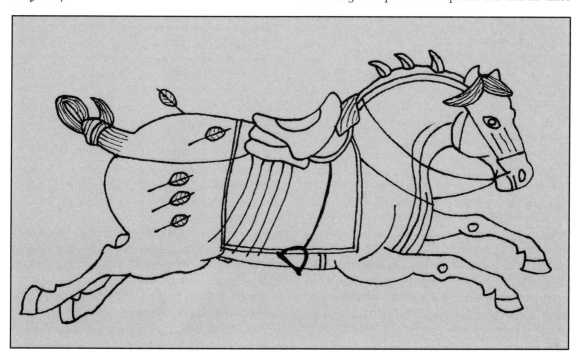

hunting. 'How can you condemn him for being too weak,' Liu Fan asked, 'when even Your Majesty's ministers cannot control your hunting?'

In 636 T'ai-tsung's beloved consort, the Empress Wen-te, died. She had been not only a wife but a trusted confidante and adviser, and the loss affected him deeply. From this time onwards, the emperor began to experience difficulties with his sons – just as his own father had. The heir apparent, Ch'eng-ch'ien, was a capable but eccentric character, who caused a scandal at court by making much of his barbarian ancestry, which the family had until then been at pains to keep quiet. The prince preferred to speak Turkish rather than Chinese, and even appeared in public wearing Turkish costume. (It is perhaps difficult for a modern reader to appreciate how offensive this was. In imperial China the way one dressed was a political statement, and the steppe nomads were not only despised barbarians, but had been bitter enemies for a generation. The impact must have been equivalent to a present-day public figure sporting a swastika.)

T'ai-tsung therefore began to favour another of his sons, Li T'ai, who soon developed ambitions to replace Ch'eng-ch'ien as heir. The latter hatched a plot to kill T'ai; this was discovered, whereupon the emperor stripped Ch'eng-ch'ien of all his titles and sent him into exile. T'ai was then caught plotting against a third son, Li Chih, and had to be banished in his turn. This left Li Chih as the only possible heir, although he was still very young and his father thought him weak-willed. These family troubles caused the emperor great distress, and one wonders whether he began to see them as a divine punishment for his own behaviour as a young man. On at least one occasion he came close to a breakdown, and even tried to stab himself – although this attempt may well have been yet another piece of showmanship, designed to make an impression on the courtiers who interrupted him.

Tang Tai-tsung's last campaign

The northern Korean kingdom of Koguryo, which had successfully resisted Sui Yang-ti's invasion, and in so doing had fatally weakened his dynasty, was nevertheless regarded by the T'ang as being within its own sphere of influence. So when in 642 a usurper overthrew the king of Koguryo, T'ai-tsung decided to intervene. The proclamation which he issued on the eve of his invasion, at the end of 644, shows that he was very much aware of the unhappy precedent, but on this occasion he saw what he regarded as a crucial difference:

> 'Ch'uan Kai-su-wen of Korea has murdered his king and oppresses the people. These things cannot be endured... The army will suffer neither loss nor toil. Those who tell how formerly Yang-ti cruelly sacrificed his soldiers without success, should know that then the king of Korea was a righteous ruler who loved his people. Their nation being united and peaceful, a ruthless invading army could not prevail against them.'[7]

This time, however, things were different. 'Righteousness,' the proclamation continued, 'must prevail over iniquity.' But righteousness was to be supported by massive force, and some very careful planning. Two generals, Li Shih-chi and Li Tao-tsung, would lead 60,000 men into Korea by the obvious overland route, across the Liao River. At the same time a diversionary seaborne landing, with 500 ships and 40,000 men, was to take place at the mouth of the Yalu River, behind the main Koguryo army.

By the time T'ai-tsung himself arrived at the front, early in 645, this stratagem had already succeeded. The Koguryo forces had been dispersed and weakened, and the T'ang commanders had turned the flank of their defensive line on the Liao River and begun reducing the fortresses which lay beyond it. The city of Liao Yang was stormed after the defeat of a relieving force by Li Tao-tsung, and several other towns surrendered without a fight. Not so An Shih Cheng, the largest town in Liao-tung Province, which was held by a skilful and stubborn Korean officer named Yang Man Choun. Here there was no sign that, as T'ai-tsung had predicted, the 'oppressed' Koreans would refuse to fight for their new master. In midsummer of 645, the emperor and his generals closed in on this last enemy stronghold in the north, and laid siege to it.

The Koreans hastily mustered another relief force, said to have numbered 150,000 troops, under Kwa Yon-so. This army comprised the last remaining reserves of the Koguryo kingdom, and Li Tao-tsung suggested that part of the T'ang forces should be used to delay its advance and keep it occupied while a detachment of 10,000 men should strike at once for the Koguryo capital, which was almost undefended. At one time, T'ai-tsung would no doubt have advocated this bold course himself, but possibly age and caution were telling on him. Or perhaps he did not regard the experience of Sui Yang-ti as being as irrelevant as he had claimed. No, he insisted, the Korean army must be defeated first, before any unsupported thrusts further into enemy territory were made. This may or may not have been sound strategy, but when it came to the battlefield, T'ai-tsung's tactical genius proved to be undiminished.

As Kwa Yon-so advanced towards An Shih Cheng, the T'ang seemed indeed to have dispersed their forces. In front of him was Li Shih-chi, formed up in line of battle with some 15,000 men, while far away on the Korean right could be seen a force of 4000 Chinese cavalry, apparently intent on blockading the city. In fact, the hilly terrain provided plenty of opportunities for other Chinese units to deploy out of sight. What Kwa could not see, as he rushed forward to crush Li Shih-chi, were the T'ang troops which were watching An Shih Cheng from concealed positions, guarding against any sorties by the defenders, and freeing the 4000 cavalry, who were led by the emperor himself, for offensive action. Neither were the Koreans aware that another 11,000

Chinese under Chang-sun Wu-chi had worked their way round their flank and were now behind them, communicating with their commander-in-chief by means of smoke signals.

Li Shih-chi's division took the initial brunt of the Korean attack, and fell back slowly across the plain. As their flank became exposed, T'ai-tsung sent up a prearranged smoke signal, then launched his charge. Kwa ordered his right wing to wheel to face this new threat, but before the manoeuvre could be completed, Chang-sun Wu-chi appeared and attacked from behind. Changing direction even once while in contact with the enemy was a difficult manoeuvre for an ancient army, amid the clouds of dust and the ear-splitting din which accompanied close combat. To do so twice was almost impossible. A succession of contradictory orders simply spread confusion, and as Chang-sun's men hit them, the Koguryo army disintegrated. Some 20,000 of them were cut down, while another 36,000, who managed to reform in the nearby hills, were surrounded a few days later, and forced to surrender. The remainder escaped, spreading panic throughout the country.

T'ai-tsung was experiencing once again the exhilaration of his youth. After so long in the claustrophobic atmosphere of the court, he was clearly enjoying himself in the field with his troops. He insisted on sharing their hardships and their rations, taking care of his own equipment, and going about armed with his beloved bow. The communiqué which he sent back to Ch'ang-an with the news of his victory concluded with a note in his own hand: 'When I am at the head of the army, what else should we expect?'

Now, it might be supposed, was the time to make a forced march to the Koguryo capital and end the war. An Shih Cheng could have been blockaded with a relatively small force, and if necessary additional supplies could have been brought over by sea, which the T'ang fleet still controlled. But the emperor insisted on taking the city. And by so doing, he was breaking one of the fundamental rules of the military art: never fight your enemy the way he fights best.

T'ang armies were well equipped and trained for siegecraft. They could deploy rams and heavy catapults, and their engineers were skilled at building siege works of all kinds. But the defence of cities was the real strength of the Korean troops. When the Chinese succeeded in knocking down a section of the wall, they found that another wall had already been built behind it. When they erected a mound of earth high enough to enable them to assault the walls, the enemy charged out unexpectedly, captured the mound, and turned it into part of the defences.

They did not always outwit T'ai-tsung, however. On one occasion, he heard the squawking of chickens from within the city, and immediately put his troops on alert. Shortly afterwards the Koreans came charging out, but were repulsed. The emperor later explained that the noise had told him that the birds were being slaughtered. In a besieged city, where supplies must be carefully conserved, there could be only one reason to kill large numbers of livestock – to provide a good meal for men about to be sent into action. So he had known that a sortie was about to be launched.

Yet An Shih Cheng still held out. After sixty-three days of siege, and with the terrible Korean winter drawing in, T'ai-tsung reluctantly gave the order to retire. The raising of the siege was accompanied by an exchange of courtesies between two opponents who had come to respect each other. Yang Man Choun came up on to the walls to see his enemy off, and the emperor presented him with a farewell gift of a hundred bolts of silk.

The Koreans did not attempt to harass the retreat, but it was an unpleasant experience nevertheless. All the bridges had been destroyed, and improvised causeways had to be constructed through the swamps by T'ang engineers. The cold weather set in suddenly, and fires had to be built along the route to warm the struggling soldiers. Even so, some froze to death. T'ai-tsung continued to share the rigours of the march, and even to assist the engineers with his own hands.

The bulk of the army returned to China, exhausted but safe, but the emperor's health never recovered. Over the next few years he became less and less able to perform his duties, and it is generally believed that at some time during the campaign of 645 he had contracted an unknown disease, which was to end his life four years later. His heir Li Chih gradually took over his day-to-day responsibilities; it was during this period that T'ai-tsung wrote for his son a book in four chapters, the *Ti-fan*, or *Plan for an Emperor*, setting out his instructions and advice on how to rule the empire.

T'ang T'ai-tsung died in the fifth month of 649, still less than fifty years of age. He was proved right about Li Chih. The new emperor, who took the title of Kao-tsung, was well-intentioned but weak. He came under the influence of his consort, the notorious Empress Wu,[8] whose extravagance and fondness for intrigue almost ruined the state.

Nevertheless the T'ang empire endured. In the 660s its boundaries reached their widest ever extent, bringing the peoples of Central Asia under Chinese control – at least for a while – as far west as Persia. In the following century, terrible rebellions threatened to overthrow the dynasty, leaving it permanently weakened. But so great was its prestige that it survived even this, and it was not finally replaced until 907. Even after that, the name of T'ang continued to be a byword for good government and military glory. Rulers such as Kubilai Khan tried to model their reigns on its precedent. Much of this strength was due to the foundations laid down by Li Yuan and his son. He may not have been the paragon of all virtue that his own annals describe, but Li Shih-min might after all have had grounds for satisfaction in the verdict of posterity.

13

GUNPOWDER

The origin of gunpowder and firearms has long been a subject of interest to historians in the West. These new weapons made their first appearance in Europe during the first quarter of the fourteenth century. Superiority in firearms was, of course, one of the reasons for the subsequent success of European conquerors all over the world. But until recently, the early history of gunpowder weapons was not widely known; even today, the theory of a European or Middle Eastern origin is repeated in some books. That the Chinese invented gunpowder has long been accepted, but Matteo Ricci – writing at the beginning of the seventeenth century – was only the first in a long line of authorities who have repeated the myth that, although they may have been the first to develop the formula, the Chinese were only interested in using it for fireworks.

The real story is much more interesting. It has its roots in alchemy and popular religion, and thus ultimately in that Taoist philosophy whose influence on the art of war has already been examined. Men seeking the elusive elixir of immortality or, more prosaically, trying to turn mercury into silver, had been experimenting with saltpetre and sulphur at least as early as AD300. By around 850, the explosive properties of this sort of mixture had been accidentally discovered. Joseph Needham, in his *Science and Civilisation in China*, quotes a Taoist book of about this date as stating:

This ceramic pillow from the Sung dynasty appears to show soldiers armed with fire-lances, semi-explosive flame-throwers which were the precursors of true handguns. (British Museum)

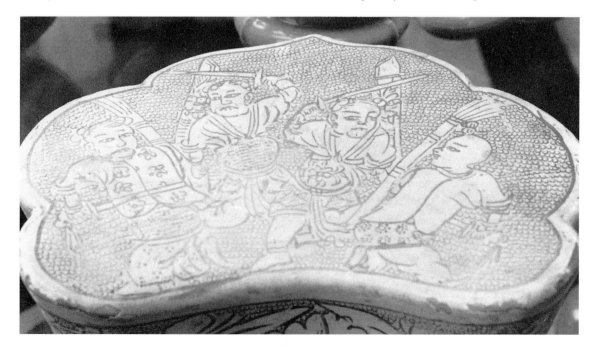

Some have heated together sulphur, realgar (i.e. arsenic disulphide) and salt-petre with honey; smoke and flames result, so that their hands and faces have been burnt, and even the whole house where they were working burned down.[1]

As yet, no practical use had been devised for this discovery, and in fact the anonymous author specifically warns his readers not to try the experiment. But seventy years later a comparable compound was being used to impregnate a slow match for igniting a flame-thrower, and by the 990s, similarly impreg-nated incendiary arrows were available in large quantities. 'Fierce fire oil' or naphtha, which had probably been introduced by the Arabs who regularly traded by sea with southern China, was also being used for mili-tary purposes by the tenth century.

Gunpowder missiles must have been a great improvement on the old fire-arrows that used burning pitch, but they were still at best only semi-explosive. The early formulae for gunpowder specified too much sulphur and carbon, and not enough saltpetre. Needham

has extracted the relevant recipes from numerous medieval works, and has clearly shown that a long period of experimentation occurred in China before the optimum proportions were discovered. By contrast, truly explosive gunpowder appears in four-teenth-century Europe without evidence of any such previous period of experiment. This strongly suggests that the technology was imported into Europe fully developed, and was not an indigenous development.

Bombs and guns

From eleventh-century China comes the first mention anywhere in the world of the use of true explosives for military purposes. The encyclopaedia known as the *Wu Ching Tsung Yao* or *Collection of the Most Important Mili-tary Techniques*, published in 1044, describes gunpowder bombs which were thrown by rope-powered artillery. The charge was enclosed in a soft case of bamboo or paper,

Cannon of the Ming period, preserved on the Great Wall. (Duncan Head)

Early Chinese firearms, as illustrated in manuals of the Ming era. 1) The 'sky-soaring poison-dragon fire-lance', from a version of the Huo Lung Ching, dating from about AD 1400. This weapon combined a central barrel firing lead shot with two flame-throwing tubes, and a crescent-shaped blade. It is thus a good example of the transition between the fire-lance and the gun. 2) A handgun from the same source, with an explosive projectile shown emerging from the barrel. 3) An iron cannon with reinforcing rings around the barrel. From the Ping Lu of 1606, this weapon is of a type which had been in use since the fourteenth century.

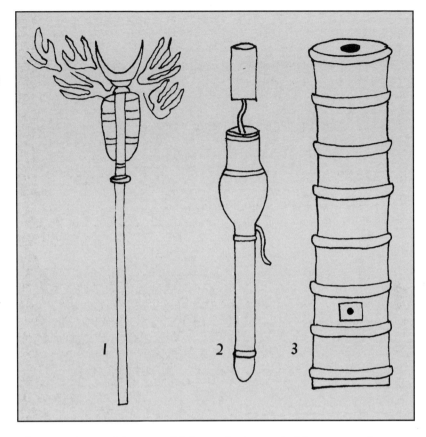

and was still not fully explosive. It would have burned very quickly, like the powder used to propel rockets, but would not have gone off with sufficient force to burst a hard casing. That next step, however, had taken place by 1221, when iron-cased fragmentation bombs were used by the Kin at the siege of Ch'i-chou. The *Kin Official History*, referring to such a bomb at the siege of K'ai-feng eleven years later, clearly describes a true explosion:

It consisted of gunpowder put into an iron container; then when the fuse was lit and the projectile shot off there was a huge explosion, the noise of which was like thunder ... the attacking soldiers were all blown to bits, not even a trace being left behind.

The apt name for this device was *chien-t'ien-lei*: 'heaven-shaking thunder'.

With explosives of this power, the way was open for the development of the true gun, which apparently had its origin in a weapon known as a *huo-ch'iang* or fire-lance. This was at first simply a firework on the end of a spear, which spewed out smoke and flames a few feet in front of the wielder, for as long as it took the charge to burn out. There is a silk banner from Tun-huang, now in the Musée Guimet in Paris, which depicts a group of demons attacking the Buddha with what are clearly fire-lances and incendiary grenades. This banner has been dated to the middle of the tenth century, making it by far the earliest evidence we have for such a weapon. If this dating is correct the fire-lance must have been successfully kept as a military secret for nearly three centuries, because it is not mentioned in the *Wu Ching Tsung Yao* or other works of the early Sung dynasty, and only starts to appear in battle accounts of the thirteenth century.

By that time, fire-lances had become quite sophisticated. Various chemicals could be added to produce irritating or poisonous smoke, and stones or similar small missiles were sometimes placed in a small bronze barrel at the end, so that they could be expelled by the force of the flames to blind or distract an adversary. Then in an entry in the *Sung Official History* for the year 1259, we read of a weapon called the *t'u huo ch'iang*, or 'flame-spouting lance':

... inside it they put a bundle of projectiles. After ignition, and when the blazing stream of flame was ending, the bundle was shot forth as if it was a trebuchet projectile, with a noise that could be heard more than 150 paces away.[2]

This is clearly a gun in all but name. By the 1280s, *huo p'ao*, or hand-held guns, are clearly described in an account of a battle in the *Yuan Official History*.

Rockets

In early Ming times, probably the most popular gunpowder weapon – at least for use in pitched battles – was the rocket. Courtiers in the Sung period had amused themselves with primitive firework rockets, but it is not until the 1340s that we begin to hear of their appearance in battle. Chinese rockets did not

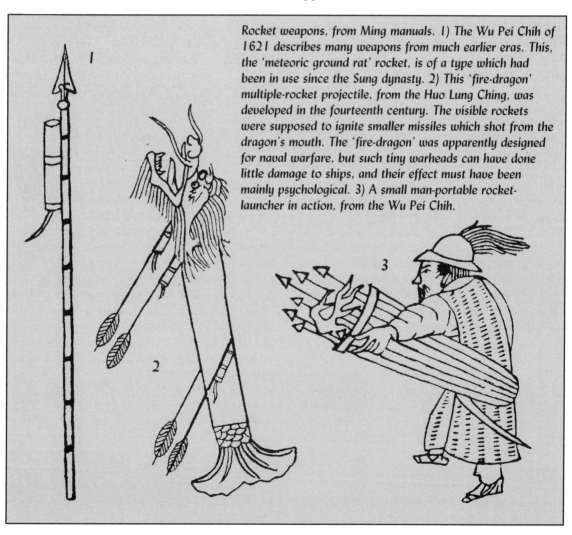

Rocket weapons, from Ming manuals. 1) The Wu Pei Chih of 1621 describes many weapons from much earlier eras. This, the 'meteoric ground rat' rocket, is of a type which had been in use since the Sung dynasty. 2) This 'fire-dragon' multiple-rocket projectile, from the Huo Lung Ching, was developed in the fourteenth century. The visible rockets were supposed to ignite smaller missiles which shot from the dragon's mouth. The 'fire-dragon' was apparently designed for naval warfare, but such tiny warheads can have done little damage to ships, and their effect must have been mainly psychological. 3) A small man-portable rocket-launcher in action, from the Wu Pei Chih.

carry explosive warheads, but were in effect gunpowder-propelled arrows. They were fired from multiple launchers, the smaller versions of which could be carried by a single man. By the 1390s, however, larger launchers were being deployed on wheelbarrows. Rockets were said to be especially effective against massed targets as their trajectory was so erratic that no one could predict where they were likely to strike. The noise of hundreds of missiles being fired together was also no doubt very impressive. They played a particularly important role in the Ming civil war of 1399 to 1402. When improved European guns became available in the sixteenth century, however, the rocket weapons lost much of their popularity. It is likely in any case that their effectiveness had always been mainly psychological, and so might be expected to decline over time as troops became more accustomed to them.

Later developments

The question inevitably arises as to why, given their head start in the development of gunpowder weapons, the Chinese failed to take full advantage of it. In fact, their weapons technology had already begun to stagnate by the end of the fifteenth century, just at the time when the Europeans were forging ahead. One reason for this failure was that the need for further improvements in weaponry was by no means obvious. Unlike Europe, which comprised a number of rival states of roughly similar strength, China's own neighbourhood contained no enemy powerful or sophisticated enough to pose a serious threat. There was thus no incentive to gain an advantage through technological advances.

Indeed, the Ming emperors were often more wary of internal enemies, and so tended to discourage the dissemination of knowledge about firearms, for fear that it could fall into the wrong hands. Furthermore, the whole ethos of the Chinese upper classes was now turning against involvement with the crude realities of warfare. Educated in Confucian thinking and steeped in tradition, they despised both military affairs and innovation in general. Thus the pursuit of improved weapons was frowned upon socially and shunned politically as a potential danger.

When foreign-manufactured guns became available in China in the sixteenth century, they were quickly recognised as superior to local designs, and soon began to replace them. It seems that Turkish arquebuses were imported into the north-west via the Muslim Central Asian state of Turfan as early as the second decade of the century. These gained a good reputation locally, but did not catch on in the rest of the country. The Portuguese, and subsequently the Spanish, introduced European guns into the south a few years later, and from that time onwards it was developments in the West which set the pace for the rest of the world. By the 1840s, when soldiers of the Ch'ing dynasty with their obsolete matchlocks were facing modern percussion-cap weapons, even the memory of Chinese superiority in firearms had long since faded.

14

CHU YUAN-CHANG:
FROM BEGGAR TO EMPEROR

'Nothing is impossible to a man of strong will.'
Chu Yuan-chang

The theme of the low-born hero, who rises from obscurity to exalted rank, has always been popular in Chinese folklore, as it has in many other cultures. But no character of fiction – nor indeed of history – ever experienced more extremes of fortune than the founder of the Ming dynasty, Chu Yuan-chang. The first twenty years of Chu's life were spent on the verge of starvation, and the last thirty surrounded by the splendours of the imperial court. The only dynastic founder to come from the very lowest stratum of Chinese society, he established a regime which ranks as among the most distinguished in all the country's history, and ended his days as probably the most powerful individual on earth.

A country in turmoil

In many ways, Chu's rise parallels the recovery of China itself. Following the military glories of the T'ang, and the artistic splendours of the Sung, a series of disasters had struck the empire in the twelfth and thirteenth centuries AD. From the tenth century onwards, China had enjoyed a boom in trade and production, creating what some scholars have called the world's first modern economy. While Europe remained locked into a world of self-sufficient feudal estates, the Chinese had mass production, paper money, gunpowder and printing. A widespread system of trade was facilitated by an advanced infrastructure of canals, roads and bridges. A large and well-educated scholar class provided a government bureaucracy which was selected by examination on the basis of ability, rather than by birth. It is not surprising that when Marco Polo returned to Italy at the end of the thirteenth century, with his tales of the wealth and size of China's cities – cities which were in fact already past their peak – he was simply not believed.

But by the time of Chu Yuan-chang's birth in 1328, things had changed. The wealthy but unmilitary Sung regime had proved unable to defend the northern frontier against successive waves of mounted barbarians from the north. First were the Khitans from Manchuria, who had seized part of the north-east in the chaos after the fall of the T'ang in 907, and could never be made to give it up. They were followed by the Jurchen – also of Manchurian origin – who conquered the Liao empire of the Khitans in 1125, then swept on into the Yellow River valley, establishing their own Kin dynasty. The Sung were driven out of northern China altogether, although they still held on in the south.

Finally, came the Mongols. Early in his career of world conquest, Chinggis Khan had gained a foothold in China by smashing the Jurchen. In 1215 he captured their northern capital of Chung-tu, on the site of modern Peking. Gradually, Chinggis and his successors pressed on southward. In 1235 the Jurchen were finally eliminated, and the Mongols, now reinforced by the resources and manpower of north China, began to close in on the Sung. In 1260, Chinggis's grandson Kubilai became Great Khan of the Mongols, and moved his capital to Chung-tu, which he renamed Ta-tu. Nineteen years later he finally completed the conquest of China, and replaced the Sung with his own Mongol Yuan dynasty.[1]

A Mongol horseman, from a Ming period painting. This man has adopted several elements of Chinese costume, and is probably typical of the soldiers of the Mongolian Yuan dynasty which was overthrown by Chu Yuan-chang. (Victoria and Albert Museum, No. E33-1964)

Kubilai was an intelligent and enlightened ruler, but most of his successors were less able, and the traditions of the nomadic Mongols provided none of the skills needed to govern a civilised empire. By the 1320s, the Yuan had degenerated into an inefficient and often brutal regime, which discriminated against the native Chinese in favour of the Mongols and their Central Asian subjects. Furthermore, the Yuan emperors' failure to understand the needs of a settled economy, and their extravagant support of thousands of Tibetan Buddhist monks, had impoverished a country already battered by the long wars of conquest. Even the Mongols – who had been settled on land which was often unsuitable for their horse- and cattle-breeding lifestyle – were bankrupt and starving. For the despised natives, conditions were far worse. Millions of people were driven to destitution by an unfair tax system, or by the unofficial exactions of almost equally desperate Mongol landlords. Hundreds of thousands of Chinese were forced to wander around the country to evade the authorities, scratching a living as best they could. Emaciated corpses lying by the roadside had become an everyday sight.

The early years of Chu Yuan-chang

Chu Yuan-chang was born in a village called Chung-li in Hao-chou district, not far from the banks of the lower Yangtze River. His father lived a hand-to-mouth existence as a tenant farmer. Most of Chu's brothers and sisters were given away for adoption, because their parents could not afford to feed them. When Chu was sixteen, his parents, weakened by privation, died in one of the epidemics which frequently ravaged the countryside in those years. The survivors of the family were unable to support the boy, and sent him to join a Buddhist monastery at the nearby temple of Huan-chueh. A few months later, in the middle of winter, the monks announced that they could no longer afford to feed the novices. Chu and his colleagues would have to leave the temple, and try to survive as best they could by begging.

For the next few years, Chu wandered around the district, begging for his food. Somehow, he survived. In fact, despite his sufferings he had grown up tall and strong, with rugged features that later historians claimed had marked him out even at this stage for distinction. However that may be, it seems that he was already developing an interest in military matters. He had been brought up with the reminiscences of his maternal grandfather, a veteran of the Sung army which had resisted the Mongols in the 1270s. In his later years, Chu preferred to forget the humiliating episodes of his youth, and he never recounted his experiences in detail. It appears likely, however, that at some stage he served briefly in the Yuan army. So

perhaps it is not surprising that his thoughts eventually turned to a military career.

The Red Turbans

As the Yuan regime crumbled, the native Chinese had begun to organise resistance. Many anti-Mongol groups operated under the cover of Buddhist religious sects. One of these, the White Lotus, combined political revolution with millenarian prophecy. It claimed that a period of chaos was imminent, which would lead to the overthrow of the Mongols. Then there would arise a 'King of Light', who was destined to restore the empire to the Chinese. In 1351, the Yuan government conscripted a huge force of peasant labourers for flood control works on the Yellow River, and White Lotus activists took the opportunity to preach their message to this mass audience.

The movement spread like wildfire. Throughout the north and along the Yangtze valley, peasant armies equipped with improvised weapons hurled themselves on the Mongol occupiers. At first they took their disorganised and complacent enemies by surprise, and won numerous victories. Equipping themselves with captured equipment, they began to organise themselves into proper armies. The rebels became known as Red Turbans, after the distinguishing headgear which they adopted.

A man named Han Shan-t'ung, who claimed to be descended from the former Sung rulers, was adopted by the triumphant Red Turbans as the prospective emperor of a restored Sung dynasty. But soon things began to go wrong for the rebels. The Yuan forces rallied, and the Red Turban leaders started to quarrel among themselves. The 'liberated' areas ended up divided among a large number of local commanders, many of them little more than bandit chiefs. All professed nominal allegiance to Han Shan-t'ung – and after 1355 to his son, Han Lin-erh – but in reality they were soon operating as independent warlords.

In February 1352, a band of rebels captured the town of Hao-chou, the capital of

Left and above: The processional way leading to Chu Yuan-chang's tomb at Nanking is lined with stone statues, representing officers of Chu's army. Their armour is of a type which had first appeared around the end of the T'ang dynasty, and remained in use until the Ch'ing. (Duncan Head)

the district where the Huan-chueh Temple was located. An undisciplined Yuan army which was sent to suppress them instead ran amok in the countryside, plundering indiscriminately. Chu Yuan-chang had returned briefly to the temple, but fled with the other monks at the approach of the Yuan troops. The fugitives returned a few days later, cold and starving, to find that the temple buildings had been looted and burned to the ground, leaving the entire community without even a roof over its head. Understandably, Chu had had enough. One day in April, he turned up alone outside Hao-chou, and announced to the sentries on the walls that he had come to join the Red Turbans.

Chu later claimed that friends among the rebels had sent him a series of messages, urging him to defect to them. It seems improbable that they would go to the trouble to seek out a destitute monk in this way, although it may be that he had already distinguished himself in some forgotten episode. Certainly Kuo Tzu-hsing, the rebel leader, welcomed him with open arms, and within a few months Chu had been promoted to command a section in Kuo's own guard. The younger of Kuo's two wives also took a fancy to the new recruit, and persuaded Kuo to give him as a wife his own adopted daughter. This lady, the future Empress Ma, remained by Chu's side throughout the rest of his eventful career.

Chu remained in Hao-chou during the following winter, when the city was unsuccessfully besieged by the Yuan, and when the siege was lifted in June 1353, he was sent back to his home village to try to raise more recruits for the Red Turbans. The continuing poverty of the villagers must have made his tales of life with the rebels all the more appealing. He came back to Hao-chou with 700 men, and a grateful Kuo permitted him to employ them as the core of his own independent command. Twenty-four of them, who had been Chu's friends in his youth, were organised into an officer corps led by Hsu Ta, who was later to prove himself an outstanding general.

Soon after this, the eager new commander was sent south to attack the city of Ting-yuan. The man responsible for this order was Chao Chun-yung, leader of another Red Turban band and a rival of Kuo, who is said to have planned to send Chu to his death against a greatly superior enemy, so leaving Chao free to murder Kuo. Chao managed to have his rival arrested, but to his amazement Chu arrived back at Hao-chou in the nick of time with the entire Yuan garrison of Ting-yuan in tow, having persuaded it to defect en masse to the rebels. Quickly assessing the situation, Chu overpowered Chao's men, and released Kuo from imprisonment.

The rebel hero

From this point onwards, Chu Yuan-chang's reputation began to grow. Over the next two years, he and Hsu Ta campaigned continuously along the north bank of the Yangtze River. By now the Yuan forces were disintegrating everywhere, and Chu continued to welcome the numerous defectors with open arms, incorporating them into his own forces. He was becoming extremely popular among the ordinary soldiers and peasants. This popularity was based largely on the discipline which he imposed on his troops who, unlike the armed mobs of the Yuan, were never permitted to plunder the villages through which they passed. As his fame grew, the process snowballed. By the beginning of 1355, when he defeated a Yuan army at Ho-yang, Chu found himself at the head of 30,000 men. Soon afterwards, two of the commanders of the Yuan naval forces on the Yangtze also defected, giving him control of a fleet of river boats.

At about the same time, Kuo Tzu-hsing died. Chu's fame had by now spread to the court of Han Lin-erh, who had succeeded Han Shan-t'ung as Red Turban 'emperor', and was trying to assert his authority. He appointed Chu second-in-command of Kuo's entire army, and thus – for the time being at least – ensured his support. At the same time, Han's endorsement lent legitimacy to Chu, who could now claim to be more than simply another rebel chieftain.

Governor of Kiangsi

The overall command was held jointly by Kuo's eldest son and brother-in-law, who had already planned their next move. On the south bank of the Yangtze, and now accessible with the help of Chu's new fleet, lay the city of Chi-ching (modern Nanking[2]). This rich prize was still held by a Yuan garrison, but its defences had been neglected, and the loyalties of its half-million inhabitants were uncertain.

Nevertheless, Chi-ching proved a tough nut to crack. The Red Turbans crossed the river in June 1355, but the city did not fall until April of the following year. By then events had once more turned to Chu's advantage. In an unsuccessful assault in October, both the joint commanders were killed, having been abandoned at a crucial moment in the battle by Ch'en Esen, one of the former Yuan officers whom Chu had recruited. Ch'en Esen himself then mysteriously died. This left Chu in control of the whole army. When his men finally stormed into the city, a grateful Han Lin-erh confirmed him as governor of the newly formed province of Kiangsi.

The apparently coincidental deaths of everyone who stood between Chu and the command of the army, all within a period of a few months, provoked comment

A close-up of one of the better preserved statues from the tombs of Chu's successors near Beijing reveals the details of how the elaborate armour was constructed and worn. (Duncan Head)

both at the time and among later historians. Not surprisingly, the *Ming Official History* glosses over the matter. Chu had a reputation as a man who valued loyalty above all else, but perhaps he considered that this applied only to his own subordinates, and not to himself. Certainly he had the air of a man who always knew exactly where he was going. And in the future there was to be another convenient death, that of the last man who obstructed his path to the ultimate prize – Han Lin-erh himself.

That was to come much later; but already in 1356 Chu was acting like a man who could imagine the imperial throne within his grasp. He announced that Chi-ching was to be his provincial capital, and renamed it Ying-tien. He continued to use the Red Turban calendar – a sign of his outward loyalty to Han Lin-erh's regime – but organised his own administration, and appointed both military and civil officials without bothering to refer to higher authority. He was now in effect an independent ruler, and from this time on his de facto 'state' is commonly referred to as the Ming, although in fact the title was not adopted until a few years later.

The Ming-Han war

By the beginning of 1360, the minor players in the lower Yangtze valley had been mopped up. The region had been shared out among three surviving states – Ming, Han and Wu. Elsewhere in the south there were five middle-ranking powers, mostly paying lip-service to the Yuan, and a large number of independent cities and local bandit chiefs. Most of North China, though still ravaged by war and roamed by Red Turban remnants, remained nominally under Yuan control. Similar arrangements had proved reasonably stable in the past – for example in the tenth century, when the T'ang dynasty had been followed by half a century of political division under the Five Dynasties and Ten Kingdoms. And now the momentum of war seemed to be slowing down, as professional armies replaced the wandering hordes of rebels. The defences of cities were also being repaired, making it less easy for them to change hands. It was by no means obvious then that the end result was going to be the reunification of the whole empire – except, that is, to two men, whose boundless ambitions were soon to restart the terrible spiral of war.

Late in 1359 the ruler of the Han state, Ch'en Yu-liang, had tried to seize a border town from the Ming, which he considered to be his weakest rival, and thus the logical first victim of his own drive for ultimate power. Chu discovered the plan, and set an ambush into which the small force which Ch'en had sent disappeared without trace. Such defiance was intolerable; so in June of the following year, Ch'en set sail down the Yangtze with an enormous fleet, determined to crush Chu once and for all. He reached the Ming riverside town of T'ai-p'ing, and manoeuvred the towering sterns of his warships up against the walls, so that his troops could jump straight on to the ramparts.

With the town in his grasp, Ch'en, now certain of victory, dropped all pretence. He announced the founding of a new imperial dynasty – to be known, naturally, as the Han – with himself as its first emperor.

This move turned out to be premature; but even in Ying-tien, most of Chu's generals shared Ch'en's assessment of the situation. In a panic they advised abandoning the capital and fleeing inland, pointing out that although the Ming could almost match Ch'en's strength on land, they had no counter to his fleet. But an officer named K'ang Mao-ts'ai came forward with another plan. He proposed to send Ch'en a message via one of his servants, who was an established double agent in the Han camp, informing him of his own wish to defect. K'ang would promise to remove the wooden bridge over the San-ch'a River, which was the only obstacle preventing the Han fleet from sailing up the river to the walls of Ying-tien and storming the city, just as they had done at T'ai-p'ing. If Chen could be lured up the narrow river by the prospect of a quick victory, he would then be vulnerable to an ambush.

Chu immediately seized on the plan, but made his own modifications to it. Perhaps he did not fully trust K'ang not to double-cross him, or perhaps he simply had in mind a better site for the ambush. At any rate, his first act was to knock down the wooden bridge, and have it rebuilt in stone. Then he stationed detachments of troops along the other small creeks and canals which led up to the walls of Ying-tien, and ordered them to drive sharpened stakes into the banks at all the likely landing spots. Now there was only one place for Ch'en to go.

Acting upon K'ang's message, the Han fleet sailed confidently into the San-ch'a, but came to a halt at the unexpected sight of a brand new stone bridge, which was too solidly built to demolish without extensive preparation. Ch'en tried to disembark his troops, but could find nowhere to land them unopposed. Temporarily baffled – and no doubt cursing K'ang Mao-ts'ai for a fool or a

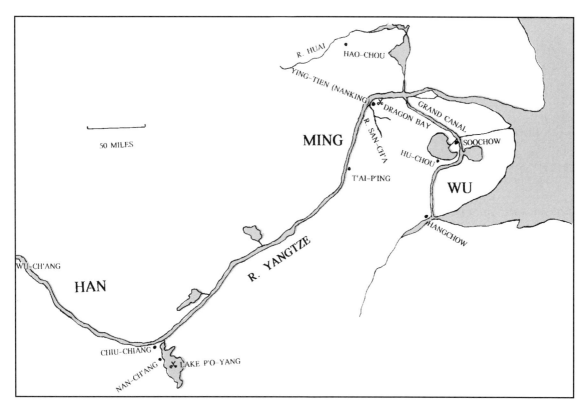

R. HUAI
HAO-CHOU
YING-TIEN (NANKING)
DRAGON BAY
GRAND CANAL
MING
R. SAN-CH'A
SOOCHOW
HU-CHOU
T'AI-P'ING
WU
50 MILES
HANGCHOW
R. YANGTZE
WU-CH'ANG
HAN
CHIU-CHIANG
NAN-CH'ANG
LAKE P'O-YANG

The theatre of war on the lower Yangtze, 1360 to 1365. The victory of the Ming over the rival leaders of Han and Wu made Chu Yuan-chang by far the strongest of the warlords still contending for the imperial throne.

traitor – he turned his fleet around and withdrew to the nearest safe anchorage. This was at a site called Dragon Bay, a few miles farther down the Yangtze, where the Hsin River flowed into it from the south. There Ch'en landed his men, built a fortified camp, and waited for K'ang to get in touch and explain what was going on.

Inland from the landing place at Dragon Bay was a wide plain, overlooked by a range of hills to the north. In the opposite direction, in the distance, could be seen the walls of Ying-tien, with an eminence known as Lion Hill just in front of them. The day of the battle was hot and sultry, with intermittent thunderstorms. Ch'en drew up his army, which was allegedly around 100,000 strong, and made ready to advance on the city. Then a red flag was spotted waving over Lion Hill. It was followed by a division of the Ming army, marching straight towards the Han. There were no more than 30,000 of them, and Chu Yuan-chang himself could be clearly seen riding at their head.

Ch'en Yu-liang was not a man to miss an opportunity like this. He ordered a rapid advance, and prepared to fall on the rival who had so rashly delivered himself into his hands. If not himself an educated man, Ch'en was surrounded by the retinue of scholars which was considered indispensable to the legitimacy of any imperial regime. Had he never been told of Han Hsin and the Ching-hsing Pass (see Chapter 8)? Or had he simply forgotten his military history in the heat of the moment? As the Han battle-line swung into the middle of the plain, they exposed their left flank to those unreconnoitred hills to the north. Suddenly, another flag – a yellow one this time – fluttered over the Ming position on Lion Hill. In response, another

30,000 Ming troops poured over the crest of the hills, and charged headlong into the rear of Ch'en's left and centre.

There was an almost immediate rout, as the surprised Han soldiers ran for their only hope of escape – the ships. But Chu's trap was more subtle than they yet realised. This far downstream, the Yangtze was tidal – a fact that an invader from upriver could perhaps not be expected to know. While they had been manoeuvring on the plain, the tide had gone out, and half the Han fleet was now aground and hopelessly stuck in the mud. Ch'en and most of his men got away, at some cost to their dignity, by wading through the stinking mud and piling on to the remaining ships, but 27,000 of the Han soldiers did not escape. Seven thousand of these had surrendered, accepting a generous offer of incorporation into Chu's army. The rest were dead; slaughtered as they ran by the exultant Ming. When the tide returned, over a hundred of the Han ships were refloated, along with several times that number of small river boats, and sailed off in triumph to form the core of a new Ming fleet.

The battle of Lake P'o-yang

The débâcle at Dragon Bay had done serious damage to Ch'en's reputation, but he was able to replace his material losses fairly quickly. Chu Yuan-chang was troubled by sporadic attacks from Wu, his neighbour on the south-east, as well as by power struggles among his own generals, and therefore could not wholeheartedly pursue his advantage. His one permanent gain was the fleet. In 1361 a Han counter-attack was thwarted by a Ming naval victory outside the walls of Chiu-chiang. Soon afterwards, Chu's forces took that city, using the captured Han ships which had been used against the walls of T'ai-p'ing. Other conquests followed, but Ch'en's main power base on the middle Yangtze remained intact.

The Ming spent the next year digesting the latest conquests along the Han border and weathering a series of internal conflicts. First, there was a rebellion by Chu's Miao troops. The Miao were southern tribesmen who had originally formed a separate army under Yuan command, before defecting to the Ming in 1360. They were brave fighters, but were not noted for their discipline. No sooner were they suppressed than most of the cities recently gained from Han tried unsuccessfully to break away.

As if this was not enough, Shao Jung, a senior Ming general who apparently felt that his role in crushing the Miao revolt had not been properly acknowledged, was caught plotting a coup. The plan was to assassinate Chu during a military review, but the plot was foiled when Chu changed his plans at the last moment because of a bad omen, and used a different gate to enter the city. (Was Chu just lucky, or was it perhaps his habit to use the omens to generate an element of unpredictability? Superstition seems inconsistent with his calculating nature.) Shao and his associates were betrayed by Ming spies and executed, but the affair seems to have temporarily shaken Chu's confidence.

Then, early in 1363, an army from Wu captured An-feng, the capital of what remained of the 'Sung' empire, and took Han Lin-erh himself into custody. Many of the new scholar class which Chu Yuan-chang had built up around him regarded this as good riddance, and tried to dissuade Chu from trying to rescue the peasant emperor. But Chu obviously considered that he was not yet strong enough to do without Han Lin-erh and his old Red Turban supporters. A question of legitimacy was involved: he was still, after all, technically only one of Han's officials. So a rescue mission was mounted. Chu and Hsu Ta marched to An-feng, stormed the city, and by a stroke of luck discovered Han Lin-erh unharmed. However, they then became bogged down in more fighting in the area, which kept Hsu Ta occupied for most of the summer.

So it was that by the middle of 1363, Ch'en Yu-liang had been permitted to regain the initiative. He had rebuilt his fleet, which was now larger than ever. Its main strength consisted of huge red-painted, three-decked 'tower ships', equipped with the usual lofty sterns, as well as with fighting towers armoured with iron plates. It is likely that many of these vessels mounted guns – a large number of cannon cast by the Han regime still survive – and each was said to be able to carry 2000–3000 men. Awestruck Ming sailors later described the giant ships as looming over them 'like mountains'.

Ch'en struck first at Nan-ch'ang, a strategically important city on the shores of Lake P'o-yang, which emptied into the Yangtze from the south. The Han force was immense – it was later said to have numbered 600,000 men – and it must have seemed invincible. But the Ming had added an extra tier to the city walls, which were now too high for the Han ships to assault. For two months, Nan-ch'ang held out against more conventional siege operations, until the garrison finally managed to get a message out to Ying-tien, asking for help.

On 15 August, Chu set sail up the Yangtze with the Ming fleet. Various sources describe this force as numbering up to 1000 ships and 200,000 men. Even if these figures are correct it must have been much smaller than the Han host which it was setting out to attack, but Chu had no choice. If Nan-ch'ang were lost, the consequences would be disastrous. Nothing else stood between Ch'en Yu-liang and the city of Ying-tien, and he could hardly be expected to make the same mistakes again. And unless Han could be stopped quickly, Wu would surely join in and force the outnumbered Ming into a two-front war. This was to be the supreme crisis of Chu's career: never before or since did he have to face such an overwhelming threat.

As the Ming fleet left the Yangtze and entered Lake P'o-yang, the Han lifted the siege of Nan-ch'ang and sailed north to confront it. The two forces met on 29 August 1363, near an island in the lake known as Mount K'ang-lang. At dawn the next day, led by Chu Yuan-chang in person, the Ming attacked. They were organised into eleven squadrons, with the heavy ships taken from the Han in the centre, and lighter and more manoeuvrable vessels on the wings. The latter engaged the enemy with stone-throwing engines shooting incendiary missiles. About twenty of the Han ships were set alight and destroyed, but in the centre their massive tower ships closed in for a boarding action, and quickly forced the Ming to retreat.

The first day's fighting ended with Chu's fleet falling back into the shallows near the lakeshore. Here some craft ran aground and had to be abandoned, but the larger Han ships dared not follow them, and so they were able to regroup. But by the next morning, demoralisation had set in. Chu had to execute a number of his more timid officers to encourage the rest to return to the fray. When they did so, they were pushed back yet again. The Ming simply could not deal with the iron-clad Han monsters in a close-quarters boarding battle. The situation must have looked hopeless at this point, but once again Chu's ingenuity came to the rescue. Observing that the enemy were advancing in very close order for mutual support, he ordered one of his officers to prepare some fishing boats as fireships. These were filled with inflammable reeds and gunpowder, and manned by picked 'dare to die' contingents. As soon as the wind shifted in the right direction, they were cut loose to drift into the middle of the enemy mass.

Because they were so close together, the Han ships could not take evasive action without colliding with one another. And as soon as one caught fire, the flames spread to the next. Bamboo sails crashed in flames on to the decks of neighbouring vessels; cannon went off indiscriminately; gunpowder stores exploded, throwing burning wreckage in all directions. Soon it must have seemed as if the whole Han line was on fire from end to end. Eventually the inferno was brought under control, but hundreds of Han ships had been abandoned, blown up or burnt to the waterline, with the loss – according to Ming historians – of some 60,000 men.

Both sides spent the third day of the battle resting and repairing damage. On the fourth day, the Han fleet, which was still numerically the stronger, advanced again – this time in open order, with plenty of space between the ships. Ch'en Yu-liang had learned a lesson, but he was still one step behind Chu Yuan-chang. Throughout the battle, Ch'en found himself being forced to react to events, rather than seizing the tactical initiative. Now the lighter and more manoeuvrable Ming vessels swarmed through the gaps in his line, concentrating against the Han monsters individually, and overwhelming them by force of numbers before their neighbours could lumber to the rescue.

At this point, with the Han fleet bloodied and frustrated, but still too strong to be decisively defeated, news came that a Ming army under Hu Te-chi had advanced overland and reached Nan-ch'ang, securing it against any further Han attacks. Chu Yuan-chang decided to take the advice of his officers and break off the action for the time being, since the strategic aim had been achieved, and the risk of defeat was still only too real. But he had not yet done with Ch'en Yu-liang. Now he intended to finish the war once and for all.

That night, the Ming fleet disengaged. Each ship following a lantern on the stern of the one ahead, they sailed north out of the lake and into the main stream of the Yangtze. Several of the captains urged a retreat all the way to Ying-tien, but Chu steadied them and kept the fleet where it was, blocking the narrow mouth of the lake, and bottling up the Han within. Ch'en dithered for a month before he decided to force his way out, and when he did so his opponent was ready.

As the Han fleet moved north, resistance suddenly melted away. With what must have been a sense of relief, Ch'en's captains sailed out into the Yangtze, and turned upstream for home. Then they looked up at the western horizon. It was black with smoke. Bearing down upon them with the current was a wall of fireships, stretching from one shore to the other. There seems to have been no attempt to deploy into line of battle. The whole Han fleet simply turned about and fled down-

stream in terror. Ming warships appeared from out of the smoke and pursued them, joined by others from garrisons farther down the river. Soon the Yangtze was dotted for miles with small groups of drifting vessels, each consisting of a mighty Han tower ship, surrounded and being bled to death by a horde of smaller enemies. Even now, Ch'en did not give up. Commandeering a small boat, he had himself rowed from ship to ship in an attempt to rally his captains. Then on one of these trips he was fatally wounded by an arrow in the eye.

That was the end of organised Han resistance. Part of the fleet surrendered; the rest escaped back to Wu-ch'ang. With this victory Chu had overthrown the temporary balance of power in the Yangtze valley, and silenced any possible rivals among the Red Turban veterans. Han Lin-erh functioned increasingly as a puppet, while the local scholar class threw in their lot more enthusiastically than ever with Chu. The perceptive among them could now see that he was the most likely candidate to found the next imperial dynasty.

Conqueror of China

It took another two years to mop up the whole of Ch'en Yu-liang's former territories, but the issue was no longer in doubt. With the new conquests, the population and military strength of Chu's state tripled in those two years. Chang Shih-ch'eng of Wu, the last major obstacle to Ming control of south China, had missed his chance to strike while his enemy was busy elsewhere. Now, he could only stand on the defensive and wait.

Early in 1364, while still engaged in the west, Chu sent Chang an unmistakable message by announcing his own adoption of the title 'Prince of Wu'. At the same time he reorganised his armed forces, establishing for the first time a formal chain of command and tables of organisation for his units. The main field army was formed into *wei* or guards regiments, each of 5000 men divided into five battalions. There were also a number of *shou-yu* or independent battalions, a thousand strong. A battalion was further subdivided into ten companies. This decimal organisation was copied from the Yuan, as was a system of appointing hereditary commanders[3]. Officers, who had previously adopted more or less any title they liked, now had proper rank titles allocated to them according to the size of the formation they led. This reform marked the final transformation of Chu's forces from a bandit horde into the standing army of a major power.

The conquest of Wu proceeded at a leisurely pace. Outlying provinces were picked off first – a strategy that Chu likened to 'clipping the wings' of his victim. Meanwhile, north of the Yangtze, a Yuan army under Koko Temur, which had been sent to aid Wu, watched inactive, paralysed by factional disputes among its officers. Far too many Yuan supporters were still blind to the peril that was looming for them, content to observe the 'rebels' killing one another, while the Ming steamroller gathered pace.

For, as usual, Chu Yuan-chang was not slaughtering anyone who could be a useful recruit to his cause. Captured and defecting Wu troops were enrolled into his armies, and were immediately turned against their old master. Impressed both by his apparent invincibility and by his leniency, the commanders of two important Wu towns, Hu-chou and Hangchow, changed sides and opened their gates to Chu. By December 1364, Chang Shih-ch'eng was being besieged by Hsu Ta in his last remaining stronghold, the great city of Soochow.

Although promised his life, and an honourable position in the Ming government, Chang refused to surrender. He personally led several sorties to interfere with the earthworks which the Ming were raising around his city, but the work went on relentlessly. When the encircling siege works were complete, Ming artillery commenced a bombardment with trebuchets and cannon. While cannonballs smashed at the walls, incendiary bombs, rockets and fire arrows arched over the defences and fell into the city, setting entire areas ablaze. The siege lasted for ten months, but on 1 October 1367

a breach was finally made in the walls, and the Ming soldiers poured into Soochow. Chang tried to hang himself, but was spotted in time, cut down and captured. A quarter of a million Wu soldiers, also taken alive, joined the Ming army.

Within a month, Chu's armies were on the move again. A combined land and naval expedition turned south along the coast, accepting the surrender of the surviving independent warlords of Fukien, while Hsu Ta and Ch'ang Yu-ch'un drove northwards into the Yellow River plain with a quarter of a million seasoned troops. Here, in the heartland of the Yuan, resistance was stronger, but the Mongol regime had long since been torn into fragments by the ambitions of its own generals, and they were unable to establish a coordinated front. K'ai-feng, the ancient Sung capital, fell to the Ming in April 1368. It was followed in September by Ta-tu, the Yuan capital founded by Kubilai Khan. Chu immediately changed the city's name to Pei-p'ing – 'The North is Pacified'. Subsequently renamed Pei-ching, the 'Northern Capital', it became the seat of government for his successors. As Peking, or Beijing, it is still the capital of China today. As for the deposed Mongol rulers, some surrendered, while others fled back into the northern steppes, there to establish a new nomad state under the name of the 'Northern Yuan'.

Anticipating victory, Chu had already taken the final step. There was no longer any need to be diffident about assuming titles. In the previous year Han Lin-erh, now clearly superfluous, had met with an unfortunate 'accident'. He had been crossing the Yangtze on a Ming ship, when he fell overboard and drowned. It is unlikely that anyone was surprised by this development – least of all Chu, who on 23 January 1368 proclaimed himself the first emperor of a new dynasty, to be known as the 'Ming', or 'Brilliant'. Following the precedent of the Yuan, he also took a reign title – a term by which he wished the period of his rule to be known to posterity. Aptly, this title was 'Hung Wu': 'Overwhelming Military Power'.[4]

Son of Heaven

The title was well chosen, for the former beggar was now the unchallenged ruler of the most populous state and the strongest armed forces on earth. Some sixty million subjects owed him allegiance, and perhaps as many as three million soldiers could be mustered beneath his banners. His triumph was unprecedented for a man of such low birth. It was also unique for another reason: in the past the centre of Chinese power had always been in the north, in the valley of the Yellow River. Every successful campaign of reunification had been launched from there, and had ended by bringing the south under the control of a capital located in the North China Plain. But during the thirteenth and fourteenth centuries, the balance of power had changed. The wars of the Mongol conquest and the subsequent Yuan misgovernment had weakened and depopulated the north, while an influx of refugees had correspondingly strengthened the south, and especially the Yangtze valley. So Chu had been able to expand from a southern base to conquer the north. This had never been achieved before, and never would be again until Chiang Kai-shek's Northern Expedition of 1928.

But the fighting was not yet over. The province of Szechwan in the far west did not fall for three more years, while Yunnan in the south-west remained in the hands of Yuan loyalists until 1382. Long before that, Hung Wu's most grandiose ambitions had had to be curbed. In the initial flush of victory, he had proposed continuing the war against the

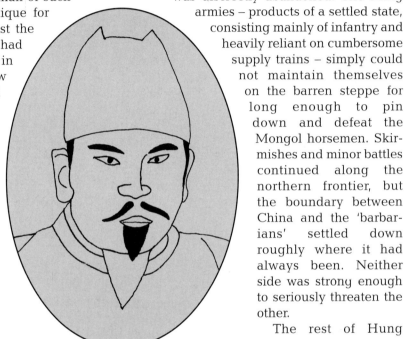

Chu Yuan-chang as the Emperor Hung-wu, after an official portrait in the Palace Museum, Taipei.

Northern Yuan and taking over the whole of Mongolia. The faithful Hsu Ta was sent on a series of campaigns which penetrated as far as Lake Baikal in Siberia – perhaps the most northerly point ever reached by Chinese armies – but in 1372 he suffered a decisive defeat on the steppe near the old Mongol capital of Karakorum, and the forward policy was discreetly abandoned. The Ming armies – products of a settled state, consisting mainly of infantry and heavily reliant on cumbersome supply trains – simply could not maintain themselves on the barren steppe for long enough to pin down and defeat the Mongol horsemen. Skirmishes and minor battles continued along the northern frontier, but the boundary between China and the 'barbarians' settled down roughly where it had always been. Neither side was strong enough to seriously threaten the other.

The rest of Hung Wu's long reign was famed in Chinese history as an age of relative peace and prosperity. Refugees returned to settle the devastated lands; millions of trees were planted to stabilise the soil; the population grew, and trade and revenue flourished. A lesser man would no doubt have rested on his laurels and enjoyed a well deserved life of luxury. But Chu worked on with his old ferocious energy, streamlining the administration, imposing military-style discipline on soldiers and civilians alike, and taking every opportunity to extend his own already awesome personal power.

His amazing success, he liked to tell his courtiers, was based on four factors. The support of Heaven, naturally; his interest, based on personal experience, in the welfare of the poor; his habit of rewarding loyalty; and his belief in discipline. With the homely country imagery that he liked to use, he told a gathering of provincial officials that the peasantry were 'like young birds learning to fly, or like seedlings newly planted. Do not pull the feathers off the one or hurt the roots of the other.' He would relate to others how, as a young officer, he had stamped his authority on his first command:

'When I was leading them out to fight, two of the men disobeyed me. I immediately ordered them to be executed. From then on, all submitted to my commands with trembling and no one dared to violate my orders. Nothing is impossible to a man of strong will.'

But Hung Wu's idea of 'strong will' had its unpleasant side, especially as he grew older. He seems, in fact, to have suffered increasingly from paranoia. He may have cherished the common people, but like many men of his background, he despised the scholar class. The Mongols had introduced the disagreeable practice of flogging their Chinese officials for a variety of offences and shortcomings, and Hung Wu continued the habit, subjecting many able men of high rank to this punishment – which was at best humiliating, and at worst often fatal. He became excessively touchy about any suggestion of setting limits to the imperial power: a passage from the ancient philoso-

The 'pig-emperor'. A less flattering caricature produced by one of Chu Yuan-chang's critics. The name 'Chu' sounds very similar to the Chinese word for 'pig', giving rise to the insulting nickname. Which of these two pictures is the more accurate likeness, we can only guess.

pher Mencius, suggesting that the popularity of a ruler depended upon how well he treated his subjects, so annoyed him that he had the monument to Mencius thrown out of the temple dedicated to the sages. Whole sections of the offending book were also removed from the syllabus for the civil service examinations.

Naturally, the living did not escape any more lightly. An army officer who was caught allowing his son to play the flute, instead of teaching him his military exercises, had his nose cut off. In 1380 and 1393, real or imagined plots against the emperor led to two great purges, in the course of which tens of thousands of people were put to death, and many more tortured. Legal formalities were largely dispensed with: for instance, the 'trial' of the former Prime Minister, Hu Wei-yung, was not begun until ten years after the defendant's execution.

Less prominent people could attract the emperor's wrath for seemingly trivial slights to his authority. One court artist found himself facing death for having painted a picture of a fisherman in a red jacket. Since red was an imperial colour, bestowed only on guardsmen and high officials, the artist must have been trying to make a subversive political point. Hung Wu was also increasingly sensitive to comments about his humble origins. It became dangerous even to mention the word 'monk' in his presence. The word 'pig' was similarly taboo, after someone scurrilously likened the imperial features to that animal.

The ultimate effect of this over-centralisation and the growing reign of terror was to weaken and cow the scholarly classes, and to discourage officials from displaying any initiative. As an example, these are Chu's instructions concerning court eunuchs, who admittedly had a reputation for intrigue, but must have included many able men:

> If you give them responsible work to do, they will cause you a great deal of trouble... Never give them a chance to excel in anything, otherwise they will grow proud and will get out of control. If they are kept in fear of the law, they will learn to become discreet, and this will keep them away from disorders.

The ladies of the court were even more restricted. For them to order necessary supplies without the emperor's approval, or even to send a message outside the palace, incurred the death penalty. The Empress Ma, however, was a steadying influence on her husband, and usually managed to find a way round the more draconian of his restrictions. On one occasion, she asked him about the attitude of the people towards the new dynasty. Hung Wu abruptly told her that affairs of state were not the concern of women. But Ma answered him back, saying:

> 'Your Majesty is now the father of the people and I am the mother. Would it be considered improper for parents to enquire how their children are faring?'

In fact, the emperor had the highest regard for his wife, and she seems to have wielded considerable influence behind the scenes. At one time, he proposed to honour her by employing her relatives as ministers, but she refused. With remarkable candour, she pointed out that her family knew nothing about government, and might be tempted to misuse the opportunity to enrich themselves.

Under later, weaker rulers, the tendency of an emperor to try to control everything himself could completely paralyse the government, but Hung Wu kept a firm grip on the reins for thirty years. One thing which he was unable to bequeath to the nation, however, was a stable succession. He had an heir whom he carefully groomed for the job, but the boy's premature death in 1392 threatened to upset all his plans for the future. The next in line to the throne was the emperor's grandson, Chu Yun-wen, but he was still a minor, and would obviously be unable to impose his will on the other imperial relatives. One of Hung Wu's weaknesses had been his indulgence towards his family, many of whom had been installed in great semi-independent fiefs in various parts of the country, and allowed to raise what were in effect private armies. The emperor must now have regretted this. He foresaw a struggle for power on his death, which might destroy the state that he had spent his life building.

It is probable that the second of his notorious purges, in 1393, was indeed a response to this threat. The ostensible cause was the excessive power and arrogance of an army general, Lan Yu, who had built up an independent personal following which the emperor may have been right to fear. But it seems clear that Lan was used as a pretext to eliminate many other potential over-mighty subjects, who could not possibly all have been involved in a plot. The eventual death toll reached 15,000.

Hung Wu died in 1398, at the age of seventy. He was succeeded by his grandson, Chu Yun-wen, who ascended the throne as the Emperor Hui-ti. The great founder had correctly foreseen that there would be trouble on his death. Civil war broke out between Hui-ti and his uncle, the Prince of Yen, and the country was thrown into turmoil for three years. Yet the empire did not disintegrate. The advantages of the unity which Chu had won for it were too obvious to all concerned. The Prince of Yen eventually prevailed, and reigned from 1402 to 1424 as the Yung-lo Emperor, leading the Ming to new heights of greatness. The dynasty would last for more than another two centuries, ruling essentially along the lines that Chu Yuan-chang had mapped out for it.

CHINESE SEA POWER

Early China was a continental civilisation, whose power rested on the agricultural development of the great river valleys. Furthermore, the Yellow River, along whose banks the earliest centres of Chinese power arose, is – as we have seen in the Introduction – unsuited to navigation. Sometimes it is shallow enough to wade across; at others, it sweeps away whole cities in its floodwaters. As a theatre of naval operations, it has never been very significant.

It is not surprising, therefore, that the first naval powers arose in the south, along the lower Yangtze. The Yangtze, at least in its lower reaches, is a much more tractable river, and is deep enough to accommodate ships for hundreds of miles upstream from its mouth. Hence the river has always been the main artery of communications in the area. This provided a stimulus to the development of large vessels which could also be used for seaborne trade, and for supplying armies operating along the coast.

The classical age

The first naval campaign of which we have any record took place in 486BC, when the state of Wu despatched a fleet under Hsu Ch'eng to link up with its army on the border

A sea battle of the Warring States era, illustrated on a fifth-century BC bronze vessel. The fighting crews of the ships appear to be standing on an upper deck above that which carries the paddlers, but details of the construction are sketchy.

of Ch'i. The combined Wu forces were attacked by Ch'i, and defeated. We have no details of the battle, but it was presumably fought at least partly at sea. The ships of this period, as depicted on contemporary cast bronze vessels, were little more than large, decked canoes, propelled by paddles. One such source shows two vessels engaged in a boarding fight, with their bows in contact and their crews striking at each other with spears, dagger-axes, and even knives. Other men are shown swimming in the vicinity, although it is not clear whether they have taken to the water deliberately in order to attack the enemy boats, or have been knocked overboard by the collision.

That more sophisticated methods of naval combat were being devised as early as the Warring States is suggested by a couple of textual sources. An account preserved in several later works, which purports to be from the reign of Ho Lu of Yueh (514 to 496BC), describes five different kinds of specialised warship, including one that carried castles, and one that was used as a ram. However this seems far too early for such advanced fleets, given the lack of any corroborating evidence, and the date of this text is also questionable on other grounds. Ramming, as known to early Mediterranean navies, was never a popular tactic in China: construction methods did not lend themselves to the fitting of an underwater ram – although strengthened bows were of course a possibility – and battle accounts tend to describe victims of a collision as being 'capsized', rather than holed and sunk.

Mo Tzu, writing in the fourth century BC, describes what was probably a more typical tactic of the period. He tells how the Ch'u navy defeated that of Yueh with the aid of a device called a *kou-ch'iang*.[1] This was used to grapple an enemy ship in order to prevent it escaping, and also to fend it off if it tried to close and board. From the description, the *kou-ch'iang* was presumably a strong pole with a hook near the end, which could be wielded by the sailors in different ways according to the tactical situation. As Mo Tzu

puts it: 'When the enemy was about to retreat one used the hook; when he came on one used the fender.' The intention was no doubt to keep the victim at a range at which the decks could be swept with close-range missile fire. Ch'u was the original home of the crossbow, and its navies may have devised this tactic in order to exploit their superiority in these weapons.

Rafts were popular in the Warring States period as troop transports. Made from the giant bamboo of western China, which has a stem up to three feet in diameter, these rafts were very buoyant and drew only a foot or so of water. They were swept up at bow and stern to facilitate dragging over sandbanks and through rapids, and so were ideal for use on rivers. In the fourth century BC, the state of Ch'u was menaced by Ch'in raiders who came down the Min River during the spring floods, travelling with the current, and moving so fast that even if the Ch'u border posts spotted them it was impossible to warn the cities downstream before they arrived. According to the *Chan-kuo Ts'e*:

> If the flat boats are used for troops, each double barge will support fifty men with grain for three months. Floating with the current one can make three hundred *li* (i.e. about a hundred miles) in a day, and although the distance is great, sweat is shed by neither horse nor man.[2]

Exactly what is meant by a 'double' barge is unclear, but they may have been constructed on the same lines as a cargo ship of the same period, the *fang-ch'uan*, which consisted of two hulls fixed together side by side.

The early imperial period

By the time the Han dynasty came to power, larger specialised fighting ships had become available. This development may be connected with Ch'in expansion along the south-east coast, where the empire incorporated peoples who already possessed a strong maritime tradition. It is generally believed that the ancestors of the Polynesians, whose spectacular advance across the Pacific was

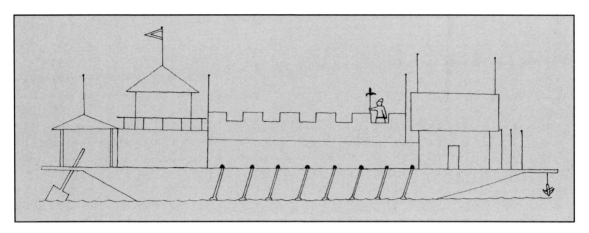

well under way by this time, came from these south-eastern coastal regions of China. Archaeologists have excavated a Ch'in period dockyard at Canton,[3] and from the width of the slipways have estimated that it was built to handle ships with a beam of up to twenty-seven feet. Such vessels were propelled by sails made of bamboo matting, and with their high bows and sterns they are recognisable as the forerunners of the modern junk. Warships could now carry fighting turrets on their decks, and unlike contemporary Hellenistic 'castles' these were probably permanent fixtures. Fleets of up to 2000 such ships are recorded from as early as the first century AD.

In the period following the Han, Chinese naval shipbuilding techniques reached new heights. Already in the first century AD the old-fashioned steering oar had been replaced by a proper rudder, and square sails gave way to a new fore-and-aft rig which permitted tacking into the wind – an advance that remained unknown in Europe for several more centuries. Hulls began to be constructed with watertight transverse bulk-heads, which not only made them difficult to sink (perhaps explaining in part the neglect of the ram), but also provided a series of strong cross-timbers on which multiple masts could be set. Ships with as many as seven masts had appeared by the third century AD.

Tomb models show that by the Han period, the smaller river boats were being rowed rather than paddled. In later ages,

A river patrol boat of the Han dynasty, recon-structed from a wooden model found in a tomb at Ch'ang-sha. By this time the rowers could be completely enclosed for protection against missiles. Note the anchor, taken from another model of the same period, which in this 'modern' form was prob-ably a Han innovation.

even large sailing ships used oars as a source of auxiliary power. Surviving illustrations of warships tend to omit sails in order not to obscure the rest of the detail, and sometimes it is not clear whether oars alone, or a combi-nation of oars and sails, were in use. Chinese oarsmen rowed standing up and facing forwards, which would have made them rather vulnerable to missiles, and so the sides of small ships were often built up to protect the rowers.

A novel variant on normal propulsion techniques was the paddle-wheel, which first appeared in the fifth century AD. The wheels were worked by means of a treadmill within the hull, which meant that the mechanism could be completely enclosed. The earliest account we have, from AD418, describes the enemy's supersitious panic at seeing ships advancing without any visible means of propulsion. At first driven by a single wheel on each side, these vessels later reached enormous proportions: one monster from the Southern Sung dynasty was said to have been 300 feet long. It was crewed by 1000 men, and powered by thirty-two paddle-

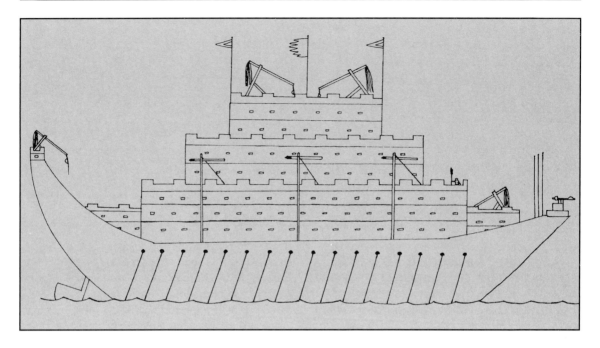

wheels. Stern-wheelers, and combined stern- and side-wheelers, were also built. Steered by stopping the wheels on each side independently, they were very fast and manoeuvrable, but were too top-heavy for rough seas, and so were restricted mainly to inland waters.

Clearly, there was considerable specialisation among warships at least as early as the Han dynasty, but the first systematic account of the various types does not appear until AD759. The *T'ai Pai Yin Ching*, published in that year, lists six classes:[4]

1. 'Tower Ships'. These were three-deckers (although five and even ten-decked ships are mentioned in later works), armed with stone-throwing engines on the top deck. The sides were protected against incendiary attack by felt or leather armour. By the Sung period, iron plates were also being used to armour ships.

2. 'Covered Swoopers'. Smaller vessels, used for swift boarding attacks in the face of enemy fire. They were completely covered over, and protected with layers of rhinoceros hide.

A Sung or Ming dynasty 'tower ship', based on textual evidence, and illustrations in a Ming edition of the Wu Ching Tsung Yao. Such a top-heavy design seems rather impractical, but these ships were intended for use on inland lakes and rivers, where heavy seas and strong winds were unlikely to be a threat. The original illustrations do not show masts or sails, although these were presumably fitted. The vessel is protected by iron plates, and is armed with stone-throwing engines, a flamethrower, and iron-tipped 'striking arms', which could be released to drop on to enemy ships and smash their superstructures. The latter devices were apparently invented by the Sui in the sixth century AD. The enormous Han ships used at the battle of Lake P'o-yang in 1363 may have looked similar to this reconstruction.

3. 'Fighting Junks'. Probably based on the standard merchant junks, these had ramparts added to the sides, and a castle in the middle of the deck. They were propelled by oars as well as sails.

4. 'Flying Barques'. Very fast vessels, with a large complement of rowers and a few élite marines, 'selected from the best and bravest'.

Flying barques were used for surprise attacks, and as a mobile reserve for emergencies.

5. 'Sea Hawks'. These appear to have been specially designed for rough weather, and perhaps for operations in the open sea. They had low bows, high sterns and 'floating boards' (presumably outriggers of some kind) on either side to provide additional stability. Their upper parts were protected by ox hides.

6. Small patrol boats, also with ramparts to protect the rowers.

The later empire

Most of the above types continue to appear in battle accounts until the Ming period, but for a long time there was no strict demarcation between warships and civilian vessels, and ordinary cargo junks and rowing boats were often converted to naval use when required. In fact, until 1132, when the Sung established the first permanent war fleet, navies were either built for a specific campaign, or requisitioned from local merchants or fishermen, with towers, ramparts and other equipment hastily added.

The 'finest hour' of the Chinese naval forces came after the Jurchen invasion of 1125, when the Sung were forced to abandon their northern capital and retire south of the Yellow River. In the first flush of victory the Jurchen pursued them, crossing the Yangtze, and driving the emperor to take refuge with his fleet off the south coast. But other naval units seized control of the Yangtze and cut off the invaders' communications with the north, obliging them to retreat. In 1161 another Jurchen army, under the deranged tyrant Hai-ling Wang, made another attempt to exterminate the Sung. This time, the barbarians augmented their forces by conscripting thousands of Chinese soldiers and sailors from the occupied north, and used Chinese experts to construct their own war fleet. But the Sung navy defeated them off the coast of Shantung, and once again blocked the Yangtze, preventing the Jurchen army from crossing.

Navies continued to play a significant part in the wars of the Mongol conquest, and in the subsequent struggles which led to the triumph of the Ming in 1368 (see Chapter 14). Early in the fifteenth century, Chinese sea power reached a short-lived pinnacle of

An early seventeenth-century drawing shows this ingenious derivative of the fireship. The articulated front section was released to drift with the current, carrying its lethal cargo of mines and incendiary weapons into an enemy fleet. The rowers shown in the original have been omitted for clarity.

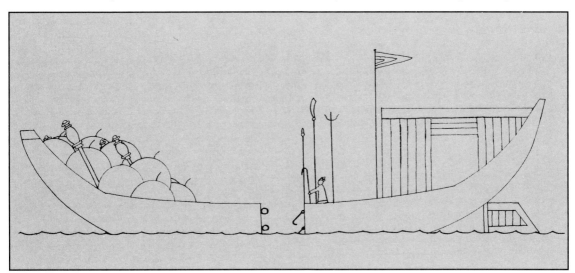

achievement, which surpassed anything that had gone before. In the 1420s the Ming navy was by far the most powerful in the world: it comprised approximately 400 large warships at its main base near Nanking; 1350 warships and a similar number of patrol boats stationed elsewhere; 400 grain transports and 250 large 'treasure ships'; and another 3000 merchant ships which could be called upon in emergencies.

Most remarkable of all were the 'treasure ships'. They were a development of a traditional design known as the *sha-ch'uan*, or 'sand ship'. These vessels were flat-bottomed, to enable them to negotiate the shallows and sand bars along the coast, and broad in the beam. When used for cargo, they had a capacity of up to 1200 tons.[5]

Between 1405 and 1433, the Ming admiral Cheng Ho made seven extended voyages to the west, utilising vessels of this type. His fleets comprised up to 200 ships, and carried tens of thousands of men. Cheng Ho sailed as far as the east coast of Africa, and the soldiers who accompanied him intervened on behalf of Chinese nominees in civil wars in Java, Sumatra and Ceylon.[6]

After the Ming had reunited the country, however, the importance of sea power declined. A powerful lobby at court favoured isolating China from undesirable foreign influences by strictly controlling overseas trade. In the sixteenth century, when Japanese and European pirates began operating in force off the southern coast, the association of seafaring with disorder became ever stronger in the minds of officialdom. Eventually, orders were issued to destroy all large seagoing ships. This policy effectively put an end to the long-distance projection of Chinese naval power, just at the time when the Portuguese and other European nations were beginning their career of seaborne expansion.

16
COXINGA: THE PIRATE KING

*'The Great Ming pacified the empire and restored its ancient splendour.
How can I meet him in heaven with my mission unfulfilled?'*
Cheng Ch'eng-kung

The Cheng family

As the Ming dynasty lost interest in the sea, the eastern coastline became increasingly vulnerable to the depredations of pirates. The first real threat came from the Japanese, who had begun raiding as early as 1307, and continued to do so intermittently for the next two centuries. Native Chinese were also often driven to piracy. In large part this was due to short-sighted government policies, which attempted to protect the empire from foreign influences by prohibiting overseas trade, and so impoverished the coastal communities which had come to depend on it.

A particularly serious out-break of disorder occurred between 1542 and 1570, when groups known as the *wou-k'ou* or 'dwarf pirates' had terrorised the provinces of Fukien and Chekiang, and even at one point threatened Chu Yuan-chang's old capital at Nanking, which was still the foremost city in South China. The appellation 'dwarf' was an insulting way of referring

to the Japanese, although in reality the *wou-k'ou* were mostly renegade Chinese, stiffened by a core of Japanese swordsmen.[1]

These bands were eventually brought under control by military operations, combined with a relaxation of the laws that

A Ming statuette of the God of War in more obviously military dress, illustrating the type of equipment which Coxinga and other generals of the period would have worn on campaign. (British Museum)

lung, who had been closely associated with the Europeans. Cheng had been baptised as a Christian by the Portuguese – who knew him as Nicholas Iquan – and he had later worked as an interpreter for the Dutch. In 1625 he acquired a fleet of junks which had previously belonged to a pirate named Li Han, and so launched his own independent career as a businessman and part-time pirate. Cheng prospered and became influential in the region, eventually attracting the attention of the Ming emperor Ch'ung-chen, whose policy it was to rule, where possible, through local magnates. In 1628, Cheng formally swore allegiance to the Ming, and was appointed commander of the south-eastern coastal region.

So pleased was the emperor with his performance that Cheng was soon awarded the title of Marquis, along with a rank in the civil service equivalent to that of a Grand Secretary. As an additional mark of favour, the emperor symbolically adopted Cheng's eldest son, Cheng Sen, as his own. The boy thus received the new name of Chu Ch'eng-kung – Chu being the surname of the Ming royal family. Ch'eng-kung later reverted to his own family name, calling himself Cheng Ch'eng-kung. After he became famous in his own right, however, he was popularly referred to by an honorific title: 'The Master with the Imperial Surname', or 'Kuo-hsing Yeh'. It was by this

regulated legitimate seafaring. But the tradition of coastal piracy was still very much alive, and was given additional impetus in the sixteenth century by the activities of European seafarers – mainly the Portuguese, and later the Dutch – who were happy to supplement their trading operations by smuggling, and often recruited local associates to help them.

In 1624, the Ming managed to raise a fleet and drive the Dutch out of the Pescadores Islands off the south coast, which they had been using as a base for smuggling. The resultant power vacuum in the area facilitated the rise of a man named Cheng Chih-

title, corrupted to suit European tongues, that he was subsequently known to the outside world: Coxinga.[2]

Coxinga's early years are obscured by the kind of mythology which often attaches itself to those who become heroes of their people. It was said, for example, that his mother was the Sea Goddess, Ma Tso-po. What is known is that his mother was in fact Japanese, and that he was born in 1623, at Hirado in Japan. His father later took him back to China, where he was educated at the Imperial Academy in Nanking. Although he was not at this stage being groomed for a military career, the young Cheng learned the arts of horsemanship and archery, as was the normal practice for noble youths at the time. Perhaps significantly, he is also said to have studied the writings of Sun Tzu.

Ming decline

By the 1640s, the Ming dynasty had been ailing for some time. Official corruption and a series of financial crises hastened the decline of the army, and popular rebellions began to sweep through the provinces.

Simultaneously, the rise of a new power on the northern frontier added to China's problems. The Manchus, as these new neighbours came to be called, were descended from the Jurchen – a people who were of course already well known to the Chinese. By the beginning of the seventeenth century, their various clans had been organised into a powerful new state, under the leadership of their Khan Nurhachi. Nurhachi now wished to extend his authority over the related tribes of the region, some of whom were vassals of the Ming emperors. In 1618, the inevitable war broke out between the Manchus and the Ming.

Initially, the Ming suffered a series of defeats, and quickly lost most of their territory north of the Great Wall. After this there was a period of stalemate until 1644, when a

A section of the Ming Great Wall near Beijing. These defences appear formidable, but the Manchu invaders – taking advantage of divisions within the empire – circumvented them without a fight. (Duncan Head)

Chinese rebel army under Li Tzu-ch'eng captured Peking, and the Emperor Ch'ung-chen committed suicide. The Ming general Wu San-kuei, who was then holding the eastern part of the wall, accepted an offer of help from the Manchus, and allowed them to enter China through the pass of Shan-hai-kuan. The Manchus quickly defeated Li Tzu-ch'eng, but then proved impossible to dislodge. They occupied Peking and announced the replacement of the Ming by their own dynasty, the Ch'ing.

Ming loyalists rallied in the south, but the Manchus fought their way inexorably towards the Yangtze River and Nanking. In the summer of 1645, Cheng Chih-lung brought his fleet up the Yangtze to oppose a Manchu crossing, but he seems to have shown little real enthusiasm for the cause. The enemy crossed the river with the aid of a diversion, and marched towards Nanking, whereupon Cheng sailed back to Fukien without firing a shot. It is likely that he was concerned first and foremost to protect his fleet, which was the basis of his own power.

Without him, however, Ming resistance was hopeless. In September 1646 the Manchus broke through the mountain passes which protected Fukien from the landward side, killed the new emperor, Lung-wu, and marched into the city of Fu-chou. Cheng Chih-lung blew up his arsenals and prepared to escape southwards by sea, but at the last moment was halted by a message from the Ch'ing government. The Manchus offered him the governorship of Fukien and Kwang-tung Provinces if he would transfer his allegiance to them.

At this point his son Coxinga, who was now twenty-two years old, appears to have made a decision that would dictate the course of the rest of his life. He had been brought up as a scholar, but he now decided to turn to the profession of arms. Although still only a junior member in the hierarchy of the Cheng clan, he began to make plans on his own account. He recruited growing numbers of personal followers, and set up a base in the offshore Hsia-men Islands, where he could train them, safe from interference by either the Manchus or his own kinsmen. Coxinga seems not to have wavered in his loyalty to the Ming, and in particular to Lung-wu, who had in fact been only the figurehead of a particular faction of Ming courtiers. In tears, Coxinga begged his father not to betray the dynasty which had so favoured him, but Chih-lung had made up his mind.

The Manchus immediately broke their word. They kidnapped Chih-lung and took him to Peking, together with 500 of his men, who had agreed to follow him. There they were kept under house arrest, while their captors tried to persuade Chih-lung to use his influence on the rest of the Cheng clan to induce them to surrender. Meanwhile, both sides engaged in a desultory campaign of raids and counter-raids, which achieved little except to deepen hatreds on both sides. Coxinga was now in charge of his own corps of several thousand men, whom he led alongside other Cheng forces in raids along the coast. So he was away from his home base of An-p'ing on the day when, early in 1647, Ch'ing raiders struck. The damage was limited, but his mother's house was destroyed. She was so distraught at this that she committed suicide. Henceforth, more than ever, Coxinga had a personal motive for his struggle.

The rise of a war-leader
The leaders of the Chengs were now Chih-lung's brother, Cheng Hung-k'uei, and his cousin, Cheng Ts'ai. They decided not only to fight on, but to take the initiative against the Manchus. In September of 1647, they advanced on Fu-chou city, and besieged it for nearly a year. Coxinga, however, was not with them. As a subordinate commander he had been despatched to the south, where he was campaigning on the borders of Kwangtung Province. He found this region in a state of anarchy, with numerous local warlords raising troops and fighting among themselves, but owing allegiance neither to the Ch'ing nor to the Ming.

Perhaps because of this instability, the people of the south flocked to Coxinga, and willingly joined the ranks of his army. Resistance was light, and his losses in battle were small. So when in the autumn of 1650 he returned to Hsia-men, he found himself in charge of what had become by far the strongest of the Cheng armies. At the same time, he was growing more and more impatient with what he regarded as the ineptitude of his colleagues. Early in the following year, he led a fleet south again to Kwangtung, but was driven back by bad weather. He returned home in a foul mood, to discover that Manchu raiders had appeared at Hsia-men in his absence, and thanks to a half-hearted defence by Hung-K'uei and another uncle, they had been allowed to devastate the islands. Coxinga at once decided to assert his authority over the Cheng operations, and ordered his men to arrest the two incompetent commanders. No one seems to have put up any serious resistance. Hung-k'uei was forced into retirement, and his colleague was executed. Coxinga was left as the undisputed leader of Ming resistance in the south-east.

Master of the China seas

The Cheng clan now owed nominal allegiance to another Ming faction – that of the Emperor Yung-li. His court, however, was based hundreds of miles inland, in the remote province of Yunnan. In practice, Coxinga was an independent ruler. He maintained the official records which Ming law required him to keep, organised his officers according to the Ming system of ranks, and kept Ming unit designations for his troops. But he soon began to bring in modifications to suit the local conditions. He introduced widespread conscription, established his own ministry to control the production of weapons and armour, and within a few years was able to equip units of picked troops with good quality iron body armour, for which they became famous. Coxinga also set up a new camp on the Chia-men Islands, where recruits could be formally trained.

In one crucial respect, however, he fell short of establishing a proper government: he had no interest in the agricultural population except as suppliers of food and manpower. He never bothered to establish a proper administration for the peasantry, simply commandeering from them whatever he required. In a way, this failing may have helped him, for it intensified the poverty of the south-eastern hinterland, and so made it more difficult for the invading Manchus to keep their armies supplied. The seafaring element of the population was in general happy with Coxinga's policy of encouraging trade, and although a few people left the area in order to avoid conscription, this was more than balanced by a flood of Ming loyalists from all over the empire, who now saw him as the last hope of the dynasty.

Coxinga's total strength was now more than 100,000 men. Fleets of up to 6000 ships are mentioned in contemporary sources, although if these figures are even close to the truth, most of these must have been very small. (One expedition in 1655 is said to have involved 5000–6000 'ships', and 60,000–70,000 soldiers. This averages out at no more than fourteen men per vessel!)

Late in 1651, Coxinga once again took the initiative against the Manchus. He sailed to the city of Chang-chou, where he blockaded the harbour, captured the Ch'ing governor and beheaded him. The Manchus responded by trying to negotiate with him through his father, whom they were still holding in Peking. They offered Coxinga the post of Regional Commander of the south-east, which meant in effect that he could keep his troops and the area that he already controlled, if he would accept the rule of the Ch'ing emperor. In his reply, he pointed out that he was far stronger in the south-east than the Manchus were, and that in any case he could not trust them, as they had broken their promises to his father, and were still keeping him under arrest.

Coxinga then went on to demand the governorship of three provinces, and the rank of Prince. This was equivalent to the awards given to Wu San-kuei, the former commander at Shan-hai-kuan, who had first admitted the Manchus to the empire, and had continued

A general of the late Ming, as represented outside the tombs of the emperors near Beijing. The Manchus quickly came to respect Chinese civilisation, preserving and treating with reverence the monuments of their predecessors. (Duncan Head)

to serve them against the Ming ever since. The claim, however, was no more than a negotiating ploy. Coxinga, as he had admitted, did not trust his enemies, and had no intention of submitting to them. He pretended for a while to accept a set of revised terms, and managed to persuade the Ch'ing to withdraw their troops from the front line in the Fukien region, in preparation for his takeover as Regional Commander. As soon as this was done, Cheng troops moved into the evacuated areas and levied contributions from the population. Then, at the last minute, Coxinga announced that he had changed his mind, and the deal was off.

When his father persuaded the Peking authorities to try again, Coxinga managed to sabotage the talks over the issue of the adoption of the Manchu hairstyle, with its shaved head and pigtail. The conquerors always insisted upon this outward sign of submission, and it had provoked considerable resistance among traditionally-minded Chinese. How important he really considered it is difficult to say, but Coxinga now announced that under no circumstances was he prepared to shave his head. In November 1654, the negotiations finally collapsed.

Not surprisingly, such behaviour infuriated the Ch'ing officials who were dealing with him. Their Chief Censor pronounced this rather two-edged verdict on Coxinga:

> 'He is prideful and ambitious, with the courage and heart of a hero, so obviously he must be constrained and controlled. Even if he comes to submission, he will harbour a "second heart"...'

Coxinga himself reacted to the end of negotiations with a flurry of angry letters. To his father, he wrote: 'Now I can only sharpen my weapons and await them.' To the Ch'ing offi-

The area of Coxinga's operations
in south-eastern China between
1656 and 1662.

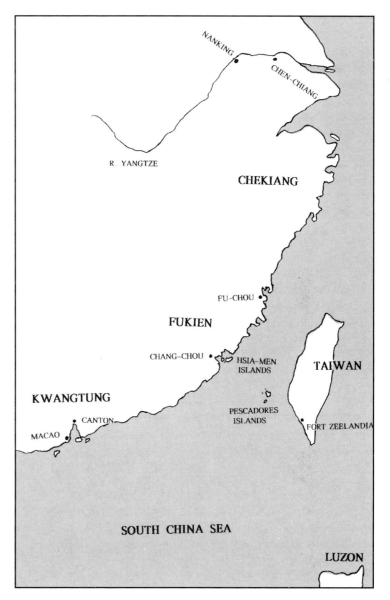

cial appointed to the thankless task of governing Fukien, he wrote complaining that it was he who had been tricked. He went on to remind the governor that China was full of people who hated the Manchus, and that they could expect many others to rebel. The Muslims in the north-west, in fact, had already done so.

In January 1655 news came that the Manchu Prince Jidu had been given command of a great army, with the task of destroying Coxinga. But Jidu's advance was painfully slow, and the Cheng had plenty of time to prepare. Coxinga ordered a scorched earth policy, including the destruction of all city walls in the coastal zone, in order to prevent the Manchus from using them as bases. Eventually, in May 1656, Jidu launched a two-pronged amphibious assault on Chinmen Island. The Manchus were still inexperienced at sea, however, and a sudden storm wrecked their fleet. Jidu's campaign collapsed, and the initiative passed back to his enemy.

Already, Coxinga had been probing northwards along the coast. Over the next three years he conducted a series of campaigns which penetrated as far as the mouth of the Yangtze River. There were successes and failures on both sides. As early as March 1655 the Cheng admiral Chang Ming-chen, who had expert knowledge of the area, had been sent to reconnoitre the Yangtze estuary. This expedition was a

disaster. Chang Ming-chen died at the beginning of 1656, the Ch'ing counterattacked and seized an island which the fleet was using as a base, and many of the sailors deserted. But Coxinga himself helped to redress the balance again in February 1657, when he defeated a Manchu army and captured three of its generals.

In June 1658, he set out on what was probably intended to be an all-out assault on Nanking, which was now the centre of Ch'ing power in the Yangtze valley. But the fleet was caught in a typhoon, and many of the ships were lost. For Coxinga personally, the worst tragedy was the sinking of the ship which was carrying most of his household: among the dead were three of his sons and six of his concubines. The expedition was forced to turn back, but Coxinga was not deterred for long, and in the early summer of the following year he tried again. All the indications are that he intended this campaign to be decisive.

High tide at Nanking[3]

In July of 1659, a Cheng fleet of perhaps 2500 ships sailed into the Yangtze. It was guided by an officer named Chang Huang-yen – one of the few survivors of the earlier northern campaign. A preliminary task for the Cheng was to hold a series of ceremonies on an island in the estuary, in honour of their guiding deities: Heaven, Earth, and the spirit of the Ming founder, Chu Yuan-chang. Coxinga read a poem which he had composed for the occasion, vowing to exterminate the barbarians.

His ships then fought their way upstream, silencing the Manchu shore batteries with cannon fire. They quickly captured the city of Chen-chiang, which the Manchus had taken from Coxinga's father in 1645. But upstream from Chen-chiang, winds and currents conspired to slow the fleet down. The heavy junks had to be dragged against the current by teams of men hauling them with ropes from the bank. Coxinga's advisers urged him to march on Nanking by land and attack it quickly, before the enemy could send reinforcements; but he was content to take his time.

He seems to have intended to encourage the Manchus to commit as many troops as possible, so that he could defeat them all at once. This would be consistent with his usual policy of seeking decisive battles; and in some ways such confidence seemed justified. He already had some 85,000 troops – far more than the Ch'ing could possibly muster. The local people came to join him in such numbers that his army was unable to absorb

them all. Officials in charge of towns and cities along the way competed to offer him their submission. But he had no time to set up a formal government, and, in any case, had little inclination for the job. Instead, he contented himself with *ad hoc* levies of money and supplies, just as he had in his Fukien coastal stronghold. He did not even bother to establish secure bases to guard a possible line of retreat, because he was absolutely certain that there would be no retreat.

On 24 August, Coxinga and his fleet at last arrived outside Nanking. Even now he would not order an attack, preferring to maintain a blockade and wait for the inevitable surrender. But in deploying his forces on land in order to surround the city, he had played into the hands of the enemy, whose mounted archers were supreme in open country. They may have been outnumbered, but the Manchus were skilled and confident soldiers, and many of them were veterans of a long and successful war of conquest. On 8 September, the defenders sallied out from one of the gates of Nanking and mauled some of Coxinga's units, before retreating back within the walls. Coxinga was still an amateur at this business of land fighting. That night he redeployed his army to face the gate in question, in case of a repeat attempt. At dawn, the Manchus came pouring out of two other gates, and attacked from the opposite direction. Taken in flank and rear, the Cheng troops fought back hard, but they were no match for the Manchu cavalry, and were cut down en masse. Coxinga escaped to the ships, but few of his men were able to join him. His army had virtually ceased to exist.

The fleet fell back slowly to cover the Cheng base in Fukien, and arrived at Hsiamen in December. The surviving soldiers were demoralised, and the popular support in the Yangtze region which they had enjoyed while they were winning had completely evaporated. Furthermore, it was obvious that the Manchus would soon be looking for their revenge. The next winter was spent in training and exhorting the troops, and concentrating them at Hsia-men for the inevitable showdown.

Dasu, a commander of the Manchu imperial bodyguard, had been given command of a new fleet. In June 1660, he broke into Hsia-men Bay and fought a great naval battle with the Cheng forces. This time it was the Ch'ing who had made the mistake of fighting on the enemy's terms. They were beaten, and retreated in confusion. Coxinga sent them a woman's handkerchief, as a combined insult and challenge to another battle. But he had noticed that the Manchu navy was better handled than previous fleets had been, and privately he considered himself lucky to have won. The enemy were learning fast, and would soon be strong enough to try again. Furthermore, the Manchus had now brought under their control the provinces of Chekiang, situated to the north of Fukien, and Kwangtung, to the south. They would soon be able to envelop him from both sides in a classic pincer movement that might be irresistible.

Fort Zeelandia

One of Coxinga's spies, who worked as an interpreter for the Dutch East India Company in Taiwan, came to him at this point with a report on the state of the Dutch garrisons on the island. Perhaps the man was simply an optimist, or perhaps he considered it wise to tell his master what he wanted to hear. Whatever the reason, he presented a wildly exaggerated picture of Taiwan's wealth and the fertility of its soil, and added that the Dutch had allowed their fortifications to fall into disrepair. Furthermore, he said, the main Dutch fleet under Jan van der Laan had just sailed for Java, leaving Taiwan almost undefended. It would make an ideal base for the Cheng to rebuild their strength before returning for the reconquest of China.

Some of Coxinga's men had been to Taiwan, and they knew that the report was wildly inaccurate. The island was too far from the mainland for reliable communications, grew scarcely enough food to support its existing population, and was notorious for its tropical diseases. One officer dared to say so, but was punished for his frankness. Coxinga had made up his mind.

Admiral van der Laan, however, was still off Macao, having stopped off there on his way south for a fight with the Portuguese. Even Coxinga was not over-confident enough to want to take on a whole fleet of Dutch warships, and so he postponed the move until the spring of 1661. Meanwhile, he wrote to the headquarters of the Dutch East India Company in Batavia, informing them that he was going to pretend to move his forces eastwards in the direction of Taiwan in order to deceive the Manchus. The Dutch should not worry, he went on, because that was just a feint, and he had no intention of attacking them. 'My real intentions,' he concluded rather ominously, 'are never known to anyone.'

The Dutch appear to have believed him, because no reinforcements were sent to Taiwan, and no attempt was made to improve the island's defences. Coxinga left about half of his troops behind in Fukien, under his eldest son and several of his best generals, and sailed eastward. In April 1661 a fleet of 800 junks arrived near the Dutch base at Fort Zeelandia, carrying 30,000 Cheng soldiers. The fleet had been held up for a week by adverse weather, and because of the spy's optimistic report on the food situation in Taiwan, it had carried no reserve provisions. While hungry Chinese sailors swarmed ashore, ransacking every grain warehouse they could find, the Dutch governor Coyett and his few hundred troops hurriedly barricaded themselves inside the fort.

Coxinga then sent Coyett a polite message, offering to let the defenders leave the island unmolested. The Dutch, he informed them, had only been allowed to occupy Taiwan in the first place by courtesy of Cheng Chih-lung, who had been governor of the region at the time. Now that Cheng's son required it as a base, he was serving them with notice to quit. Naturally Coyett refused to comply, and so the siege began.

Coxinga's first task was to surround and isolate the fort. He landed artillery on the shore, and kept up a bombardment on the southern side as a demonstration, although the Dutch guns prevented his own from getting close enough to do much damage. Then he sent a fleet of junks to sail up a river on the northern side of the fort. According to some local Chinese, the defenders had decided that this river was too shallow for ships to use, and so had not troubled to guard that approach.

Chinese junks, however, were designed for river work, and they drew less water than European vessels of comparable size. They negotiated the river without difficulty, and landed their troops well inland. These joined up with more of Taiwan's Chinese settlers, and blockaded Fort Zeelandia from the landward side. But Coxinga soon realised that he was still too weak to risk an assault. Supply convoys from the mainland had failed to arrive, and the food situation was becoming ever more serious. He was forced to detach large numbers of men to clear fields and sow rice, while fevers and other diseases ate further into his strength.

In August, with both sides almost starving, a Dutch fleet arrived and broke through to the fort with supplies and reinforcements. This must have been discouraging to the besiegers, but it seems that it was even more so to the Dutch. On his way in, the commander of the Dutch fleet had been able to see the true size of Coxinga's forces, and the experience had shattered his nerve. He offered to take a message from Governor Coyett requesting help from the Ch'ing government in Peking, but instead of delivering the message he gathered his ships and fled to Siam. By December, with no further help in prospect, the Dutch soldiers began to despair. There were only about 500 defenders left, many were sick, and food and ammunition were once again running low.

Some of the Dutch climbed over the walls and deserted to Coxinga, informing him of the weak points of the defences. So on 25 January 1662, the Cheng artillery began a concentrated bombardment of one of the redoubts. This soon collapsed, and Coxinga's men stormed it. With a section of the walls in enemy hands, Coyett agreed to surrender. In recognition of a gallant defence, Coxinga stuck to his original terms, and allowed him and his men to leave for Batavia with everything but their weapons.

Failure and death

Coxinga was now free to establish his own regime on the island, which he organised along the lines of a Ming prefecture, with a tax system and a formal alloca-

A Chinese war junk, from an eighteenth-century drawing. The larger vessels of Coxinga's navy, as well as the forces hastily raised by the Manchus to oppose him, must have been very similar in appearance.

tion of land to his followers. Farmers and scholars were encouraged to migrate from the mainland to escape from Manchu rule, and a start was made on building a new merchant fleet. But civil administration was still not Coxinga's forte, and it continued to be neglected in favour of what was in effect military rule. All adult males were forced to train as soldiers, supervised by a corps of military officials who outnumbered their civilian counterparts by about six to one.

Taiwan remained an armed camp, dedicated to taking the fight back to the Manchus. Yet it must quickly have become obvious that this was impossible. It would require all the resources of the Cheng 'state' merely to survive in this strange environment, where the harvests were poor, and tropical fevers continued to strike down the unacclimatised Chinese. Coxinga had secured his base, but now he was effectively trapped there.

At one point, he conceived a wild plan to augment his strength by capturing the Philippines. He sent an ambassador to demand tribute from the Spanish authorities there, but the scheme backfired. There were already many Chinese settlers on the islands, and the colonial government had long been wary of them. The arrival of an embassy from Coxinga sparked off such displays of public enthusiasm among these Chinese that the Spanish became frightened, and slaughtered many of them. Coxinga then decided to send an invasion fleet to avenge the massacre, but events overtook him, and this fleet was destined never to set sail.

All these frustrations worsened Coxinga's temper, and he began to resort to ever harsher measures against anyone who criticised or defied him. Meanwhile, those whom he had left behind on the coastal islands of Fukien, deprived of his stern discipline, began to desert to the Ch'ing. In March 1662 he sent orders to his son, Cheng Ching, and his other commanders to evacuate Hsia-men and the other islands and join him in Taiwan. They simply ignored him. Soon afterwards he was informed that his father had been

executed in Peking, while at about the same time the last Ming emperor, Yung-li, had been captured and also put to death. There was now no longer a Ming dynasty to restore.

Finally, word came that Cheng Ching had fathered a son. What would seem to be good news at last sent Coxinga into a mad rage. The mother, it turned out, had been a wet-nurse to Cheng Ching's infant brother. Thus, according to traditional Chinese thinking, she was already a member of the family. Accusing his son of incest – which was technically true, perhaps, but an exceptionally harsh interpretation of the law – Coxinga ordered the immediate execution of his infant grandson, both parents and also, for good measure, his own wife, whom he blamed for allowing the affair to take place. His officers brought him the head of the child's mother, but refused to lay hands on the others, so he ordered the disobedient soldiers to be killed as well. No one, it seems, took any notice.

We are told that at this point Coxinga fell ill. His increasingly strange behaviour, and his growing failure to impose his authority, must lead to the suspicion that he had been ailing for some time. Probably some jungle fever had been slowly weakening him since soon after his arrival in Taiwan. He took to his bed in June 1662, and died soon afterwards. The master of the China seas was only thirty-seven years old. He died a Ming loyalist to the last. His last reported words were: 'The Great Ming (i.e. the founder, Chu Yuan-chang) pacified the empire and restored its ancient splendour. How can I meet him in heaven with my mission unfulfilled?'

With Coxinga's death, the long struggle was almost over. In 1664, Manchu troops overran the last Cheng strongholds in Fukien. The Cheng clan held Taiwan for another two decades, but in 1683 the new rulers of the mainland finally collected a fleet and conquered the island. The name of the Ming would endure as a rallying cry for disaffected Chinese until the end of the nineteenth century, but the last hope of restoring the reality had died with Coxinga.

POSTSCRIPT: CHINA'S MILITARY TRADITION AND THE MODERN WORLD

The course of China's history since the Manchu conquest has been as dramatic as that of any preceding era. Under the Manchus, the empire reached its widest ever extent – eventually incorporating the Mongols, the Tibetans and many of the Muslim peoples of Central Asia. Few of these peoples, however, were happy under Chinese domination and, especially in Taiwan and Central Asia, the Ch'ing found themselves bogged down in a series of indecisive counter-insurgency campaigns.

In the nineteenth century, the newly industrialised European powers subjected the empire to repeated humiliations. They defeated its obsolete armed forces on numerous occasions, extorted territorial and other concessions from the Ch'ing government, and only just stopped short of partitioning the entire country among themselves. In 1911 the Ch'ing dynasty was overthrown by its internal opponents, and was replaced by a republic. This upheaval led to decades of internal strife – first between imperialists and republicans, then among competing warlords, and finally between the nationalists of the Kuomintang and the Communists. The situation was still further complicated after 1931 by a brutal Japanese invasion.

When the Communists led by Mao Tse-tung finally overcame their enemies and seized power in 1949, they were faced with the task of dragging an impoverished and backward country into the modern world. Many of Mao's increasingly hare-brained policies at first made the economic and political situation worse. But at least the Communists, by their victory over the foreign imperialists and their protégés, had given the Chinese people back their pride. And gradu-ally, they learned through bitter experience the art of government. Today, although its administration remains oppressive and corrupt by Western standards, China has one of the highest rates of economic growth in the world. Its armed forces, which until recently had to rely on crudely made copies of 1940s vintage Russian equipment, are re-equip-ping, reorganising, and replacing outmoded doctrines with a combination of modern military science and the best of their own indigenous traditions.

In the mid-1990s, the armed forces of the People's Republic of China comprised nearly three million men and women, plus at least an additional 1,200,000 armed militia. Some 2,200,000 of these personnel were serving in the People's Liberation Army, making it by far the largest army in the world. The PLA still has a long way to go before more than a small proportion of its soldiers are equipped and trained for modern mobile warfare, but this 'small proportion' is still large enough to dwarf the armies of most potential opponents. The People's Republic can currently field ten armoured divisions, with a total of some 10,000 tanks, at least 2,800 armoured personnel carriers, and tens of thousands of artillery pieces.[1]

The Chinese navy is also modernising and expanding, and the appearance of the first aircraft carrier is imminent. China has also been in possession of nuclear weapons for several decades, and is undoubtedly developing improved delivery systems for them, including ICBMs. The country is widely tipped to be an economic and military superpower of the twenty-first century.

Is there any place in this new world, then, for the ancient Chinese military heritage? Do the warlords of old still have anything to teach their modern successors? It appears that the answer is yes. There is very much more to military power than an impressive collection of hardware – as the late President Mobutu of Zaire and Iraq's Saddam Hussein, among others, could testify. An army is also a reflection of the society which has produced it, and its effectiveness depends heavily on the cohesion of that society, and the regard in which it holds its armed forces.

We have seen how the Chinese upper classes of the later imperial age, following Confucian dogma, came to despise the military arts, and how for a time this attitude hampered progress. Contact with this scholarly élite encouraged many early foreign observers to regard the Chinese as an innately unwarlike people – an attitude that has persisted in some quarters to this day. But no one who has met him in battle has ever cast doubt on the bravery and determination of the ordinary Chinese soldier. The Japanese in the sixteenth century, and again in the Second World War; the British in the Opium Wars; and the Americans in Korea in the 1950s – to take just a few examples – have all paid tribute to the way in which Chinese armies have repeatedly compensated for their inferiority in equipment by exploiting speed of manoeuvre, skill at camouflage and deception, and sheer courage.

The reasons for the superiority of one fighting man over another are of course extremely complex, but there can be little doubt that the motivation produced by awareness of a long and illustrious military tradition plays a part. The regimental system of the British Army is based on exactly this principle. The enormous self-confidence of the Chinese soldier undoubtedly owes much to awareness of the achievements of the past. And in the late twentieth century, Confucius has been largely eclipsed as a national symbol by more robustly practical figures. Recent decades have witnessed the revival of what amounts almost to a personality cult around the figure of the First Emperor, Ch'in Shih Huang-ti. This began under Mao in the

early 1970s, and continues to testify to the importance which the Chinese government attaches to the example of history.

Shih Huang-ti is undoubtedly the best known today of the warlords whose stories are told in this book. Several of the others, especially those associated with the founding of the great dynasties – Liu Pang, Li Shih-min and Chu Yuan-chang – are also very much household names. But more potent than any of them as a symbol of past military glories is the semi-mythical figure of Sun Tzu. The Communist regime, which swept away so much of the country's past, has never ceased to acknowledge the influence of what we have described as the 'Taoist school' of military thought. Of course, its indirect and subtle approach was particularly appropriate for the guerrilla warfare which Mao was forced to adopt in the early stages of their civil war.

As a child, the young revolutionary is said to have been fascinated by stories of the exploits of Ts'ao Ts'ao, and other ancient heroes who rose to prominence from obscure beginnings. Mao also had high regard for Sun Tzu, and consciously echoed his teachings in many of his own works. He once stated:

> 'We must not belittle the saying in the book of Sun Wu Tzu... "Know your enemy and know yourself and you can fight a hundred battles without disaster."'[2]

As a result of such endorsements, the old tradition of editing and commentating on the Military Classics received a new lease of life under the Communists. For example, a leading strategist of the Civil War period, Kuo Hua-jo, produced several editions of Sun Tzu's *Art of War*. The first of these, issued in 1939, was studied in the People's Liberation Army during the Second World War as a textbook.[3]

New translations – or, as often as not, reworkings of old translations – of Sun Tzu continue to appear regularly in China, just as they do in the West. The People's Liberation Army of the 1990s, although it is now discarding much of Mao's doctrine on guer-

rilla warfare, remains steeped in the Sun Tzu tradition. There is today a society in China dedicated to the study of the 'Art of War'. Its president – a serving Major-General in the PLA – has recently published his own commentary on the classic.[4] Other army officers have produced their own interpretations of Sun Tzu, illustrated with examples of battles ranging in time from the founding of the Shang dynasty to the Civil War of 1945–49.[5] A recurring theme in such books is the relevance of the tactical and strategic principles devised in ancient times to the superficially very different conditions of today.

China's history as a tourist attraction: crowds of visitors on the Great Wall. Such symbols of past military greatness do much more than bring in tourist revenue: they also act as powerful symbols of the country's enduring strength. (Duncan Head)

It is to be hoped that the handful of examples presented in this book have shown that Oriental military history has as much to offer as the better known experience of the West. Certainly it is full of lessons which the Chinese heirs to this tradition have not neglected.

NOTES

The main sources for each of the biographical subjects are indicated in the Suggested Further Reading list under the relevant headings.

Introduction
[1] The changing course of the Yellow River is mapped in more detail in Blunden and Elvin, *Cultural Atlas of China*, p. 16. *The Historical Atlas of China*, Vol. 1, includes numerous maps which show how dramatically the coastline and drainage patterns have changed since classical times.

Chapter 1
[1] For the archaeology of Shang chariots, and other military aspects of the Shang dynasty, see K. C. Chang, *Shang Civilisation*, Yale University Press, 1980, pp. 194–200.
[2] Sawyer, *The Seven Military Classics of Ancient China*, p. 130.
[3] Legge, *The Tso Chuan*, in *The Chinese Classics*, Vol. 5, Book 1, p. 28.
[4] Sawyer, *Military Classics*, pp. 76–7.

Chapter 2
[1] Sawyer, *Military Classics*, p. 131.
[2] This subject is treated in detail in R. L. Walker, *The Multi-State System of Ancient China*, Shoestring Press, Connecticut, 1953.
[3] Confucius, *The Analects*, Penguin Classics edition, Bk XIV. 15, p. 126.
[4] ibid. p. 127.
[5] Sawyer, op. cit., p. 245.
[6] Confucius, op. cit. pp. 126–7.
[7] For Tso Ch'u-ming's account of the battle of Ch'eng-p'u, see Legge, *The Tso Chuan*, pp. 209–10.

Chapter 3
[1] Lao Tzu, *Tao Te Ching*, Book 2, Chapter L.

Penguin Classics edition, p. 111.
[2] Griffith, *Sun Tzu: The Art of War*, Book VI, pp. 96–7.
[3] ibid. p. 101.

Chapter 4
[1] Sawyer, *Sun Pin – Military Methods*, Chapter 1, p. 81.
[2] Griffith, *Sun Tzu: The Art of War*, Book VI, p. 109.
[3] Sawyer, *Sun Pin*, Chapter 4, p. 96. Sun Pin remarks on this doctrine: 'This is the way I took P'ang and captured Imperial Prince Shen' (i.e. at the battle of Ma-ling).
[4] Ssu-ma Ch'ien, *Shih Chih*, Chapter 23: Biographies of Lu Chung-lien and Tsou Yang. Quoted in Sawyer, *Sun Pin*, p. 52.
[5] The question of the size of ancient and medieval Chinese armies is a controversial one. From the Warring States onwards, chroniclers regularly quote figures in the hundreds of thousands, or even millions. Modern commentators generally find such figures utterly incredible. It is difficult, however, to dismiss many of them as total fabrications. In the second chapter of his *Art of War*, Sun Tzu insists on careful calculations of relative strengths, and goes so far as to estimate the cost of an army of 100,000 as 'one thousand pieces of gold a day'. A passage in the *Chan-kuo Ts'e* explicitly contrasts earlier forces of only 30,000 or so with the much larger armies required for the warfare of the third century BC. On the other hand, it is certain that at times, 'ten thousand' or 'a hundred thousand' could simply mean 'a lot'. Perhaps the best resolution of the dilemma lies in a remark by the Han dynasty historian Pan Ku, that the men recruited for one campaign 'were altogether more than forty thousand and were called a

hundred thousand'. This would obviously not represent a fixed ratio, but perhaps on average, a reduction of the very large figures by a factor of two and a half or three would be a reasonable compromise.

[6] Crump, *Chan-kuo Ts'e*, *The Book of Ch'i*, Chapter 121, p. 154.

[7] Sawyer, *Sun Pin*, Chapter 3, p. 89.

[8] ibid.

[9] ibid. p. 91.

[10] ibid. Chapter 22, p. 192.

[11] ibid. Chapter 31, p. 236.

[12] ibid. Chapter 20, p. 186.

[13] This theory is discussed in the Introduction to Griffith, *Sun Tzu*.

[14] Sawyer, *Sun Pin*, Chapter 30, p. 231.

Chapter 5

[1] Crump, *Chan-kuo Ts'e*, *The Book of Chao*, Chapters 239–42, pp. 296–306.

[2] Sawyer, *Sun Pin*, Chapter 32, p. 240.

[3] Griffith, *Sun Tzu*, Chapter 5, p. 92.

[4] Crump, op. cit. *The Book of Han*, Chapter 387, p. 460.

[5] See R. C. Rudolph, *The Minatory Crossbowman in Early Chinese Tombs*, Archives of the Chinese Art Society of America, Vol. XIX, 1965.

[6] The full list is given in Ranitzsch, *The Tang Army*, p. 18.

Chapter 6

[1] See J. J. L. Duyvendak, *The Book of Lord Shang*, Arthur Probsthain, 1928.

[2] Crump, *Chan-kuo Ts'e*, *The Book of Han*, Chapter 393, p. 466.

[3] *Wu Ch'i's Art of War*, Chapter 2. Quoted in Griffith, *Sun Tzu*, p. 155.

[4] 1,489,000 to be exact. See *The Cambridge History of China*, Vol. 1, p. 40.

[5] ibid. p. 94. The story of Cheng's illegitimacy, along with the later burial of the scholars, is dismissed here because the passage in the *Shih Chih* has been shown, on semantic grounds, to be a later interpolation. This does not, of course, necessarily mean that it is not true – merely that the rumour may have been remarkably persistent, and hence still current many years afterwards.

[6] Ssu-ma Ch'ien, *Shih Chih*, Chapter 88. Quoted in A. Waldron, *The Great Wall of China*, Cambridge University Press, 1990, p. 17.

[7] ibid. Chapter 110. Quoted in Waldron, op. cit. p. 17.

[8] Waldron, op. cit., provides a fairly comprehensive survey of the changing status of the northern frontier defences from Ch'in times to the present.

[9] The 'Magic Canal' is described, with photographs, in R. K. G. Temple, *China – Land of Discovery and Invention*, Patrick Stephens, 1986, pp. 181–2. It is a graphic example of how far ahead of their time the Ch'in engineers were.

[10] The K'ang-hsi Emperor of the Manchu Ch'ing dynasty reigned from AD1661 to 1722. His sixty-one-year reign was the longest of any Chinese emperor, and among the most illustrious. See J. D. Spence, *Emperor of China – Self Portrait of K'ang-hsi*, Jonathan Cape, 1974.

[11] See the discussion in *The Cambridge History of China*, Vol. 1, p. 94.

[12] Apart from the works listed in the bibliography – especially Cotterell, *The First Emperor of China* – several other popular publications, often lavishly illustrated, have appeared on the subject of the terracotta army. The most up-to-date is probably Zhang Wenli, *Terracotta Figures and Horses of Qin Shihuang*, Northwest University Press, Xian. See also A. Cotterell, *The First Emperor's Warriors*, published in London by the Emperor's Warriors Exhibition Ltd., 1987.

Chapter 7

[1] Legge, *The Tso Chuan*, in *The Chinese Classics*, Vol. 5, Book VII, p. 319.

[2] Most of this chapter is based on the translations in Sawyer, *Military Classics*.

[3] Ssu-ma Ch'ien, *Shih Chih*, Chapter 55. Quoted in Sawyer, *Military Classics*, p. 282.

[4] Sawyer, *Military Classics*, p. 132.

[5] ibid. p. 138.

[6] ibid. p. 267.

[7] Ssu-ma Kuang, *The Chronicle of the Three*

Kingdoms – Chapters 69–78 from the *Tzu Chih T'ung Chien*. Trans. A. Fang, Harvard University Press, 1952, p. 16.

Chapter 8

[1] In his biography of Hsiang Yu, Ssu-ma Ch'ien rather implausibly credits Hsiang personally with every one of these 'kills'.

[2] The 'imperial' colour connected with the Han dynasty was changed several times, giving rise to some confusion. Liu Pang's rebel armies originally used red for their flags and emblems, but after the establishment of the dynasty black was adopted, following Ch'in practice (in Chinese astrology, black was the colour associated with water). In 104BC this was changed to yellow, as part of a major overhaul of the dynasty's image under the Emperor Wu-ti. After the restoration of the Eastern Han in AD25, the imperial colour reverted to red.

[3] Han Wu-ti, the famous 'Martial Emperor', reigned from 141 until 87BC.

Chapter 9

[1] For the Tung Shou tomb, see Dien, *A Study of Early Chinese Armour*, p. 20, n. 89.

Chapter 10

[1] Yu-wen T'ai was a member of the Yu-wen clan of the Hsien-pi, and one of the leading figures of mid-sixth-century China. As a minister and general of the state of Western Wei, he was the architect of the victory at Sha-yuan (see Chapter 9).

[2] For the military aspects of the Yueh-chih, see V. P. Nikonorov, *The Armies of Bactria, 700BC–AD450* (2 vols.), Montvert Publications, 1997.

[3] For an account of this extraordinary battle, derived from the *Wei Official History*, see Jenner, *Memories of Lo-yang*, pp. 92–3.

[4] Griffith, *Sun Tzu*, Chapter VI, pp. 96, 97, 100.

Chapter 11

[1] The sources for the 'War of the Heavenly Horses' are the *Shih Chih*, Chapter 123, translated in Watson, *Records of the Grand Historian*, p. 274; and Pan Ku's *Han Shu*, or *History of the Former Han Dynasty*, Chapters 61 and 96. These passages are translated in F. P. Hulsewé, *China in Central Asia, the Early Stage: 125BC–AD23*, E. J. Brill, Leiden, 1979. These accounts are so similar that one must have been copied from the other, but it is not clear which was the original.

[2] This campaign, together with the whole series of wars between T'ang China and Tibet, is treated in detail in C. Beckwith, *The Tibetan Empire in Central Asia*, Princeton University Press, 1987.

Chapter 12

[1] This issue is discussed in *The Cambridge History of China*, Vol. 3, pp. 155–6.

[2] The account in Fitzgerald, *Son of Heaven*, is based firmly on the Ssu-ma Kuang tradition, and presents such a eulogistic picture of the young Li Shih-min as to seriously try the reader's patience. It is nevertheless a detailed and highly readable story. I have tended to rely on it for the battle and campaign narratives, but to regard its treatment of the relations between Shih-min and his father and brothers with considerable scepticism.

[3] Sawyer, *Military Classics*, p. 322.

[4] Li Shih-min's tomb was adorned with carved reliefs depicting six of his favourite chargers. These were accompanied by verses extolling their accomplishments, and detailing the wounds which they had received in battle. For example, 'Shih-fa-ch'ih', the chestnut which Shih-min rode at the battle of Ssu-shui, was hit in the rump by no fewer than five arrows. From the evidence of these reliefs, it appears that Shih-min's horses did not go into battle wearing armour. This surprising deviation from earlier practice is perhaps to be explained by the growing importance of mounted archery, under Turkish influence, and the consequent need for speed and agility.

[5] For the battle of Ssu-shui, see Fitzgerald, op. cit. pp. 80–9.

[6] A member of the Yu-wen clan, and hence of Hsien-pi descent. Forty percent of the offi-

cers of the Sui army had been of non-Chinese origin, and many of these continued to serve under the T'ang.

[7] Quoted in Fitzgerald, op. cit. pp. 190–1.

[8] The Empress Wu founded her own short-lived 'Chou' dynasty, which governed from 690 until 705, when the T'ang was restored.

Chapter 13

[1] Needham, *Science and Civilisation in China*, Vol. 5, Part 7, p. 112.

[2] ibid. p. 226.

Chapter 14

[1] For the career of Kubilai, see M. Rossabi, *Khubilai Khan: His Life and Times*, University of California Press, 1988. D. Nicolle, *The Mongol Warlords*, Firebird Books, 1990, Chapter 2, also has an interesting account of Kubilai's military career.

[2] Nanking, or Nan-ching, means 'Southern Capital'. The city remained the capital of the Ming dynasty until 1402, when the Yung-lo Emperor moved north to Peking, the 'Northern Capital'.

[3] For Yuan military organisation, see C. C. Hsiao, *The Military Establishment of the Yuan Dynasty*, Harvard University Press, 1978.

[4] As well as a personal name and a reign title, Ming emperors also possessed a 'throne name', by which they are referred to in some sources. Chu Yuan-chang's throne name was Ming T'ai-tsu.

Chapter 15

[1] For the *kuo-ch'iang*, see Needham, *Science and Civilisation in China*, Vol. 4, Part 3, pp. 681–2.

[2] Crump, *Chan-kuo Ts'e, The Book of Ch'u*, Chapter 195, p. 245.

[3] *Ancient China's Technology and Science*, Foreign Languages Press, Beijing, 1983, pp. 486 - 488.

[4] Needham, *Science and Civilisation in China*, Vol. 5, Part 7, pp. 685–6.

[5] For sand ships, see *Ancient China's Technology and Science*, pp. 479–80.

[6] The career of Cheng Ho and the political background to his expeditions are covered in detail in L. Levathes, *When China Ruled the Seas*, Oxford University Press, 1994.

Chapter 16

[1] For the *wou-k'ou*, see R. Huang, *1587 – A Year of No Significance*, Yale University Press, 1981.

[2] A commonly encountered variant is 'Koxinga'.

[3] Struve, *Southern Ming*, pp. 186–9, covers the Nanking campaign in detail.

Postscript

[1] These figures are based on data from *The Military Balance*, published by the International Institute for Strategic Studies, 1995.

[2] Mao Tse-tung, *Selected Works*, Lawrence and Wishart, 1955, Vol. 1, p. 187.

[3] The influence of Sun Tzu on Communist doctrine is discussed in more detail in Griffith, *Sun Tzu*, pp. 45–56.

[4] Xie Guoliang, *Sun Zi: The Art of War*, Beijing, 1995.

[5] See for example Tao Hanzhang, *Sun Tzu's Art of War – The Modern Chinese Interpretation*, trans. Yuan Shibing, Sterling Publishing Co., New York, 1992.

SUGGESTED FURTHER READING

Primary sources in English translation

The Tso Chuan, in Vol. 5 of *The Chinese Classics*, trans. J. Legge. Oxford University Press, 1872.

Chan-kuo Ts'e, trans. J. I. Crump. Clarendon Press, 1970.

The Seven Military Classics of Ancient China, trans. R. D. Sawyer. Westview Press, Boulder, Colorado, 1993.

Sun Tzu – The Art of War (also includes *Wu Ch'i's Art of War* in an appendix), trans. S. B. Griffith. Oxford University Press, 1963.

Sun Tzu: Art of War, trans. R. D. Sawyer. Westview Press, Boulder, Colorado, 1994.

Records of the Grand Historian: Chapters from the Shih Chi of Ssu-ma Ch'ien, trans. B. Watson. Columbia University Press, 1969.

Pan Ku, *The History of the Former Han Dynasty*, trans. H. Dubs. Kegan Paul, Trench, Trubner and Co, 1944.

Ssu-ma Kuang, *The Chronicle of the Three Kingdoms*, trans. A. Fang. Harvard University Press, 1952.

Yang Hsuan-chih, *A Record of Buddhist Monasteries in Lo-yang*, trans. Yi-t'ung Wang. Princeton University Press, 1984.

General works on Chinese history and military affairs

Blunden, C. and Elvin, M., *Cultural Atlas of China*. Phaidon, 1983.

Dien, A., *A Study of Early Chinese Armour.* Artibus Asiae XLIII 1/2, 1981–2.

—*The Stirrup and its Effect on Chinese Military History*. Ars Orientalis XVI. University of Michigan, 1986.

Kierman, F. and Fairbank, J., *Chinese Ways in Warfare*. Harvard University Press, 1974.

Loewe, M., *Military Operations in the Han Period*, China Society Occasional Papers No. 12. The China Society, London, 1961.

Needham, J., *Science and Civilisation in China*, Vol. 5, Pts 6–8 – 'Military Technology'. Cambridge University Press, 1989 onwards.

Nicolle, D., *Attila and the Nomad Hordes – Warfare on the Eurasian Steppes, 4th to 12th Centuries*. Osprey Elite No. 30, 1990.

Peers, C. J., *Ancient Chinese Armies, 1500 to 200BC*. Osprey Men-at-Arms No. 218, 1990.

— *Imperial Chinese Armies (1), 200BC to AD589*. Osprey Men-at-Arms No. 284, 1995.

— *Imperial Chinese Armies (2), AD590 to 1260*. Osprey Men-at-Arms No. 295, 1996.

— *Medieval Chinese Armies, 1260 to 1520*. Osprey Men-at-Arms No. 251, 1992.

— *Late Imperial Chinese Armies, 1520 to 1842*. Osprey Men-at-Arms No. 307, 1997.

Tan Qixiang (ed.), *The Historical Atlas of China* (8 vols). Cartographic Publishing House, Beijing, 1981 onwards.

Ranitzsch, K-H., *The Army of Tang China*. Montvert Publications, 1995.

Rawson, J., *Ancient China – Art and Archaeology*. British Museum Publications, 1980.

Robinson, H. Russell., *Oriental Armour*. Herbert Jenkins, 1967.

Schafer, E. H., *The Vermilion Bird*. University of California Press, 1967.

Smith, B. and Weng, W. G., *China – A History in Art*. Studio Vista, 1973.

Toynbee, A. (ed.), *Half the World – The History and Culture of Japan and China*. Thames and Hudson, 1973.

Yang Hong, *Weapons in Ancient China*. Science Press, Beijing and New York, 1992.

Watson, W., *China* ('Ancient Peoples and Places' series). Thames and Hudson, 1961.

Zhongmin, H. and Delahaye, H., *A Journey Through Ancient China*. Muller, Blond and White, 1985.

On Dukes Huan and Wen
There is no detailed treatment in English of the careers of these two men. My main source has been Legge, *Tso Chuan*. See also Cotterell, *The First Emperor of China*, cited below.

On Sun Pin
The principal source is the translation of the *Sun Pin Ping Fa* and the comprehensive historical introduction in:
Sawyer, R. D., *Sun Pin – Military Methods*. Westview Press, Boulder, 1995.
A complete translation of Ssu-ma Ch'ien's biographies of Sun Tzu and Sun Pin appears in Griffith, *Sun Tzu*.

On Ch'in Shih Huang-ti
Apart from the relevant chapters in Ssu-ma Ch'ien, several of which appear in Watson, *Records of the Grand Historian*, the career of the First Emperor has been well treated in several works, notably the following:
The Cambridge History of China, Vol. 1: *The Ch'in and Han Empires*. Cambridge University Press, 1986.
Bodde, D., *China's First Unifier*. E. J. Brill, Leiden, 1938.
Cottrell, A., *The First Emperor of China*. Macmillan, 1981.

On Liu Pang and Hsiang Yu
The civil war following the collapse of the Ch'in has not been as well covered in secondary works as either the Ch'in or the Han dynasties. The primary sources are the biographies of Hsiang Yu, Liu Pang, Ch'en She, Han Hsin and other protagonists in Ssu-ma Ch'ien's *Shih Chih*. These are translated in Watson, *Records of the Grand Historian*.

On Ehrchu Jung
For this story, I have relied mainly on Yang Hsuan-chih. *Buddhist Monasteries*, and:
Jenner, W., *Memories of Lo-yang – Yang Hsuan-chih and the Lost Capital, 493–534*. Oxford University Press, 1981.

On Li Shih-min
The relevant portions of the T'ang histories and the work of Ssu-ma Kuang are not currently available in full in translation. The most important secondary sources are:
The Cambridge History of China, Vol. 3: *Sui and T'ang China, 598–906*. Cambridge University Press, 1979.
Fitzgerald, C. P., *Son of Heaven – A Biography of Li Shih-min*. Cambridge University Press, 1933.

On Chu Yuan-chang
The Ming founder also suffers from a lack of primary sources in translation. However, there are good accounts in:
The Cambridge History of China, Vol. 7, Part 1: *The Ming Dynasty, 1368–1644*. Cambridge University Press, 1988.
Chan, A., *The Glory and Fall of the Ming Dynasty*. University of Oklahoma Press, 1982.
Yong Yap and Cotterell, A., *Chinese Civilisation from the Ming Revival to Chairman Mao*. Weidenfeld and Nicolson, 1977.

On Coxinga
This tangled story has been reconstructed mainly with reference to the following, in addition to the works cited above under Chu Yuan-chang:
Goddard, W. G., *Formosa – A Study in Chinese History*. Macmillan, 1966.
Spence, J. (ed.), *From Ming to Ch'ing*. Yale University Press, 1979.
Struve, L., *The Southern Ming, 1644–1662*. Yale University Press, 1984.

INDEX